LV

FEB 11, 2016

D1020245

A LONG WAY FROM TIPPERARY

A LONG WAY
FROM TIPPERARY

A Memoir

JOHN DOMINIC CROSSAN

HarperSanFrancisco
A Division of HarperCollins*Publishers*

3 1336 10124 6305

A LONG WAY FROM TIPPERARY: *A Memoir.* Copyright © 2000 by John Dominic Crossan. All rights reserved. Printed in the United States of America. No part of this book may be used or reproduced in any manner whatsoever without written permission except in the case of brief quotations embodied in critical articles and reviews. For information address HarperCollins Publishers Inc., 10 East 53rd Street, New York, NY 10022.

HarperCollins books may be purchased for educational, business, or sales promotional use. For information please write: Special Markets Department, HarperCollins Publishers Inc., 10 East 53rd Street, New York, NY 10022.

HarperCollins Web site: http://www.harpercollins.com

HarperCollins®, 📖 ®, and HarperSanFrancisco™ are trademarks of HarperCollins Publishers Inc.

FIRST EDITION

Library of Congress Cataloging-in-Publication Data
Crossan, John Dominic.
   A long way from Tipperary : a memoir / John Dominic Crossan.—1st ed.
   p. cm.
   Includes index.
   ISBN 0–06–069974–4 (cloth)
   ISBN 0–06–069975–2 (pbk.)
   1. Crossan, John Dominic. 2. Catholic ex-priests—United States—Biography. 3. Catholic ex-priests—Ireland—Biography. 4. Theologians—United States—Biography. 5. Theologians—Ireland—Biography. I. Title.
   BX4668.3 C76 A3 2000
   220'.092—dc21   [B] 00-020477

00 01 02 03 04 ❖ RRD(H) 10 9 8 7 6 5 4 3 2 1

To
my mother
Elizabeth Farry
and my father
Daniel Joseph Crossan
for those earliest years

Contents

Not Where I Expected to Be

Dawn on Sunday, June 4, 1967. The road emerged from the sheltering confines of the Judean hills, and the full glare of the rising sun hit the front seats of the taxi. The driver was moving very fast, too fast even for empty roads, down from the Old City of Jerusalem into the Jordan valley, over the river's bridge, and eastward to Amman across the desert plateau. All of that still belonged, for one last day, to the Hashemite Kingdom of Jordan.

I sat in the front next to the driver, sat in utter silence from the front gate of the French Biblical and Archeological School to the departure drop at the International Airport. He was staying and I was leaving, although I think *fleeing* is the more appropriate, technical term. Jordanian tanks were digging in as fixed-gun emplacements on the north side of the road as it finally descended onto the valley floor. They would be lethal if Israeli soldiers streamed down the road. They would be fatal if Israeli jets screamed out of the sun. I had only one thought, clear and sharp to this day, but then chanting through my mind like a mantra: What a shitty way to end a stay and leave a country!

I had lived for two years at that famous French school just outside the northern wall of the Old City, halfway between Damascus Gate and Mandelbaum Gate. That latter pseudogate, too, had only one day left. In the preceding weeks shopkeepers taped their windows and drivers painted their headlights down to narrow slits. The Jerusalem Airport was closed to lengthen its runway for the new Boeing 747s, and that left Amman, presuming the Jordan bridge intact, as the only airway exit before war broke out. Embassies and consulates told their nationals that, unless they had to stay, they should get out; hereafter, they would be on their own. The United Nations Command removed its dependents from Israel and Jordan across the Galilean border into Lebanon and on to Beirut or Cyprus. There were many Irish families among them, wives and children of army officers under U.N. auspices on the Israel-Jordan demarcation line or of nonmilitary personnel at U.N. headquarters in the old British Mandate's Government House south of Jerusalem. I knew several families very well after two years. I had been at their parties for other Irish U.N. officers from the demarcation line between Turks and Greeks on Cyprus, appeared on Jordanian TV with them for St. Patrick's Day, gone on trips with them north to Damascus and south to Aqaba, and baptized some of their children at the traditional site of Jesus' baptism in the Jordan river. (High noon in July, with the young mother's back tight against the retaining wall in an attempt to get some shade. We heard no heavenly voice, we saw no descending dove, but we all had, directly or indirectly, some very cold beer from the big white cooler in the back of the big white Jeep.) Then one day, they were all gone, and I did not get a chance to say good-bye to any of them. I still feel it to this day: the dawn, the sun, the mantra.

It was already late to be leaving and, of course, much later than I then knew. It was late not because of either bravery or stupidity on my part. I was a monk with a vow of obedience, and I had to wait for permission from my religious superiors in America. Much more important, I was a monk with a vow of poverty, and I had to wait for airfare from my financial superiors in America. But early or late, Amman Airport for a flight to Rome was not where I was supposed to be that day. I was supposed to be on my third and final visit to Israel during the first two weeks of that month, and by June 4 I should have been somewhere in Galilee, maybe even at Nazareth. I never got there and recognized the irony immediately, since I was not only a monastic priest, but already a New Testament scholar with a focus on the Gospels. I had no idea then how great the irony of that lost chance, that nonvisit, was to become.

Between 1965 and 1967 I had been everywhere and seen almost every ancient site in the Middle East. Everywhere except Galilee and Nazareth, where Jesus lived for most of his life. At various times and in no hurry I had spent weeks in Greece and Turkey, Lebanon and Syria, Iraq and Iran, Morocco and Tunisia, Egypt and the Sinai. Great trips, weird trips, unforgettable trips.

In Egypt, I climbed to the top of Mount Sinai for the tradition, the top of the Great Pyramid for the view, and the top of the Nile Hilton for the bar. In Morocco, I drove along the royal road from Casablanca to Marrakech to Fès to Rabat on a trip that was to last four days, but never got farther than the La Mamounia Hotel in Marrakech. I thought I felt sick, but it might just have been that beautiful outdoor pool with the Atlas Mountains as a distant backdrop (*Que sera, sera*). In Iraq, from Baghdad to Babylon I was on a good, paved road. But then from Babylon at noon through Ur at dusk to Basra at midnight, where a paved road appeared in the *Hachette Guide's* fantasy, there was packed earth in the Iraqi government's reality. I had a cheap ride in a new Mercedes on delivery to the Gulf; the driver waited at a rest stop and then followed an oil truck across the desert as it headed for the excess-gas fires flaming along the coast.

In Turkey, the English-speaking travel agent in Antakya got a prepaid driver and "car" to take me through the Cilician Gates in the Taurus Mountains to stops at Lystra, Derbe, and Iconium, Pauline sites with nothing much Pauline (or anything else) to see, and on to a final destination at Antalya's airport. The driver slept in the car every night, drove slowly and pointedly up every mountain, and tried to make me pay for the gas at every pump. When we stopped each day for lunch, I let him order and indicated that I wanted the same. Somewhere south of Konya on our last day together he began by popping a large pepper in his mouth. I did the same, felt my tongue explode, and poured a whole glass of water in my mouth to put out the fire. Across the table, my driver was chewing contentedly, looking me straight in the eye, and smiling.

In those days Jordan controlled both Transjordan and the West Bank. Since I was living in Jordan, it was easy to visit any of the West Bank areas, and the Old City of Jerusalem itself was a daily walk. I had been a dozen times to Bethlehem with colleagues or visitors. I had been a dozen times to the site where Jesus was born according to parable, but never to Nazareth, where he was born according to history. I had not planned it that way, but that was how it happened. I had been everywhere except Galilee. I had seen everything except Nazareth.

In those years tourists were allowed to cross Mandelbaum Gate in only one direction, leaving Jordan for Israel or Israel for Jordan. They could not return. But certain foreign residents in Jordan, for example, ordained ministers or field archeologists, were allowed double crossings, over to Israel and back, but not too often and only on carefully prearranged and preauthorized dates. It was also imperative never to get an Israeli stamp on your passport, or entry into countries such as Syria or Iraq would thereafter be denied. An Irish citizen like myself carried two passports, one stamped "Valid for travel to Israel" and another for everywhere else, especially for Arab countries hostile to Israel.

To make a double crossing you had to get permission well in advance from both Jordan and Israel (yes, contact with Israel was possible even from the Jordanian side), present yourself at checkpoints on either side of no-man's-land (euphemistically, Mandelbaum Gate) at the designated hour going and returning, remember carefully which pocket you had which passport in, and get the right stamps in the right places. To avoid pushing my luck, I had planned three double crossings during my time in Jordan, one for the south, one for the middle, and one for the north of Israel. I had no trouble with the first two in 1966, and I was holding the most important northern one for the first two weeks of June 1967. I had permission to cross on June 1 and return on June 14. I was not where I expected to be that June 4.

To be elsewhere than expected started far back at the beginning. I should have been born in Galway, but started life in Tipperary instead. In 1934 my parents were living in Portumna, County Galway, where my father was working in the Hibernian Bank. The nearest town with maternity facilities was Nenagh, across the Shannon, in County Tipperary. I am grateful to them for the decision to go there, since it gave me the very appropriate title for this book. *A Long Way from Galway* would not have worked quite as well. Being where I had not expected to be or becoming what I had not planned to become is now a pattern of life I have come to recognize and accept. Again and again, things started out to be this and ended up by being that, started to go here and went instead there. Ireland to America, monastery to university, priesthood to marriage, academic scholarship to public discourse.

Those who planned my life thought, as I did, that they could make me both monastic priest and seminary teacher. They found, as I did, that it would have to be one or the other. Every institution, even a church, needs research and development, marketing and sales, promotion and public relations. Every institution, especially a church, needs to know which is which, who is where, and when it is doing one and not the other. Religion, Christianity, and Roman Catholicism were my life, but I worked at reformation and reconstruction as both were going out of fashion, having been in for but a fleeting moment. Eventually, after nineteen years, I left the monastic priesthood to get married. Even if I could have stayed and married, I would not have done so. By then the more profound conflict was not between my vow of celibacy and marriage, but between my vow of obedience and scholarship. The truth may make you free, but it may also make a lot of other people extremely annoyed. Margaret and I were married. We swore ourselves to one another till death do us part. Death did.

Monastic priest to academic scholar and then academic scholar to public intellectual. We scholars speak to one another in a language dense with technical terms and bristling with footnotes, references, disagreements, and qualifications. That keeps the amateurs away, leaves us free to choose our subject without external interference (unless we need grants), permits us to say more and more about less and less, and tempts us to carve out our own tiny kingdom where nobody else may safely enter. For religious scholars that system has special advantages. It protects us from thinking anything relevant enough for public controversy and, if we think up something like that, from formulating it in a way that any outsider could understand. If one is, as I am, an expert on the historical Jesus and earliest Christianity, it may be wiser to avoid conflicts between faith and history in one's own heart, one's own church, and one's own public community. Stay peacefully academic and let the ivy round your walls curl comfortably around your conscience.

An academic scholar is not the same as a public intellectual. It is quite possible to be either one or the other. It is also possible to be both. A public intellectual in religion is, however, a rather special case, an endangered species from the past and an uninvented species in the present. We have high-profile religious hucksters and frauds, cheats and criminals, pederasts and rapists. We have high-profile religious activists and ministers, pacifists and preachers, saints and martyrs. But public religious intellectuals are much harder to find. They live publicly and openly where reason intersects with revelation and history intersects with faith, and they answer equally and honestly to both those imperious demands. Their job is to think out loud about religion in general or Christianity, for example, in particular, and to so do within public discourse and not just denominational confession. For me that role means speaking as publicly as possible about the Gospels and the New Testament, the historical Jesus and earliest Christianity, in language true to both their ancient first-century situations and their modern twenty-first-century continuations. And "as publicly as possible" is not a question of volume, but of clarity, not of spin and hype, but of honesty and accuracy. The purpose is not indoctrination, but education. And education means awareness of all your options. The hope is for debate without caricature and argument without derision.

After joining DePaul University in 1969, I spent my first twenty years teaching required courses to undergraduate students and in writing scholarly books for academic audiences. I loved that combination and neither sought nor wanted any other situation. I was one of the very, very few scholars in the whole world whose professional life was focused exclusively on the historical Jesus, that is, on the reconstruction of Jesus' life as lived in the first century's first quarter, long before it was creatively recorded and necessarily reinterpreted by the Gospel writers in that century's last quarter. It was not unusual for experts on early Christianity to write a book about Jesus, but it was very unusual, then or even now, to devote one's entire professional career to that subject. I did not understand that strange omission until the 1990s, when the Jesus Wars made it clear that historical Jesus research is open-heart surgery on Christianity, and maybe also on civilization itself. You may have a quieter life on some other topic, some lesser subject, like Paul, for instance. In any case, with my academic colleagues as primary readers, I was far, far away from any wider audience, any public conversation, any general lay interest.

I was still imagining an exclusively academic reception committee when I wrote *The Historical Jesus: The Life of a Mediterranean Jewish Peasant* in 1991, but that was when everything changed. Peter Steinfels, religion reporter for the *New York Times,* was fascinated by two graduates of Rome's Pontifical Biblical Institute who were professors at Catholic universities, one a priest and one an ex-priest, with two books on the historical Jesus coming out that same fall. He put the story on the front page of the paper for Monday, December 23, and it appeared not only there, but in papers using the New York Times Wire Service and abroad in the *International Herald Tribune.*

With that public launch my book stayed for six months among the top ten religion best-sellers in *Publishers Weekly,* and when it peaked there as number one in June 1992, I thought I now had my fleeting minutes of instant fame. But something was happening out there that I still cannot fully understand. There were very many Christians, apparently, for whom nineteenth-century rationalism had broken into secularism and fundamentalism, twin extremes that richly deserved each other. Those centrist Christians demanded both reason *and* revelation, both history *and* faith, both mind *and* heart. They knew that history was not just history anymore and that Jesus research opened up all the theological and religious questions worth asking. It also, in fact, appealed to ex-Christians, para-Christians, and post-Christians.

Far from sputtering out like another passing fad, interest in the historical Jesus grew steadily as the 1990s progressed. The 1996 Easter covers of *Time, Newsweek,* and *U.S. News & World Report* were on the historical Jesus, as were television programs like A&E's *Mysteries of the Bible,* PBS's *Frontline* "From Jesus to Christ," and ABC's news special with Peter Jennings. I was involved in all those endeavors and tried to stay both on the cutting edge of that scholarly research and on the leading edge of its popular interpretation. I wrote about one million words on the historical Jesus in the 1990s, had three more books on that *Publishers Weekly* list for several months apiece, and found myself translated into nine foreign languages including Korean, Chinese, and Japanese. All of which gave me a swelled head? That is probably for others to judge, but I do not think so. First, I do not take myself too seriously—my subject yes, passionately, myself no, generally. Second, sometimes I felt like a cause of that interest, but mostly I felt like its effect, and in any case, I had learned from windsurfing that you are never totally in control, that all is balance and cooperation, and that you ride the wind and the wave you are given ("Christianity and the Art of Windsurfing"?). Third, and this above everything else, I was moved and humbled by invitations from parishes to come not just for one-hour celebrity lectures, but for full-weekend seminars, Friday night and all day Saturday to Sunday morning. Many if not most such discussions were also preceded by group study of the books involved.

There is, however, a somewhat tired jibe that scholars often make about others' reconstructions of the historical Jesus (not about their own, of course). That is not Jesus, they say; it is simply your own face at the bottom of a deep well. It comes to me in this customized version: You see Jesus as an exploited and oppressed first-century Jewish peasant because you are thinking about, sympathizing with, and projecting backward upon him and his companions the fate of nineteenth-century Irish peasants.

It is quite true that I wanted to introduce forcibly the question of social class into discussions of the historical Jesus, to distinguish how differently things looked from the bottom up than from the top down. If you consider those perspectives equal in their views or irrelevant in their differences, compare these two sets of statistics. One set: When the *Titanic* sank on April 15, 1912, 32 percent of the passengers lived and 68 percent died. Another set: When the *Titanic* sank on April 15, 1912, 94 percent of the first-cabin women and children lived and 47 percent of the steerage women and children died. Gender mattered, but so did class. Yes, I wanted to know if Jesus was an illiterate peasant (unlike me) or a learned scholar (like me), because social class matters for point of view and awareness of injustice. If he came from a peasant hamlet, he was probably a peasant laborer. Although, of course, if it looks like a duck, walks like a duck, and quacks like a duck, it might be a camel in disguise.

That aside, it is easy enough to rebut the face-in-the-well dismissal. Are you yourself not involved in some similar process in another deep well? Or, better: Have you ever seen anything down a deep well? Or, best: If you did, is not the water changed by the face and the face by the water? Is not such interaction, inevitable in *any* historical reconstruction of *any* historical figure, profoundly interesting for either good (like Jesus) or evil (like Hitler)?

That last response raised for me the question addressed in this present book. Aside from the self-serving function of that deep-well crack when aimed only at others, it still has a valid core that applies to us all. For me it goes like this. How has my own life influenced my understanding of the historical Jesus? How does my role as a temporary background bit player clarify or distort my view of the leading character in a very long running and still ongoing religious drama? You will notice immediately my somewhat vertiginous situation. I have to reconstruct my own life, reconstruct that of Jesus, and ponder the interaction (another reconstruction?) between them. And that is the purpose of this book.

How does the general heritage that I carry as part of a first postcolonial generation, and indeed of a European colony within Europe, qualify my vision of the first-century Jewish homeland still under imperial control? Did I decide that Jesus disliked the Roman Empire because I disliked the British Empire? Was it truly that last-century Irish peasantry, destroyed by Penal Laws and Poor Laws, potato blight and famine disease, nonviolent legal resistance and violent armed revolt, that shaped my view of the first-century Jewish peasantry, also swept by catastrophe and cataclysm, also saved by death and Diaspora?

Apart from that historical baggage, what of more individual and personal influences? I am an ex-monk and an ex-priest— does that prejudice me against religion in general or Roman Catholicism in particular? Against the priesthood, the Bible, religious denomination, or denominational authority? Maybe I just need the historical Jesus to attack Christianity and fill a vacuum left over from all that ex-"hood"? Was I fleetingly hurt or permanently angry from that transition? Maybe you should know this right away: My passport, still Irish after half a century in this country, gives my first name as John and my middle names as Michael Edmund. When you entered a traditional religious order, your secular identity disappeared and you were renamed (like those people in the Bible), so, in 1950, I became Brother Dominic, O.S.M. When I left nineteen years later, I kept that name: John I was, Dominic I became, John Dominic I am. Hurt, anger, hate? I do not think so, because I cannot find those feelings anywhere in my heart, but I will let you judge for yourself.

This book is about a series of transitions, from Ireland to America, from priesthood to marriage, from monastery to university, and from academic scholar to public intellectual. It is especially about the transition from a very traditional Roman Catholic faith, accepted fully and internalized completely but undiscussed, uninvestigated, and uncriticized, at the start of this century to a self-conscious and self-critical Roman Catholic faith for the start of the next one (Rome was not rebuilt in a day). It is most especially about the continuity across all those transitions and across that last one in particular. That is what I find most deeply operative in my life—not a series of dislocating and discontinuous transitions but, no matter how difficult they were at the time, beneath them an abiding serenity, a continuity as a person, a scholar, and a Christian. Throughout this book, therefore, I am constantly looking in two directions at the same time, at the reconstruction of my own life and my reconstruction of the historical Jesus. For example, even when I talk about my own parents and my own earliest recoverable years, I will be asking simultaneously what effect those events and memories have on how I see the parents of Jesus and the infancy of Jesus.

I did not, as I said, set out to be a scholar, let alone a biblical scholar. It was thrust upon me by others, but I accepted the role with enthusiasm. So also with the role of public religious intellectual. I did not plot it, expect it, or set out to acquire it. It too came from others, but it too was accepted with enthusiasm. Since it was neither my idea nor my plan, I have been quite comfortable with the controversies accompanying that role. Actually, the eye of the storm is a rather peaceful place to be. The trick is to stay in the eye.

Reactions to me are necessarily diverse. One letter says: "If Hell were not already created, it should be invented just for you." That does not scare me, and besides, the postmark is far away. But another prays: "Thank you God for Dominic. We really need him." That does scare me, a little. Reviews can be just as divergent. One in the *Los Angeles Times* Sunday book review describes my latest book, *The Birth of Christianity,* as "a self-absorbed academic exercise, the product of a cramped and airless world in which theories feed on theories, scholars are endlessly commenting on the views of other scholars, and words intertwine without a footing in historical reality." But another, in the *St. Louis Post Dispatch,* concludes that "Crossan can be credited with the

exceptional command of the tools of a first-rate public intellectual." I understand those disagreements. In the last thirty years I
have written over fifteen books about the historical Jesus. All that
probing and dissecting, excising and reconstructing is, as I mentioned earlier, a little like conducting open-heart surgery on
Christianity, and responses differ between those who consider it
medical malpractice and those who consider it overdue remedy.
For me it is surely time, especially as we enter a new millennium,
to distinguish in public debate between spirituality and sentimentality, between religion and Prozac, between baptism and
lobotomy. Besides, if people have had enough chicken soup for
the soul, how about some Irish stew for the mind?

After a decade of interviews in newspapers and magazines, discussions on radio and television, lectures in parishes and seminaries, colleges and universities, I now recognize a group in this
country who claim a center of the road between the extremes of
secularism and fundamentalism. They are also dissatisfied, disappointed, or even disgusted with classical Christianity and their
denominational tradition. They hold on with anger or leave with
nostalgia, but are not happy with either decision. They do not
want to invent or join a new age, but to reclaim and redeem an
ancient one. They do not want to settle for a generic-brand religion, but to rediscover their own specific and particular roots.
But they know now that those roots must be in a renewed
Christianity whose validity does not reject every other religion's
integrity, a renewed Christianity that has purged itself of rationalism, fundamentalism, and literalism, whether of book, tradition,
community, or leader. I did not set out to speak to those people,
because I did not know they existed until about 80 percent of my
mail told me they did. That, once again, was not where I expected to be, but happily am.

I started this Prologue at home, but held this last paragraph
until today. The irony of living in Jerusalem from 1965 to 1967
and traveling all over the Middle East, but never visiting Galilee
and Nazareth, was compounded by writing and lecturing on the
historical Jesus from 1967 to 1999, but still never visiting Galilee
and Nazareth. Today is exactly thirty-two years to the month, the

week, and possibly even the day when I had expected to be in Nazareth for the first time. I deliberately finish this Prologue in this place and on this date to emphasize one point. I have, again and again, ended up where I did not plan or expect to be, but if I had to do it all over again, I would do it all over again. But it is still a long way from Tipperary.

Nazareth, Israel

June 11, 1999

A LONG WAY FROM TIPPERARY

CHAPTER 1

The Most Exciting Game Around

In 1944 I turned ten and never again spent a full year at home. After that it was boarding school, monastery, America. In questions during lectures and interviews with journalists I am never asked about that boarding school, but often about that monastery. That is a first mistake. And I am seldom asked why I became a monk, but rather why I became a priest. That is a second mistake. But that question comes up at some point in almost every interview: Why did I become a priest? It is a question to me at sixty-five about me at fifteen, but also a question from the American late 1990s about the Irish late 1940s. And quite often the question is prompted by one or more of these three inquiries.

Was I particularly pious as a boy? No, at least not in any sense of that word I knew then or have come to recognize since. I did become an altar boy at the early age of eight, but I recall that choice primarily in response, as it were, to a series of dares. Could I learn by heart the Mass responses in a Latin I did not then understand? Could I handle the thurible at Benediction so that the priest got the incense on the hot coals and I did not get the hot coals on him? Could I light the tall (very tall) candles on the high (very high) altar by stretching the lit taper one-handed above my head to connect with a wick I could not see, preferably without setting any altar linens on fire in the process? It may have been piety, but I thought of it as fun, as adventure, as seeing the inside of something mysterious, and maybe even, at eight and after, as a sort of instant adulthood.

Were my parents influential or even forceful about my becoming a priest? Wasn't it an honor to have a priest in the family, especially for an Irish mother? No doubt, but before I left for America, my father said, "Just remember, if this doesn't work out, your home is here and you can always come back home." By fifteen I had already lived away from home for four years at boarding school, and my family accepted the independence earned by that experience. I made up my own mind about the priesthood, and they supported me with a respect I did not appreciate fully until nineteen years later.

Were the priests who ran my boarding secondary school significant as mentors or models for my decision? That question, posed by a Canadian journalist with an Irish Catholic background, stopped me cold for a moment. I realized, only at his question, that I had never, ever, considered becoming a diocesan priest like my teachers at St. Eunan's College in Letterkenny, County Donegal. I both admired and respected them as good teachers and fair disciplinarians, but I never imagined myself like them either as parish pastor or schoolteacher. It was somewhat of a shock to realize, and only from that prompting question fifty years later, that becoming their type of priest had never entered my mind for a moment. Yet those were the priests I knew best over seven years from altar boy to schoolboy.

Why I became a priest is actually the wrong question, although I only realized that after I tried to answer it. What I wanted was to enter a monastery and become a missionary, to become a monastic (priest) and a missionary (priest). Monastery and mission were in the immediate foreground, with ordination and priesthood as necessary and accepted concomitants. The diocesan priesthood that I knew best from everyday experience was never of any interest to me. Not piety but adventure was what fired my imagination at fifteen years of age. If somebody had told me that I was giving up my life to God, and I don't remember anyone ever doing so, I would not have been impressed. If somebody had told me that I was giving up my life for others, and I don't remember anyone ever doing so, I would not have been impressed. What impressed me was that monastic life meant challenge, that foreign mission meant adventure, and that God clearly had the best game in town, the most exciting game around (still does fifty years later, though the field has changed). That was what attracted me, moth to flame.

It might be more seemly to invoke personal piety, spiritual commitment, or religious dedication as driving forces in that long-ago teenage determination. But my clearest recollection suggests none of those emphases. The attraction was that of adventure, divine adventure to be sure, but adventure first and foremost. The diocesan or parish priesthood was not an option because that was never my idea of adventure. And, already from long before, it was as the lure and challenge of adventure that I had begun to see life itself.

In spring 1998, American public television aired a program, "From Jesus to Christ: The First Christians," and I was one of a dozen scholars interviewed and identified on camera. A priest from California wrote me a few days later with this question: "I am very curious to know if you and I were in the sixth class with Brother Grennan in 1943–44 in Naas, County Kildare. Was your father Dan, who worked in the Hibernian Bank with my father Stephen? If it's the same, you have a brother Dan and a sister Aileen." I replied affirmatively, and we continued reminiscences by e-mail. What struck me was how much he remembered and how little I did about our years together in primary school during the late 1930s and early 1940s. He recalled the names of each year's teacher complete with details about his teaching abilities and caning proclivities. "Kindergarten, first, and second grade were in one room," he recalled. "Everything was in Gaelic, even English as far as possible." That I had totally forgotten. In fact, I had only a few random and fragmentary memories of *any* classes in the Christian Brothers' school at Naas.

I knew that I had skipped the second and fifth years, but such jumps were not at all unusual in the Naas system. I could hardly forget that, since I was thereafter two years younger than my classmates for the next dozen years (for example, secondary school completed by sixteen, ordained by twenty-three, doctorate by twenty-five). But little else comes back even when prompted by my friend's e-mail details. And I wonder about those silences in memory.

I grew up in Naas, with memories of other locations lost to earliest infancy. I left Naas one day in the summer of 1945, and all contact was broken until that letter over fifty years later. My classmate, on the other hand, had gone on to secondary school at nearby Clongowes Wood College, the Jesuit school made (in)famous by James Joyce's *Portrait of the Artist as a Young Man*. He had also kept in fairly close contact with his Naas roots and promised, in closing, "I will visit next year and advise with the latest."

Maybe, I thought, that was the explanation. My complete break at the end of primary school, my relocation from Naas, County Kildare, to Ballybofey, County Donegal, had simply obliterated memories that his continued contact had kept fresh and vibrant. The only problem is that I have lots of other memories from those primary-school years in Naas. I have, for example, no difficulty recalling running full speed after a golf ball down the stairs and not stopping before hitting the inside of the front door. The door had a flapped slit for a letter box and two blunt screws protruding over an inch on either side. I took the left one just below my right eye and still have a slight indentation there to aid my memory. A half inch higher might have radically changed my life. In those days a one-eyed applicant would not have made it into the priesthood.

That, of course, is a special memory. I have lots like it from my primary-school years, but not about primary school itself. I recall only what interested me, and the classroom did not do so. No doubt it was adequate, maybe even excellent, just not memorable, at least not for me. What, then, from those years was memorable?

We are back with adventure of two kinds, outside and inside, summer and winter, fields and libraries, woods and books (movies too), minor personal adventures and major vicarious ones.

Between our home and Naas itself were some scattered houses, one large development, and a high railway bridge. (The bridge is gone now, but from its top I could see the town hall clock, and if it was after six-twenty, I would be late as altar boy for the six-thirty Mass.) That slight separation from the town meant that near our house was a large wood, a disused quarry, fields with sheep and cattle, and, finally, the Naas racecourse. What I remember from those years is not education but adventure, that is, the regular endangerment of limb, if not life, in what we described to our parents as "playing outside." For my sister, myself, and other friends from the terrace, play meant this. We waited in the wood until the crows settled down at sunset, then climbed way up into their trees and sent the whole rookery cawing back into the air. We went around the quarry rim and found ever new places to climb down to the bottom. Some were relatively safe, some were much more interesting. We raced across the fields to see if a bull would bother to chase us and, if it did, whether we could make the hedge in time. We watched the butcher herd sheep into the pen and grab one by its back legs to drag it out to his cart. It looked so easy. We did the same when he was gone, and I got kicked hard against the rails. It was not as easy as it looked. But especially we "went to the races" on the one Saturday a month when they were held.

The racecourse was set amid open fields and was only separated from them by an ordinary low wooden fence. We could stand in the field right at that fence. And, best of all, those races had jumps. Once we reached our position, we had to stand without movement lest we frighten the horses. But proximity and immobility only added to the excitement. So we stood at the jumps and waited for falls. If you see races on television or even from distant grandstands, you do not know how it feels when the whole earth shakes with a dozen horses pounding past only a few feet in front of you. The jump where we stood was a high flat hedge with a water-filled ditch on the other side. A horse could falter in midair when it finally glimpsed the water in clearing the fence. If it faltered, it fell. And if it fell, it was quite likely that it would bring down a few others as well. So we waited and hoped. We could hear the leather strain, almost smell the sweat, see the whips strike, almost touch the horses—and we could feel the earth tremble. In our last years at Naas, my father sometimes took me with him up into the grandstands (as assistant bank manager he got two free tickets). I could never tell him that it was boring up there, that even the use of his binoculars could not compensate for feeling the ground shake beneath your feet.

We could play outside in the late light of summer until bedtime, but the early dark of winter finished outside activities by five at the very latest. And if outside meant fields, inside meant books. There were, of course, comics, but at threepence apiece the newer "Beano" and "Dandy" or the older "Boys Own Paper" were not good investments for how fast they could be finished. Then I discovered libraries, or more accurately, I discovered my father using libraries. Libraries, books, and reading were about imitation before they were about entertainment, let alone education. They were about my father rather than about my teachers. At what age?

One of the two or three earliest memories I can date precisely is about a library. My father had driven over to nearby Newbridge, and I am sitting with the rest of the family outside its library awaiting his return. I recall a white building with black letters located close to the Liffey bridge that gave the town its name. The major question is why on earth I should remember that event in any case. And here the date may be significant because it was, at the latest, September 1939. When World War II broke out in Europe, Ireland rationed petrol on a need-for-use basis. My father jacked up our Vauxhall car in the garage behind the terrace, took off the wheels, let the axles down on four butter boxes, and went out to buy a bike. That Newbridge trip had to be, at the latest, before the start of the war, when I was about five and a half years old. Maybe, and it can only be a maybe, my father went there that day to return books for the last time. Maybe, and it can only be a maybe, I recall that particular drive because it was suffused with the crisis atmosphere of the war's inception. But how awful to remember others' carnage only as one's own inconvenience.

I have many more memories of the Naas library but cannot date them any more exactly than before I was eleven. It did not have a full building to itself like the one in Newbridge, but was located upstairs in the town hall. I went there with my father, but since imitation ruled, I wanted as soon as possible to get books from adult sections like he did rather than from those sections reserved for children. The *Tarzan* books by Edgar Rice Burroughs and the *Saint* books by Leslie Charteris are what I remember best. My father read mostly history, biography, and discovery, but especially as those were subsumed under the guise of travel, adventure, or exploration. A factual account of Howard Carter's discovering Tutankhamen's tomb and a fictional tale of an archeologist incurring a mummy's curse were both on the same shelf. A typical example from the four-sided swivel bookcase in the corner of our living room was H. Rider Haggard's *King Solomon's Mines*. After we left Naas and I was on Christmas holidays from boarding school, my diary has these brief reports: "Got *The Sky Hawk* in bookcase and read it all day. Finished it in bed" (Tuesday, January 13, 1948) and "Read *The Flying Dutchman* today. Life of Fokker" (Wednesday, January 14, 1948). I was then almost fourteen, and those titles were exactly what my father would have read and exactly what I would have chosen to imitate him.

Reading in bed was a long-established protective device. During the long winter evenings in Naas, the fire-warmed living room was the only place to be. But if I had planned to read and neighbors dropped in to talk to my parents, I was trapped. I was expected to stay in the living room, listen quietly to the conversation, and speak politely only when addressed. If I had a particularly good book and didn't want to chance interruption, there was only one solution. Immediately after tea, by seven at the latest and before any knocks on the front door, I disappeared upstairs to bed. It was cold in the rest of the house, but my mother wrapped our pajamas around hot-water bottles (crockery, not rubber!) by four in the afternoon, and with a little practice, it was possible to get fully undressed at night (and dressed in the morning) while totally under the bedclothes. Then I could turn on the bed light and read without any chance of disturbance. That was how, one night when I was about eight, I finished Jules Verne's

Twenty Thousand Leagues Under the Sea. Under the sea and under the bedclothes.

Fields and woods outside in the summers, libraries and books inside in the winters. What I was doing then was simply having fun. What I see now is exploration and adventure, outside my house or inside my mind. I wonder which of those exercises was more important for my later life as a scholar. Was it more important to be early literate or early fearless? What do you learn from trying to climb as high as you can in the tallest tree you can find? You dare not slip going up, and when you have reached the top, you still have to come down backward blind. And even though you go exploring trees together, you climb your own tree alone. In any case, my memory recalls both reading books and climbing trees with equal insistence and forgets so much else as if it had never happened.

Thinking about why I didn't become a diocesan priest helps me remember about adventure, and thinking about why I didn't become a banker helps to confirm it. I spent my youth in adoring imitation of my father. He was a bank official, yet I never, ever, considered becoming a banker just like him.

There were, in those days and before recent amalgamations, about nine main banks in Ireland, most with head offices in Dublin and branches throughout the country. Even a small town could have a few such competing offices. Banking was a very good job, permanent, pensionable, and well unionized. You began not by earning a university degree, but by taking each bank's competitive exam for the number of openings available that year. When you had worked up through the ranks of clerk, cashier, or accountant, you became a manager, and then the size and importance of the branch's location determined later promotional steps. A bank manager in a small Irish town had high social status, but not a high individual salary. A manager knew the exact financial standing of everyone around, decided loans to people far wealthier than himself, and lived in a big house next to or above the bank on the town's main street. My father never wanted a city branch in Dublin, because then you lost your free house, got a house allowance instead, and had to pay income tax on it. And you could no longer just walk downstairs to work.

I knew a fair amount about banking, especially after my father became a manager and we lived above the bank in Ballybofey. I was often in there when it was not open to customers, but operational behind the scenes. Evenings I learned to type in my father's private office and learned to hunt and peck so fast that I have never since progressed beyond that limited capacity. Mornings I watched the porter open the walk-in safe and bring the huge ledgers to their daily place on the officials' high sloped desks. That was before accounts were kept mechanically, let alone electronically, and those ledgers, three feet high, a foot and a half wide, and a foot thick, must have weighed about fifty pounds. One day, with the bank closed for the semiannual balance and everyone there until it was done, my father had me write up one of those ledgers. It was not for current accounts, of course, but for recording checks before they were forwarded to their home banks for clearance. Later that year, an inspector noticed the unfamiliar handwriting and commented to my father wryly, "Your son, I presume." Banking was always interesting, sometimes fascinating, but never an exciting enough lure for a lifetime.

The bank was flanked by a left door into the house and a right door into the office. We lived behind (kitchen, pantry, larder) and above it (dining, living, bath, and bedrooms) with an internal-access door from bank to house. We children were not supposed to enter the house through the bank during customer hours, but to use our own door, which meant knocking, waiting, and being patient. But if you ran through the bank very fast, Daddy might be inside his private office, and what he didn't know wouldn't hurt you. A beautiful mahogany counter ran the full length of the bank, separating customers from officials at writing-level height and allowing passage through a hinged countertop and swing-in door at the right end. Those were usually left open since my father's private office was outside the counter. As I recall one particular day when I was twelve years of age, the pain is still sharp in my memory. I am running full speed through the bank into the house, but this day the door is open while the counter flap is down. There is space above it, space below it, and at eye level it merges completely with the wood paneling behind it. I took it full force across my forehead, went down hard, and the rest is completely lost. (I begin to see a pattern here—run as hard as possible against an immovable object, take it in the face, and see what happens.)

Maybe that concussion explains my disinterest in banking, but I doubt it. My father never hinted or suggested and probably never hoped or expected that I would follow him in that direction. Neither did he ever talk against banking, and my younger brother followed him both in name, Daniel Joseph, Jr., and in profession (but in the Northern, not the Hibernian, Bank). My father enjoyed his job, appreciated its security and status, but knew my imitation of him worked at a deeper level. Here is how it operated, apart from those libraries and books already mentioned.

We went walking together. During the war, when I was about nine or ten and our car was up on those butter boxes in the garage, my father and I went for long walks. He recited poetry to me, and I memorized and recited it back. His taste in poetry, like his taste in prose, was more functional than classical. The poems were about lives more interesting than our own, not about bankers in business suits, but about exciting adventures in faraway places. They were not the British poems of romanticism or the Irish poems of rebellion, but poems of storied adventure in other times and faraway places. It was, in other words, different from school stuff and did not feel like homework disguised as conversation.

The poets were not Shelley and Wordsworth, but Robert Service and John Masefield. Service was easier for me than Masefield because I had the development of the story as well as the rhythm of the lines to help. No problem, then, with Service's "The Shooting of Dan McGrew," in which a bunch of the boys were whooping it up in a Malamute saloon, the kid that handled the music box was hitting a ragtime tune, and back of the bar, in a solo game, sat Dangerous Dan McGrew, while watching his luck was his light-of-love, the lady that's known as Lou. More problem with Masefield's name-now-gone poem about a quinquereme from Nineveh and sunny lands of azure (or was it Asia?) carrying ivory, apes, and peacocks, and sweet white wine.

It is, above all the others, Rudyard Kipling's homage from the cockney archetype Tommy Atkins to the Indian water carrier Gunga Din that stays in my mind to this day, most verses more or less intact:

> *When the sweating troop train lay*
> *In a siding all the day,*
> *And the heat would make your blooming eyebrows crawl . . .*
> *I shan't forget the night*
> *When I fell behind the fight*
> *With a bullet where my belt-plate should have been. . . .*
> *He pillowed up my head,*
> *And he plugged me where I bled,*
> *And gave me half a pint of water green. . . .*
> *He carried me away*
> *To where the dooly [spelling? meaning?] lay*
> *And a bullet came and plugged the beggar clean. . . .*
> *You're a better man than I am, Gunga Din.*

I can still remember most of it even now, although I hear one line rather differently today: "And for all his dirty hide / he was white, clear white, inside." I know that poem because it was given to me as a challenge. I got sixpence for learning it all by heart from my father's recitation by the end of our two-hour walk. Over fifty years later not only do the words come back, but with them the footpath along the north side of the Naas-Dublin road, the main houses along it on either side, my father's step, my father's stick, and my father's voice. Gunga Din, my madeleine. The sixpenny piece is gone into the new Irish coinage, the Dublin road is gone into the new Naas bypass, and my father is gone into loving memory. But those walks and those poems I remember, sharp and hard and clear, and I recall not a bit of what I was doing in school at the same time.

We went shooting together. Not really hunting, it was more like .22 target practice at unfortunate rabbits, crows, and pigeons. I was not, of course, supposed to use the .22 by myself and certainly not anywhere near the house, let alone the town. Here are two diary entries from the Easter holidays of 1948, when I was home from boarding school, after our move from Naas to Ballybofey. This one, for Monday, March 29, was all right: "Shot a few crows from the sliding roof of the car." This one, for Thursday, April 1, was decidedly not: "Shot and wounded two homing pigeons breaking one of their wings. Dickens of a row. How was I too know they were homing pigeons. That shook them anyway." In the former case I was out with my father. In the latter case I had taken the gun, without permission, into our backyard, within the town, and hit a neighbor's pigeons resting in the big tree behind our house. I love that entry, with its minor misspelling and terminal defiance for the alleged pigeons.

We went driving together. When I was fourteen and fifteen, the deal was this. If I learned fully how the car's engine worked, my father would teach me to drive (a new black Vauxhall from the mid-1940s, which replaced the older maroon one from the early 1930s). I did, he did, and I was thereafter allowed to drive as long as he was with me. At fifteen, away at school, I sent off an application for a driver's license. There was no test, and it cost me only a small fee (I recall it as ten shillings) and a big lie. I wrote my birth date as 1933 rather than 1934 to bring me up to the mandatory age of sixteen. I also took the number on the car's key and wrote Vauxhall for a copy. I came home for the Christmas holidays of 1949 with my own key and my own license and mentioned casually that I was thinking of having lunch with a school friend who lived about twenty miles away in Donegal town.

"When were you thinking of doing that?"

"Next Monday or Tuesday."

"How were you thinking of getting there?"

"I was thinking of taking the car."

So, complete with "legal" license, I got to drive for the first time all by myself. It was, as I knew and he knew and each of us knew that the other knew, calculated from the start for just that single result. I returned home around five o'clock and saw my father just outside town, walking along the Donegal road to meet me.

His days were spent effectively and competently in the business of the bank, but that was not what fired his imagination, and what fired his imagination sparked mine as well. That was where the imitation lay, from poems heard, from books read, from things done, and, oh, I almost forgot, from movies seen together. Two of the earliest I can remember were *The Four Feathers* and *For Whom the Bell Tolls*. (Years later I saw that last film again and something was missing. Ingrid Bergman still wanted to know where the noses go, but a scene in which men had to run a gauntlet of wooden flails was cut.) What my memory *does not* recall and what my memory *does* recall from those primary-school years in Naas are equally important. They show that my focus was not on academics but on adventure, in local exploration and in faraway imagination, and on paternal imitation. The moment of transition in 1945, when I left Naas for Ballybofey, primary school for secondary school, and home for boarding school, confirms that emphasis.

In that year my father was called for an interview at the bank's Dublin headquarters, and we knew that meant promotion to his own branch. ("We" means my elder sister and myself. Daniel was four years younger, and we neither requested nor recorded his views on such important matters.) What interested us was this: Where would the new branch be? It could be anywhere in the republic, but anywhere had to be somewhere. So where would it be? As soon as Dad knew, he was to phone the bank in Naas, and they would send a messenger to our house. I remember the day but not the date. It was Holy Thursday, just before Easter, and I was walking home from altar-boy duties at the church. The porter from the bank passed me on his bicycle and announced, "Your Da is manager in Ballybofey, County Donegal." By the time I got home, he had already arrived with the message, but there was not much more information. What I recall very clearly is my sister and I on the floor in our living room with a big atlas opened before us. Where was Ballybofey, and above all else, was it on the coast, where we could swim in the ocean every day that summer?

Naas itself was not far from the coast, but Dublin city stood in the way east to the Irish Sea. Ballybofey, we found, was not on the coast. It was on the main road from Donegal town to Letterkenny, but as we consoled ourselves illogically, it was just about equal distance from most points on the westward circle of Donegal's Atlantic coast. Swimming in the ocean was still possible, so the whole promotion was not a complete loss.

One aspect of that scene still strikes me as strange fifty years later. Contemporary parents often find that relocation reduces their children to tears, reproaches, and controlled rebellion. They dislike leaving their known environments, losing their close friends, and changing schools. Such forms of resistance were not part of our time and place. But neither were we so embedded in parental life that relocation was accepted passively. We had our own very definite response to that move, and I still recall it quite clearly. We found the process exciting, the change exhilarating, and the future opening up to difference and surprise. I probably did miss my friends in that relocation, but what I recall now is not the sorrow of parting, but the excitement of moving. Indeed, what I remember about those friends is our adventures together, and those prepared me to see relocation as but another, bigger adventure. That excitement overrode departures and farewells.

In autumn 1945, without either of us having much say in the matter, my paternal imitation program reached a major milestone. I started secondary school at St. Eunan's College, Letterkenny, County Donegal, as my father had done a quarter of a century earlier.

His parents, John Crossan and Rose McLaughlin, were living then in the townland of Lisnenan, just outside Letterkenny. My father was their first child, and they had two other children, Mary and Annie (Nan). Their 1903 marriage certificate gives the groom's "rank or profession" as "attendant in Letterkenny asylum" and, a year later, in 1904, my father's birth certificate lists the "rank or profession of father" as "asylum attendant." My father's 1929 marriage certificate records the "rank or profession of father" as "farmer." In those days, apparently, individuals did not have mothers and brides did not have ranks or professions. That sequence, attendant to farmer, is also the proper order of emphasis for sustenance and support. The farm would not have been enough. It was a very, very small one, but I have vivid memories of it from the late 1930s and early 1940s.

The house was a single-story, whitewashed cottage separated from the connected chicken shed and donkey stable by an intervening wall, but with continuous outside walls around and continuous thatched roof above. There was no running water inside, but a well with an iron pump at the front of the house and an outhouse toilet at the back of the house. The heating of water and cooking of food were done over a turf fire with cast-iron pot, pan, and kettle hanging from a single arm which swung over or away from the fire on a pivoting upright attached to the right side of the open hearth. (Irish brown bread made in such a pot gets a quarter-inch crust all around it, and you won't get that any other way.) There were no pigs, sheep, or cattle, no crops in the two small hilly fields, but a lot of chickens, one goat, and one donkey (no horse), which drew the trap for transportation. Its fascinating otherness made it a place whose every inch I still recall when elsewhere towns and even cities are gone forever from memory. My Auntie Nan went out in the morning with her bucket of grain and called out, "Here, chick chick, here, chick chick"; the hens came running and got fed. I did the same later with a bucket of water—the hens came running and got wet. Years later she told me they stopped laying for a week after my every visit.

When in 1991 I subtitled *The Historical Jesus* as *The Life of a Mediterranean Jewish Peasant,* a Jewish scholar found that last term "unsuitable" and an Anglican scholar thought it was due to my "Irish roots." Strictly speaking, my father's parents were not peasants, since peasants are small farmers whose surplus is expropriated by others. My paternal grandparents were a post-peasant generation, but had, in any case, little surplus to be expropriated by anyone. I loved visiting their home because it was so different from our own ordinary one in Naas, but so also was my maternal grandparents' home.

The 1883 marriage certificate of Michael Farry and Bridget Rogers gives the groom's "rank or profession" as "tradesman," that is, a shopkeeper. By the time I remember visiting the shop, run then by my mother's sister, Auntie Ter, there was another auntie in a shop next door and another auntie in one across the road. The house next door was a draper's shop (boring!), but those facing ones were general shops for a market town. They had large yards and storage sheds behind, they had all sorts of mysterious stuff that farmers needed, and there were horses and cars in there all the time. You had three houses to check for dessert each night and, besides all that, a blacksmith's shop next door (other side from the drapery bore), whose fire I can see and anvil I can hear to this day. Those two worlds, that of the Lisnenan farm and the Ballymote shops, were equally fascinating, equally visitable, equally exciting, and I see no preference in roots or memory for farmer over tradesman or either over banker. But it may well be true that I took from Ireland's history a sense of justice and injustice that Judaism and Christianity did not have to create, but only confirm. Those are Irish roots I recognize. Back, in any case, to 1945.

Since my father lived in Letterkenny, he attended St. Eunan's as a day boy, but I went there as a boarder. Going to boarding school was not a privilege or distinction either within the family or the society. Aileen started boarding school in Sligo that same autumn, and so did Daniel a few years later in Dundalk. Do not imagine the aristocracy of British or American elite boarding schools. St. Eunan's was a simple necessity of economy and geography. The many small towns of rural Donegal could not each afford a decent secondary school, so one major boarding school in a town like Letterkenny could serve the twenty or so students from that town as day boys and the hundred or so others around the county as boarders. St. Eunan's was founded in 1906 as a preparatory seminary for future priests but was soon turned into a general-admission secondary school. Expansions were made regularly thereafter: in 1931 for a new study hall, professors' suites, and student dormitory; in 1952 for a new chapel; and in 1980 for new classrooms.

In the political geography of Ireland's disunity, County Donegal is the northernmost part of the country, but a part of "southern," not "northern," Ireland! (Aileen and I once climbed far out on the rocks off the Malin Head of Donegal's Inishowen Peninsula to see how far north we could get in Ireland. They were, of course, wet, slippery, seaweedy, and dangerous rocks. That was probably the unspoken point of it all.) The county is surrounded by the Atlantic to the west and "the North" to the east and has only one main road connection to "the South" through the narrows where ocean and history squeeze closely together near Donegal town. I do not know if it was, in the 1940s, the poorest county in Ireland, but it must have been one of them. St. Eunan's was as good a school as there was in Ireland, because it did not depend on local taxes, salaries, curricula, standards, or exams. It was part of a national system with national exams, the Intermediate and Final Certificates, after the third and fifth years of secondary school. Those exams were centrally set, students were designated on them only by number, and any teacher who wanted to correct a bunch at so much per exam could get them from the National Board of Education. Nobody, by the way, used true-false, multiple-choice, or machine grading. My point is simple. I remember little of my primary-school education, but I presume it was good. I remember a lot of my secondary-school education, and I know it was very good. Put another way, I am very grateful that a secondary school in a poor area of Ireland was not a high school in a poor area of the United States. If it were, my life would have been a little different.

I look back today with profound respect for the pedagogy of St. Eunan's College. We studied, for example, one Shakespearean play per year in English class and learned all the main soliloquies by heart. Such memorization was not the end, but the presupposition, of learning. The examination question might be something like this (admittedly, from vaguest memory): "When Shakespeare was writing his plays, the religious atmosphere did not allow too much causality for supernatural interventions. Discuss, quoting freely." That question, and others like it, had to be answered without a book and strictly from memory. So you ran bits and pieces of *Hamlet* or *Macbeth* through your mind and recognized that Hamlet said "Oh, my prophetic soul" when his father's ghost told him he had been murdered (so the ghost only confirmed what Hamlet was already thinking) or that Macbeth responded to the witches, "Thou marshal'st me the way that I was going" (so the witches only confirmed what Macbeth was already thinking). There you had it; now pad it all out into a nice, short composition. We memorized poems and soliloquies, and we studied thick books of past questions; we knew those would never be asked again, but they were the type of ones we would have to face. We learned to memorize precisely, to think creatively, and, as a bonus by-product, to write, if we became writers later, with the rhythms of English poetry humming away quietly somewhere in our subconscious. Decades later, while waiting for the start of faculty meetings in the department of religious studies at DePaul University, a Hindu colleague and I amused ourselves by reciting in unison the poems we had memorized in secondary school. She had learned them from Irish nuns in India, and I had learned them from Irish priests in Ireland. Both of us had learned exactly the same ones as the residual inheritance of the British empire in two of its very different outposts.

At the time, of course, none of that impressed me the least little bit. Neither did this, though it awes me now: St. Eunan's was a classical secondary school with five full years of Latin and Greek, but it was also in Donegal and all courses, save English, were in Gaelic. We learned Caesar and Cicero, Homer and Sophocles by reading them in Latin or Greek, thinking them into English, and translating them into Irish. The auxiliary (but permanent) classroom at the rear of the study hall had six long bench seats with six students side by side in each. The teacher sat at a small desk in front on the same level as we did (the teacher's first mistake), and unless you were dumb enough to sit in the front row (the student's first mistake), it worked like this. A student was called on to parse, translate, and explain a line, let us say of Sophocles' *Philoctetes*. You sat with your elbows on the desk, your furrowed brow held by your two hands, and *mirabile dictu,* the interlinear pony slid onto your lap open at the right page. If the teacher stood up, and that seldom happened, the pony disappeared just as miraculously. You read the Greek, checked the English pony (there were no Irish ones), and translated into Irish. You also knew how to do it so that the teacher would have difficulty deciding whether you had not done the Greek homework (inexcusable) or did not know the Irish language (excusable).

I fully appreciate the school's pedagogy only now in retrospect, and the same is probably true for its sociology. Set apart from the main building was a smaller and newer one with around twenty toilets for fore and another twenty for aft (urinals and arsenals, to us). We called it "Pluck" (no idea why) and at its side was a tap about two feet from the ground presumably for the regular hosing down of the establishment inside. At the start of each year everyone stood in tight circles around that tap, and the new students were ducked under it while being given their official nicknames. Because of my size I got Charlie McCarthy, which was much too long and never stuck. And that was as close to hazing as ever happened at St. Eunan's. It was not really hazing, although there was a certain amount of pushing and shoving as you broke out through those circles after baptism. But this was clear to me even then: I was the ideal object, the perfect target, for bullying—young, small, slight, and still in short pants.

To my eternal gratitude the social structure of the school made bullying impossible. The pedagogical units were, of course, by class (first year, second year, and so forth). But the social units were not by class, but by "bus." You belonged primarily and indelibly to your local or regional group, to, as it were, the autobus that brought you there. Everybody belonged to one bus or another, and I belonged to the Ballybofey bus. But a bus would usually have a mixture of years within it, so that it was not possible for an older bully to get at a weaker boy. To have done so within a bus would have been an unthinkable violation of regional identity and local cohesion. While it could have happened in theory, it never did in practice. When, for example, recreation did not involve formal games but simply walking around the perimeter of the grounds (always counterclockwise), you walked with your bus. It was a magnificently simple system that precluded bullying, since even the most vulnerable boy was encased in the protection of some preestablished group. I had already read enough about bullying in the public (i.e., private) schools of England and of younger students as "fags," or servants, of older ones to recognize the value of an alternative system. I never wondered at the time how it got started, but I have one guess about it today. Between 1957 and 1959 I was taking my doctorate at Maynooth College, the two-hundred-year-old national seminary of Ireland in County Kildare. The seminarians there took their recreational walks around the grounds sorted into dioceses, and I wonder now if our priest teachers at St. Eunan's brought over that idea by sorting us inaugurally into towns and townlands. I am, in any case and whatever its source, deeply grateful for that protective system, because the injustice of bullying does not teach one justice, but revenge at best and brutality at worst.

The bus system established the basic and guaranteed social units, but it did not in any way exclude particular or special friendships that cut across bus boundaries. For most of my time at St. Eunan's, I had a best friend a year ahead of me and from a completely different bus. I walked the circuit of the grounds with him and not with my own bus during nongame recreation. But if we had a row or were temporarily not speaking to one another, it was perfectly acceptable for each of us to revert to our home bus. A friend might come or go, but a bus was there forever. The special-friend system was a very nice complement to the basic local-bus system, and it was years before I realized something unusual about it. Nobody seemed the least bit afraid of homosexuality. I was utterly oblivious to that possibility in my early teens. A few years later, the monastery's emphasis was very different, although, in the beginning, I still did not know what the fuss was all about. You were never allowed to go into another student's room, but had to stand and talk from outside the opened door. And "special friendships" were absolutely forbidden as destructive of community. Despite the boarding school's unconcern with the possibility of homosexuality and the monastery's concern with its avoidance, I never ran into it or even heard about it in either place.

For the last three of my five years at St. Eunan's, I had my own room. Many students preferred companionship in two- or three-person rooms, but I wanted my own because I read for at least an hour after lights-out at ten o'clock every night. I pulled the covers over my head, went into a comfortable fetal position with the bicycle lamp at my chest and the open book against my knees, and nothing showed through the glass transom above the door. Rooms or cubicles, by the way, were only for sleep; access during the day was only with permission.

There was no hazing or bullying at St. Eunan's, but there was discipline and punishment. Mostly quite well deserved. But only when you got caught. I remember canes and straps, but cannot recall which was from the primary-school Christian Brothers and which was from the secondary-school diocesan priests, or whether both were from both. The cane was what you can imagine and was administered to hands or buttocks. The strap was more special. It was about eighteen inches long, an inch and a quarter wide, and a half inch thick. If struck by the wide side, your hands were very, very sore. If struck with the thick side, your hands were very, very numb. I read my diary's entry for Friday, February 27, "Doc using cable in 2B classroom." I hear a faint echo from long ago and recall that we called that strap a cable.

A shark can sense the tiniest amount of blood in a large area of ocean, but the blood must first be out of its owner. Boarders are better than sharks. We could sense the slightest weakness in a professor, could know with a terrible accuracy whom we could persecute and whom it would never enter our minds to tempt. There was, for example, a teacher nicknamed Flash whom we tortured mercilessly. One night he was walking up and down the aisles of the study hall during second study. As he approached the raised stage at the front, somebody seated at the back of the adjacent aisle bowled an ink bottle down the aisle to shatter against the dais. And somebody got away with it. We would never even have dreamed of trying something like that on, say, Arty the president. This is my diary for Friday, April 16, 1948: "Steve is giving a concert down in the Devlin [Hall] tonight. All the pros away. Every bed including the Doc's pulled out. Racket up stairs." Translation, if needed: All the professors were away; students went upstairs before bedtime and pulled all the bedclothes onto the floor, even those of the dean, who was a priest; after bedtime and lights-out, all sorts of noise. So far so good. But then comes Saturday, April 17. "Arty threatened that if names of kicker-upper rackets were not given to him—no film. Got list. Picture 'Bad Man of Brimestone.'"

Once, however, we went after Flash and got Arty instead. The refectory had long tables that marched down the room parallel to one another. They were tight to the wall at one end, but had a wide aisle for serving at the other. The professors ate at a separate table, with separate food, at a separate time. But one of them always walked up and down that aisle, praying his breviary and keeping an eye on us as we ate. Flash was doing that when the racket began. Somebody, somewhere, kicked up full strength against the underside of one of the tables. Crash of table and rattle of dishes. Flash whirled, and then it happened from the other direction. It was kept up, now here, now there, and it was impossible even to tell where it was coming from, let alone who was doing it. You could hardly be sure if the person next to you hadn't done it. All eyes stared ahead, the racket continued as Flash shouted and threatened, but we knew it would be nothing but bluster and we would get away with it, as always. But then we ran out of luck. Arty passed by the refectory on his way out the front door. He did not waste a second demanding culprits and confessions. He just said, "All chairs will be removed from the refectory for the next week, and you will eat your meals kneeling on the hard floor. See if you can kick the table kneeling down." (You can't, by the way.)

Refectory, chapel, and study hall were the only rooms where all the students were together at the same time. A larger outside chapel replaced the smaller inside one years after I left, but it was in the study hall rather than the chapel that my future was set.

That was where I decided to be a monk, a missionary, and therefore a priest. That was where adventure in faraway places finally caught up with me.

We spent a lot of time in that study hall, and its character is important in what happened. There were three study periods each night and another in the morning before breakfast, each about an hour or so long. The hall had seven or eight rows of lidded desks and wooden chairs, with fifteen or so desk-chair units per row. There was a very wide platform at the front, which also served as a stage for a Gilbert and Sullivan operetta each December. There was a special, tall step-up desk at the back to the left of the entrance door. The first two study periods were monitored by a priest at that desk to the rear. The last two were monitored by a fifth-year student as first prefect on that stage up front and another as second prefect at that desk to the rear. The geography of authority's distribution was important and is accordingly very clear in my memory to this day.

You were allowed to do nothing, absolutely nothing, but study in that study hall. It was work only and silence only. Whether you had your assigned work done or not, you were not allowed to read anything else. For about four hours each day. The one exception was Irish novels, but that found few takers. We were allowed to read English novels in the library on days too wet for outside sports, but nothing except assigned work could be read in the study hall. That was excruciatingly difficult to endure since I got my work done early, liked to read voraciously, and clearly had to beat a system that absurdly closed.

The prefects did not have to enforce the work-only policy. They were there for the silence-only policy. If a student acted up they had the right to "biff" him by standing behind his chair and boxing his ears. It was not wise, on those occasions, to put your head down on the desk and cover your ears with your arms. That was simply asking for worse. It was, in other words, quite acceptable, as far as the prefects were concerned, to read illegally during the third and fourth study periods. The question was how to beat the first and second ones. This is how it was done.

At the end of recreation periods we clustered on the stone steps and stone balustrades of the main doors waiting for the bell to bring us inside. You could pass those minutes by taking a coin and scratching it against the granite until only the central figure remained. You could, with time and patience, eventually get the hen and chicks on the heads side of the large Irish penny in clear profile with no metal around them. You could also take a piece of broken mirror and smooth it until it was exactly the size of a monocle, exactly the size you could hold firmly within a circle made by your thumb and forefinger.

In the study hall I sat near the front with elbows on desk and head in hands as if concentrating intently. But I was actually keeping that tiny mirror beside my eye and focused on the priest on that high desk at the back. It was my own personal, up-close, rearview mirror. As I completed every few sentences, I flicked my eye sideways to the mirror and checked for movement at the rear. If the priest started to walk up and down the rows, I did not move my shoulders at all; I simply slipped novel and mirror into my coat's inside right pocket and continued studying with hands to head. If a person got caught once, it was not just a case of some appropriate punishment, but of being watched thereafter until it became too dangerous to try. For the record, I was never caught, and for the amount I read, that was something of an accomplishment. It took a lot of books (I read all of Agatha Christie's Penguin volumes), a small, round mirror, and shoulders that never moved.

During that third study period, career recruiters were allowed to address us. But only one such career was ever presented. There were no farmers, bankers, doctors, lawyers, engineers, or anything else except priests, and not diocesan priests or parish pastors, but monastic and missionary priests. All such speakers had two things in their immediate favor. They were replacing study, and if you wanted to read novels and ignore them, you were quite safe, as the dean would not come in and interrupt their talk. But they were usually very interesting in any case, with fascinating tales of dangerous worlds far away. It was, whatever your intentions, great entertainment and hands down better than study in any case. A student who wished to talk about a possible vocation to the priesthood could meet with them afterward in private. For me those conversations were often disappointing. I wanted to talk about the great big world out there, and they wanted to talk about my sex life. That was not just prurient interest. If, they explained, I wanted to be a priest, I could not be too involved sexually: with girls (mentioned), with boys (not mentioned), or with myself (mentioned a lot). Generally speaking, however, my sex life was nonexistent at that age.

Sometime when I was around thirteen or fourteen, my father asked me if I knew about sex. I said, "Of course."

"How do you know? Who told you?"

"Nobody in particular. I have seen dogs, I have seen cattle, I know how it works."

I omitted one detail. My father sometimes went on bank business to visit important customers in their homes and took me along for the ride. That was how I first saw Clongowes Wood College. It was also how I first saw a stud farm, whose name I have long forgotten, but it was somewhere in Kildare's horse country. While he was inside I wandered outside and saw a stallion mount a mare and work very, very hard at earning its stud fee. It scared the living daylights out of me, and I never mentioned it to my father. But, as far as I was concerned, I knew all about sex. I knew how it was done. Information about female and male anatomy given later in the monastery classroom simply confirmed that I knew all about that. There was just one problem. I had it backward, and it took me a few years to appreciate my mistake. We were not allowed to read novels in the seminary except during two weeks of communal vacation at some lake in nearby Wisconsin. I was about twenty and reading a novel on one such annual vacation. My memory is vague and uncertain on the details, but I think it was *The Big Sky* and I think it involved a prostitute. I am quite sure of what happened. I was stopped cold by the simple statement that he felt her breath on his face during intercourse. I learned a little late, and all in theory, about face-to-face intercourse.

Nobody in rural Ireland's 1940s felt any responsibility to supply mixers, dances, or social get-togethers for secondary (let alone primary) students. And the general atmosphere was not as overtly sex-saturated as contemporary America's. Movies, for example, were nationally censored, but by selective excision rather than total exclusion. There was a girls' boarding school down the road from ours, but the two student bodies never met. Certainly not collectively and officially. We had day boys, of course, and they had day girls, students who went home after second study around eight each evening. We had our tea then and recreation for a while before the last study period. Individual contact was possible through such day-student intermediaries, but to be caught was to be expelled. Risks were probably taken in the space between the two boarding schools and in the dark between the two study periods, but I do not even recall second-hand knowledge, let alone first-hand experience of them. My own minimal experience was limited to some kissing and some fumbling, not so much up clothes or down clothes as through clothes. I could reassure those priest recruiters, or, more politely, vocational directors, that I was not so sexually involved as to be an impossible candidate for lifelong celibacy. Celibacy, in fact, did not seem much of a lifestyle change at fifteen or sixteen.

It was not that I was uninterested in sex, just much more interested in stamps. Movies, novels, poems, the challenge of distant times, the lure of faraway places—all that came visually together in stamp collecting. They were about history and geography more than acquiring and collecting. Stamps also had a definite entre-preneurial edge to them that I had completely forgotten.

Two subjects dominate the pages of my 1948 diary. The first one is our teachers' health. Sickness meant a free class that day, no homework that evening, and more time for illegal study-hall activity. Each cold is recalled with clinical precision. Monday, May 24, records this: "Steve in bed today & Arty bulled about it." General translation: The vice president was sick and the president, in announcing it to his classes, let us know his displeasure. Personal translation: Steve probably had a good book and want-ed undisturbed reading time. Tuesday, May 25, continues with this: "Steve up today. Arty and Steve went to funeral of Fr.

Mulreiny's sister in Killybegs. Steve not in study." No priest monitor, in other words, for first and second study periods. More, and safer, study-hall novels. But the second subject is collecting stamps, and that receives more space than even professorial illnesses and absences.

There are two pages for addresses at the front of that tiny pocket diary, and the six numbered entries are all of British stamp dealers. Pride of place, at number one, goes to the slightly misspelled philatelic services of Stanly Gibbons, 391 The Strand, London E.C.2. After the addresses comes a single page for telephone numbers, but there is only one entry. In the *Name* column is Miss Mary Crossan, 34 Eaton Place, London S.W.1, and in the *Exchange No.* column is Sloane 3031. She too is there as part of stamp collecting, because without a responsible adult in England, they would never send stamps "on approval" to a teenager in Ireland. Throughout the succeeding five months, day after day that diary records getting, choosing, and paying for stamps from British dealers.

When, in those early teenage years, I talked with visiting priests about monasteries and missions in personal interviews after last-study vocational addresses, I could answer their questions with complete honesty. Yes, I knew about sex. No, I was not sexually involved with anyone including myself. They never asked about stamps, although I would have been very happy to discuss them too. But why, finally, did I choose the Servites from all those who extended invitations?

Unlike other medieval orders, which had been in Ireland for centuries, the Servites, whose monastery was in Benburb, near Armagh, in Northern Ireland, arrived there only in 1947 as an extension of their American province. So I heard of many others before finally hearing about them. Father James Keane, O.S.M., was a charismatic speaker and a formidable organizer, and he had used both those talents to bring the then Opposition Leader, Eamon de Valera, across the border into Northern Ireland (which de Valera had said he would never do) for the new monastery's foundation as Our Lady of Benburb Priory. But the main attraction for me was neither charisma nor efficiency. Most of the priests who talked to us of faraway places were not themselves from there, but from Ireland itself. But Father Keane was from America. Others talked about going abroad after ordination, six or seven years in the future. But Father Keane spoke of studying abroad immediately, of going to Louvain, Rome, or Chicago for our philosophical and theological studies. There would be only a single year of novitiate at Benburb and then we would have to go elsewhere for further seminary courses.

It was that, as best I can recall, that did it. Movies, poems, novels, and stamps, the lure of travel and adventure, the challenge of monastery and mission, but especially the immediacy of it with the Servites—all came together into an inevitable decision. I never seriously considered any alternative. I had read *The Citadel* and thought, for a week or two, about becoming a doctor. I had read *How Green Was My Valley* and did not think, even for a second or two, about becoming a miner. I knew a fair amount about a profession like banking. No attraction there. I knew a fair amount about the diocesan priesthood. No attraction there. At the age of sixteen, adventure was the attraction, and from all I could see, God had going the best adventure around, and the Servites were the fastest way into it.

CHAPTER 2

Only Through a Glass Darkly

Around noon on Wednesday, April 14, 1948, I sat in the car beside my father waiting to follow a hearse to the cemetery. The story consumes four days, April 11–14, in my diary:

Got news today that Auntie Mary died in London this morning at 4, after an operation for appendicitis in a nursing home in Guildford, Surrey. Paralysis set in after the operation. She received Holy Communion before she died. A lot of cuttings in the English papers today about Mary. Three photographs. The remains came from England by ship and were met in Belfast this morning by hearse. It arrived here at 2. Grave covered with wreaths and flowers. Two friends came over with it.

My mother was not in the car. She had gone by bus to Aileen's boarding school in Sligo to tell her personally about Auntie Mary's sudden death. There was just my father and myself sitting in our postwar black Vauxhall, waiting for the hearse from Belfast. It was my first experience with death, and it was the death of a relative not so much accepted as adored. She swept across our childhood like a resplendent being from another world, and indeed, she was usually coming to us from afar. She had been in Egypt in the late 1930s, for example, as the governess of an English family there on political appointment. I have no remembrance of who or what they were. But Aileen and I still have house gifts she brought our parents from that time abroad. Aileen has a rosewood box with three stoppered crystal jars for perfume (it still recalls, nostalgically, Port Out Starboard Home). I have three embossed brass containers with calligraphic inscriptions from the Qur'an. She had died without any warning of sickness, and I presume that what my diary heard as paralysis might well have been peritonitis.

There was also a telegram of sympathy from Lord Mountbatten, but I have no memory of why and only a dim recollection that Mary was somehow important in the British Red Cross during World War II. Her obituary in the *Times* of London in those distant days when births, marriages, and deaths got the left half of its front page says only this: "CROSSAN—On April 11, 1948, at Guildford, Mary Crossan, founder and organizing secretary of the Returned British Prisoners of War Association. Requiem at Westminster Cathedral 12 noon to-morrow (Tuesday). R.I.P." Most of the details of Mary's death are dim, if not lost, and that citation is from current microfilm, not distant memory. But two images always remained.

I am standing across from a newly dug grave in a very unkempt cemetery. I see tall, uncut grass. It is near a boundary wall or hedge (boundary stays, rest blurs). The grave diggers and their shovels are on one side, slightly back, and the small group of mourners are around me on the other side. This is Donegal in the late 1940s, and funerals lack cosmetics. In the pile of newly dug earth I can see, and still see quite clearly, large fragments of bone from earlier burials in that same family plot. It was not "alas poor Yorick" time, but it was bone for sure and forever. We stayed there until the grave diggers had refilled and mounded the earth, eventually moving the wreaths to cover it completely. I have neither memory nor evidence of that experience creating any early revelation of my own mortality. I was fourteen and still immortal. Even granted that the less than two square inches of daily diary space did not allow much room for emotion, here is the next day's entry: "Free day today. Busty has started baseball here and we played today. Steve is showing a picture on Saturday night."

The second image may have had deeper and longer-lasting influence. I do not recall a word my father said to me as we sat outside Letterkenny on the main road from Belfast waiting for that hearse. Maybe he talked deliberately about Mary. Maybe he talked deliberately about everything else. If I even heard, I do not remember. This was what I thought, was unable not to think, and was even more unable to utter: If Auntie Mary could die, then my father could die. I did not think of it so much in terms of their ages. Actually, I always thought Mary was his older sister, probably projecting onto them my own sibling relationship to Aileen. It was only in checking genealogical records much, much later that I discovered she was about two years younger than he was. None of those details entered into the terribly new eyes with which I looked at my father that day in our car. If she could die, he could die. If she could die suddenly, unexpectedly, without any warning, then so could he. What, then, would happen to us, to me?

My father died at sixty-seven when I was thirty-seven. But what if he had died at forty-four when I was fourteen? It is not just how I would have developed without his influence, it is how my mother would have survived as the widow of a bank clerk with three young children in late 1940s Ireland. The house we lived in was very, very nice, beside and above the bank on the main street of Ballybofey. We would have had to leave it immediately. In the front of my father's official diaries from the Irish Bank Officials' Association were printed the general bylaws of that good, strong bankers' union. But this, as I look at them now, is all it has on that subject: "The following minimum scale of ex-gratia Death Grants is payable to the widows or other dependents of officials who die during the normal period of service: Between 5 and 25 years' service—one year's salary." I do not know what life insurance my father would have carried, but even at best, I think I know what would have happened to us, had he died when we were young. My mother had worked in the family shop and lived in the adjacent family home before she was married. Her sister Ter (for Theresa) was managing both and, in something of an Irish tradition for the youngest daughter, was also taking care of her bedridden mother until she died in August of that same 1948. My mother would have returned to Ballymote, County

Sligo, to work once again in that family shop, to live in a household not her own, and to defer to three older married sisters with one shop next door, another across the street, and a third toward the other end of that small town. For her it would have been back to an earlier life she had hated, a life from which she carried anger and unhappiness until the day she died.

My thoughts that day stayed silent and unspoken, but this is now the question I take from them: How did those earliest relationships with my father and mother and that earliest understanding of myself as son color and influence how I later reconstructed the earliest relationships of another family, a family with whom, in one way or another, I was to spend the rest of my life?

We were a banker's family, and that profession impacted directly on our lives because promotions meant relocations. In my first years I had already been in three different counties: born in Nenagh (Tipperary), lived in Portumna (Galway), moved to Naas (Kildare). By the time I entered the monastery I had been in all four of Ireland's ancient provincial divisions: born in Munster, lived in Connacht, primary-schooled in Leinster, and secondary-schooled in Ulster. When I left for America, my family lived in one place, Ballybofey (Donegal), but when I returned the first time they had moved to Trim (Meath) and by the second time to Dublin. The result of such frequent family moves, much less normal in Ireland then than in America now, was that home was not a family place, but a family group that moved with the rhythms of my father's job around several small towns in Ireland. But, for the next fifty years after secondary school, I was much less involved with my own family, distant in space, than with another one far more distant in time.

It is a family we Irish Roman Catholics invoke as "Jesus, Mary, and Joseph." It is used as a prayer during times of danger, but also as an expletive in anger. Always without siblings for Jesus. Always in that sequence. Always with Joseph unimportant except as material support for Mary or paternal cover for Jesus. But I spent twenty years of monastic life in devotion to Mary as a heavenly figure who had called seven Florentine noblemen to found the Servites, short for the Order of Servants of Mary, in the early thirteenth century. (As students we joked that it must have been miraculous, since seven Servites never again agreed on anything.) And I then spent thirty years of academic life in research on Jesus as an earthly figure worshiped by some contemporaries who believed him divine, but crucified by some contemporaries who believed him criminal. My sequence was first Mary, then Jesus. Joseph, once again, was a forgotten figure, an unnecessary father.

After thirty years and half as many books interpreting the historical Jesus, I wonder in this book how what I was and what I became must have filtered and fixed my understanding of Jesus. I wonder in this chapter how my own inaugural family experiences assisted and distorted my understanding of Joseph as father, Mary as mother, and Jesus as son (and even or especially as Son). That is also a more general Christian question. If you call God your "Father," why do you do so, and what vision of paternity lurks at the back of your mind or in the depths of your soul? How did it get there, and do you know what it is? I emphasize that I am not interested in a psychoanalysis of my own family relations and even less in those of Jesus' family long ago. I ask only this: How have my own experiences in family and faith influenced my understanding of Jesus' family and faith, and how has that interaction been reciprocal, not just from present to past, but from past to present?

Years ago I was on a panel with some other priests, and one of them said that he could not believe in God except as Father. I said nothing but wondered why I could never have made that statement. It was not because relations with my own father were too bad to allow such metaphoric projection, but because they were too good to require it. I wondered but did not ask about my colleague's relations with his own father. Was my attitude just a personal idiosyncrasy or a more general situation? How did Jesus' relationship to Joseph as father affect his emphasis on God as Father, and how did my relationship to mine affect my reaction to that question? In response, I begin with two memories of my father, one from around 1940 and the other from around 1970. Each happened only once, and it was not necessary for either to be repeated.

The first memory is from the late 1930s or early 1940s. We were living in a six-house terrace just outside Naas, County Kildare, about twenty miles west of Dublin, and my father was working up to assistant manager in the local branch of the Hibernian Bank. The story involves the girl next door, and there is pain surrounding her memory, but it was not located in my preadolescent heart. She was about a year and a half older than I, and her family was politically important. Aileen and I watched from behind the front-room curtains as Prime Minister Eamon de Valera visited their home. (Our younger brother, Daniel, was still too young to have been a participant or even a target in whatever we should not have been doing at any given time.) That visit interested us but did not impress us. What impressed us was that she was being educated at home and did not go to school. That was clear evidence of a deprived childhood. Worse, she was not allowed out with us and other classmates to explore the woods below the terrace, to climb the highest tree you dared, and to know the difference between going up where you could see the way and coming down where you had to feel for it. That was how courage was established, and what was life without courage?

She was having lunch in the garden with her governess, and when the latter went in for the next course, we asked her over to the fence to show us what type of soup she was eating. Into which I immediately dumped a handful of black dirt from our flower bed (I, not we; we plotted, but I acted). It was small, mean, spiteful, and unfair. The governess came round, of course, to our front door and complained. My mother said, "Just wait until your father gets home from the office." My father said, "Get upstairs to the bathroom." He still used a straight razor in those days, and the strop for sharpening it hung on the inside handle of the bathroom door. I do not know whether that was the first or even the last time I encountered that strop, but it is the only time I remember. I knew the beating was fully deserved because I had broken two basic rules. First, never let your parents know what you did. Second, never let any adults who might get back to your parents know what you did.

An update. I knew from Aileen that the girl next door had become an important journalist. I interrupted this story to look up her name on an Internet browser. Although married and the mother of five children, she kept both maiden and married names, so it worked. I found an interview with the *Irish Times* that was only four months old. It said that "she grew up on the outskirts of Naas, where her father had a small clothing business." I knew that, of course, although I remember shoes, not clothes. But I did not know that she was "a dauntingly productive public servant" and "one of the most respected figures in national life." She studied in Rome in the early 1950s, and "Rome's extremes of wealth and poverty shaped her politically. Her sense of justice was often outraged by the inequalities she saw." By the time I had finished that review of her life, I knew that we were wrong back then not only in our particular action, but even in our general judgment. You can learn courage from a tree in a wood, but also apparently from a governess in a garden.

The second memory is one I can date almost to the hour, around two o'clock on Tuesday, June 2, 1970, but it needs some background. In 1963, at fifty-nine, a heart attack forced my father into immediate retirement, diminished activity, and the constant expectation of another one at any time. The medical restrictions were severe. He had to lose fifty pounds. He could not take a drink or climb the stairs. He had to keep those nitroglycerin tablets always at hand. He recorded events, tersely and unemotionally, in the Irish Bank Officials' Association Pocket Diary for each year. The coded reference for those tablets in his diary is 1T or 2T with single or double underlining. Medical restrictions told him to be careful walking in the cold and damp of Dublin's winter. He wrote on Thursday, January 16, 1969: "2T out in frost to Credit Union. Really not very necessary, but to stop anything. 1 before going out in frost—walk 50 yards, 1 before going home in frost—walk 50 yards." Medical restrictions told him to be careful driving in the noise and stress of Dublin's traffic. He wrote on Saturday, April 26, 1969: "2T—traffic and hard to park in city. 1 before lunch. 1 after." (There was no hint of anger or even complaint in those diaries or in his letters despite all that was gone. He, like so many of his generation, had never learned to whine.)

Aileen and Daniel, married and with growing families, lived on the southern outskirts of Dublin. My parents moved nearby to a house with a downstairs bedroom. Two of their children were always there for assistance and support. That was not the problem. The problem was that I came back each year to visit. A visit meant excitement over all the things we could do together. A visit meant frustration over all the things we could not do together. They were, of course, exactly the same things. Those medical restrictions said to avoid excitement and frustration. Not to stay with my parents might cause offense. To stay with them might cause stress. Not to come could hurt. To come could kill. Margaret Dagenais and I were married in August 1969 and made our first visit home together in June 1970.

My father was no longer allowed in heavy traffic, but to give up driving forever would have been an ultimate indignity. During our visit that June, on a day "dull and dry," he decided to drive us up into the Dublin mountains. We were already in the car, just about to leave, and he went, without saying a word, back into the house. I waited a few minutes, then followed. He had gone upstairs to get his camera from a storage closet and made it back to the hall, but as I came in, he was sitting on a bottom step with the bottle dropped on the floor and the nitroglycerin tablets scattered round his feet. I helped him get some in his mouth and then asked a rather vapid question.

"What would have happened if I had not arrived in time?" It was inane, but if you articulate a fear, maybe you can tolerate it better.

"Well then," my father said, "I could not have died in the arms of a better man."

I have never received and do not expect ever to receive a greater compliment. It makes any acclaim quite negligible and any criticism quite tolerable. Afterward, the trip still proceeded, my father still drove, and the only concession was to visit his doctor that evening. But the terse and unemotional record in his diary said only this for Tuesday, June 2, 1970: "Dublin Mtns. run. Spasm of shortage of breath. Saw Dr. Brennan." That visit was the last time I saw my father alive. He died nine months later from a second and immediately fatal heart attack.

• • •

When I read, in the New Testament, that Jesus called God "Father" or when I hear, in a seminar, that my colleague can believe in God only as "Father," I recognize that my own early experiences filter that title into a very different consciousness. It is not, on the one hand, just general distaste for patriarchal hierarchy and the delusion that God must be, literally or metaphorically, male rather than female, father rather than mother. If, in fact, you want the parent metaphor for God, I think father is much more appropriate than mother. It is the mother who is publicly knowable, visibly provable, and legally certifiable. You do not need faith to know a mother. You need faith to know a father, because he is known only on the mother's word and sometimes not even then (at least in the days before DNA testing).

It is not, on the other hand, an inability to appreciate what Jesus meant by using "Father" for God. Matthew interprets it quite clearly and accurately by saying, "Call no one your father on earth, for you have one Father—the one in heaven." If there is only one Father, then we are all children on an equal level. The title asserts, in other words, the radical equality of all human beings as children of this God as "Father." Still I wonder why someone who spoke primarily of "the Kingdom of God" called God "Father" rather than, say, "King of Heaven and Earth." Granted all that, I also wonder how personal experiences refract my interpretation of Jesus' own relationship with Joseph as father and God as Father. How, for example, does it influence the way I hear the following two New Testament stories?

The first story is in Mark's Gospel and begins with the strange statement that Jesus' family "went out to restrain him, for people were saying, 'He has gone out of his mind.'" That might just be nasty name-calling, but it might also indicate that Jesus healed in a state of ecstatic trance as do so many other indigenous healers. In any case, what is interesting is how that term *family* is specified as the story continues. Jesus is sitting inside a house surrounded by a crowd when "his mother and his brothers" arrive and he is told that "your mother and your brothers are outside, asking for you." But Jesus refuses to acknowledge his family by asking the crowd around him, "Who are my mother and my brothers?" and then telling the crowd that *they* "are my mother and my brothers! Whoever does the will of God is my brother and sister and mother." Four times, as if with emphatic drumbeats, Mark identifies Jesus' family as "mother and brothers," and even in that last specification, there is still no mention of a father. Why is that? I can only imagine one answer to that question: Joseph was already dead. That would explain his absence in Mark's tradition, but it does not indicate how long he had been dead. That question arises from a second Markan story.

This incident concerns Jesus' fellow villagers in Nazareth. They ask suspiciously about where Jesus got the wisdom of his teaching and the power of his healing. They ask, "Is not this the carpenter, the son of Mary and brother of James and Joses and Judas and Simon, and are not his sisters here with us?" Joseph, once again, is not even mentioned, and even more surprising, Jesus is identified through his mother rather than through his father. He is identified as "son of Mary" and not as "son of Joseph," the normal designation in a patriarchal society. Why is that? The best explanation for the absence of Joseph from Jesus' patronymic in that second story is that Joseph was already long, long dead. He was so long dead that "son of Joseph" had ceased to be a useful description. It might also indicate that there was no family of Joseph alive at Nazareth to render that patronymic meaningful and/or that the family of Mary was more extant and prominent in the small world of village kinship. Joseph, it would seem, was already long irrelevant even to the local memory of a tiny hamlet within a patriarchal system.

How long ago is long, long ago? Did Jesus, in other words, grow up without a father? And from what age? If you take the story of Jesus' virginal conception as a literal, factual, historical narrative, Jesus was Mary's firstborn son. And he had at least six siblings according to that second story above. It mentions four brothers, who are all named, and at least two sisters, who are left unnamed in the Mediterranean's tradition of polite condescension toward women. Taken literally, then, Jesus' birth story in Matthew and Luke would have Joseph alive for *at least* the time required to father *at least* six siblings after the birth of Jesus—a span, maybe, of about twelve years? (I think of my own maternal grandparents, married in 1883 when he was twenty-three and she was but nineteen. They had nine children between 1884 and 1903, an average of one every two years. Michael Farry died in 1918, presumably from exhaustion, and his wife, Bridget, survived him for another thirty years, presumably from relief.) If, on the other hand, those Gospel birth stories are to be taken not literally, but symbolically, not about the biology of Mary, but about the theology of Jesus, then,, of course, Jesus could be the youngest as easily as the oldest sibling. Or anywhere in between.

Think back once more to that first story. The Mediterranean first-century world was based on honor and shame, especially in the intensely confrontational world of the small village, where the family protected its honor constantly in full view of public opinion. If Joseph was dead and Jesus was the eldest son, then Jesus was the head of his family. Would, could, should his "mother and brothers" dishonor him and themselves by moving to "restrain" the head of the family "gone out of his mind"? Is that what you would do to the oldest or to the youngest son? I know those questions allow only guesses for answers, but I cannot avoid asking them. And they all lead up to this one: Did Jesus lose his father at a relatively early age? I wonder then, against the background of my own paternal experiences, if the absence of Joseph led Jesus to emphasize God as Father in a way that I could never do. My earthly father was all I could ever wish for in a father, and I do not give that name too lightly to another, not even to a heavenly Father, not even to God. That has everything to do with my own personal sensibility, but it colors how I imagine the situation of Jesus and Joseph long, long ago.

I never knew the day, the month, or the year of my mother's birth. I never knew her age. She never told us, and we did not probe the subject. We did not celebrate even our own birthdays and were not at all curious about our mother's. But I always thought she was the youngest in her family, and so, Aileen agrees, did she. And since she was the youngest, we could not use comparisons to locate her in the sequence of sibling births even if we had thought to do so. We were not, however, even curious about it then, and it is only in the last few months that I have realized some of the implications in her silence.

She was private, intensely private, about her early life. She told only a few incidents, fragments rather than narratives, but those few were told over and over again. She never told detailed stories about early home, family, or siblings or about early desires, hopes, or fears. I had, as a child, known the home, the family, and the siblings of her public youth. But neither as child nor adult had I known the desires, the hopes, and the fears of her private youth. There were only a few glimpses, and when I recall the two main ones now, I hear resentment and disappointment I was then too young to recognize. She was the second youngest of nine children, with two brothers, six sisters, and a father dead when she was seventeen. One brother, the first child, already sixteen when she was born, died later from a motorcycle accident in America. The other brother, born just before her, was four when she arrived. Her twin and oft-told tales involved that second, unmarried brother and an older, married sister.

Her brother Mikey had promised, she said, to take her with him to America. But he was dead by age thirty-nine, an alcoholic, and the sadness in the retelling of that promise was for a lost brother and a lost dream. I wonder, she usually concluded, how things would have turned out had I gone there. In September 1951, when my one-year novitiate concluded, my family visited me at the Servite monastery in Benburb, County Tyrone. I told them that I was going to study in a monastic seminary outside Chicago for the next six years. There were a lot of tears that day, but I wonder if my mother was crying because she was now losing a son or because she had long ago lost a brother, because I was going to America or because she had never gone there.

She was once sent to live in Galway city with her married sister Winney because she was "a little wild." What, I now wonder, did that mean in small-town Ballymote, County Sligo, in the early decades of this century? Was it punishment or prevention? It was not pregnancy, because she once told me that my father had to explain "everything" to her after they were married. That revelation came in June 1969, when I was thirty-five and leaving the monastic priesthood. She was worried that some of those "Hollywood-type women" might seduce me, and we were discussing my immediate future. It was said and gone in an instant, and even though I was older then, I was still too naive to ask leading questions or too preoccupied with myself even to recognize the invitation.

I never knew how, why, where, or when those events took place. I never knew what age my mother was when they happened. They are more passing glimpses than detailed narratives or circumstantial stories. But their very lack of detail as well as their repeated performance gave them almost a mythical simplicity. They formed a tandem archetypal scenario of detention and liberation, but the detention had been a fact and the liberation only a hope.

My father spent the last eight years of his life with a weakened heart. My mother spent the last twelve years of her life with a weakened mind. After his death, she spent the rest of her life in and out of a nursing home succumbing slowly but surely to senile dementia. Margaret and I saw her every year on visits home to Ireland, and either my sister or brother was usually with us. They both knew the necessity of identifying themselves so that she could assert that she knew quite well who they were. My brother's routine always made her laugh. "Do you know who I am? I'm your son Daniel who lives in Dublin. I'm the good son who visits you every week. Do you know who this guy is? He's your other son, John, who lives in America. He's the bad son who only comes to visit you once a year." It always worked, every time. She laughed, teased back, and assured us that she knew exactly which was which. But she knew us more as past memories than as present realities, and our careful coaching could disguise but not assuage that fact. In those final years I could have asked her about her youth and her responses would have been quite accurate. The questions and answers about the past were not the problem. It was the questioner and answerer in the present who roved in and out of contact.

Once, when we had said good-bye, left the room, and were almost to the car, Margaret ran back for a scarf she had forgotten.

My mother had just talked with Margaret intelligently for over an hour, but now, only a few minutes later, she did not recognize her. She said, "Who are you? You're a lovely girl. Are you married yet?" I kept those phrases then as sad confirmation that my mother no longer knew who we were. I keep them now for another reason as well.

There are traces in memory, warm still with frustrations never forgotten, never forgiven. There are also records and graves, marks on paper and cuts on stone, cold, hard, and impersonal, but intractably there when memory is gone and the story is silent. I have checked them to write this, and they tell me now that Elizabeth Farry was born on March 1, 1901, and that she married Daniel Crossan on June 3, 1929, in Ballymote. There, I realize, is a second date I never knew. I had always known my father's birthday as March 18, 1904, and I now read my mother's birthday as March 1, 1901. She was three years older than my father. Did that discrepancy in age disturb her, disturb others? She was twenty-eight years old when they were married. In that time, in that place, was that a late age to be married, for her, for others? Was that why she never told us those dates? Was she embarrassed by them? Did that all come out as past, present, and future merged together toward the end of her life, in those three sentences: "Who are you? You're a lovely girl. Are you married yet?" Was she talking to Margaret, then in her forties, or to herself, long ago in her twenties?

There are questions about my mother's youth I was once too young to ask, then too absent to ask, and finally too late to ask. There are also questions about my own youth, about her and myself, that I did not know enough to ask. When I think of parental influence, I am always immediately conscious and explicitly detailed about my father rather than my mother. That, if I am right about Joseph, may have been the opposite of the parental influences playing on Jesus' youth. But, of course, the most important maternal influences would have happened earlier than the paternal ones I can recall.

My mother was a housewife in the traditional sense of that term and she was good at it, but I do not think she liked it. When the family went for day trips or annual holidays to Buncrana on the narrow Lough Swilly inlet of the northern Atlantic, we children would have only one topic of conversation. When were the high tides each day? If the tide was in, you could go off the diving boards and swim across deep waves to the offshore raft. If it was out, you would have to walk across wet sand and shallow water forever it seemed and still never get out to the deep channel. The ideal day had high tides at about eight o'clock so you could swim twice at near full tide, once after breakfast and once before tea. That was our always-topic, but Mam's always-topic was this: It will be so nice to sit down and have your meal served to you. But not liking housework did not mean avoiding it or doing it badly, so that while my father's influences were those of remembered particularities, my mother's were those of unremembered regularities. And together those influences made me strong enough for boarding school at eleven, monastery at sixteen, and immigration at seventeen.

Here is one example of what I mean by "unremembered regularities." I do not recall it, but my diary records it for Sunday, May 9, 1948. I was in my third year at boarding school and it was obviously visiting Sunday (every second one was, as I recall). The diary reports: "Got a lb. of butter from home." Background on breakfast, just for an example. It consisted, day in and day out for five years, of porridge, tea, bread, and butter. We sat at those large tables of sixteen students apiece, with two portions of butter per table, one for the top eight, the other for the bottom eight. Each portion was divided by a student on a rotating basis, then passed around for others to take their share, but whoever cut it up got it last (a rather basic guarantee of distributive justice!). You got enough, spread thinly, for two slices of bread, and that extra pound, secreted to the table in small tobacco tins, would have greatly extended the ration's range. But that reminds me of all the other "tuck" brought by my mother from home each and every visiting Sunday. Her care was regular, consistent, inevitable, and therefore almost forgotten as I try now to reconstruct my youth. But this is certain: When I think of home activities, I think immediately of my father; when I think of school visits, I think immediately of my mother.

Aileen says that Mam was too much of a perfectionist. I reply that I didn't notice it. "You were one of two sons," she responds. "I was the only daughter, and it took me years to empathize with Mam's early frustrations and disappointments so that I could forgive her for what she imposed on me." That agrees not only with standard mother-daughter tensions lacking in mother-son relations, but it links back to Mam's own family situation. From the age of seventeen and the death of her father to the age of twenty-eight and her marriage to Dad, she lived in unhappy proximity to her mother and older sisters with only the four-year-older Mikey as savior and support. Aileen is surely right about that perfectionism, but I did not bear the brunt of it because I was male. But, finally, it does agree with my very earliest memory, one I can date exactly to May 10, 1938.

I can be so precise because that was the day my younger brother, Daniel, was born. But the memory is not of the excitement when the new baby was brought home for the first time. Neither is it about the start of sibling rivalry as another son arrived in the house. Let me be clear, by the way, about my sibling experiences. Aileen and I agreed from the start that Daniel's only purpose on earth was our amusement. As soon as he was mobile we persecuted him not fatally, but regularly. Examples. First, there was money. When visiting aunts and uncles gave us children money at departure, Aileen and I took our pennies, the old Irish ones in color like American cents but in size over an inch across, polished them bright with sand, and swapped two or three of them with Daniel for a shilling, the color and size of an American nickel, then worth twelve pennies. We showed him that there were about six chickens on those big bright pennies, but only one bull on his small dull shilling. "We are only doing this because we love you, but don't tell Mam or Dad because you know we are supposed to keep gifts and not get rid of them."

Then, there was food. "We have a new game, Daniel, in which you close your eyes, stick out your tongue, and have to guess what food we put in your mouth. We will let you go first because you're the youngest." And on that unsuspecting tongue we planted a spoonful of Coleman's mustard, a lethal concoction our father mixed directly from powder by adding water. The old penny and the old shilling are gone now, but so, to deepest sorrow, is our younger brother, dead from a heart attack before he reached the age of fifty. There were also reprisals. I once jumped out from under the tablecloth on hands and knees, and Daniel, instead of being appropriately frightened, just kicked me in the mouth. I see that chipped bottom front tooth every morning in the mirror and am grateful beyond words for its presence.

This is what I remember of that day in May over sixty years ago. When I awoke, my parents had left for a Dublin hospital to have Daniel, and the mother's helper who came in every day was in charge of the house. I do not remember anything in particular about excitement or unusual activity, although that must have registered as background. What I recall in a still vivid image is wandering into my parents' bedroom and finding the whole room in disarray, with the bedclothes thrown aside and the bed unmade. I had never seen the room like that before or probably afterward either. It was always neatly tidied before it was opened for the day. I leave to others any analysis of oedipal ecstasies in that first memory. What I see is confirmation of Aileen's judgment that Mam was a perfectionist who never left her bed unmade or her bedroom disordered. Maybe I got some mildly neurotic tendencies for orderliness from my mother, but that only made life easier in boarding school and monastery, where one did not leave a bed unmade or a room disordered. I never experienced from my mother the criticism that Aileen knew all too well and I never even recognized at the time. But as I think now of my relations with my own mother, I wonder how they influence my understanding of Mary and Jesus, especially since, if Joseph was long gone, she would have had to have been the more significant parental figure.

Some contemporary scholars, like some ancient opponents, consider Jesus a bastard born to Mary as a result of either fornication or adultery. The earliest form of that accusation is from the Greek anti-Christian polemicist Celsus writing in the last quarter of the second century. He said, basing himself on an earlier Jewish source, that Mary "was pregnant by a Roman soldier named Panthera and was driven away by her husband—the carpenter—and convicted of adultery . . . so that in her disgrace, wandering far from home, she gave birth to a male child in silence and humiliation." Furthermore, Jesus "fabricated the story of [his] birth from a virgin to quiet rumors about the true and unsavory circumstances of [his] origins." Clear enough. But it is a very serious modern mistake to take ancient name-calling and story mongering as historical data and factual information.

In ancient polemics, rhetoricians attacked philosophers and philosophers attacked one another, pagans attacked Jews and Jews attacked one another, Jews attacked Christians and Christians attacked one another. Such rhetorical invective was then called *vituperatio*, and we recognize it today as negative campaigning, character assassination, or politics as usual. In all such strife, accuracy and truth yield swiftly to libel and slander. The immediate background here is not the later polemics between Christianity and Judaism as separated religions, but the earlier attacks and counterattacks between Christian Jews and non-Christian Jews as divergent factions *within* Judaism itself. It is simply part and parcel of first-century acrimony between Pharisees and Sadducees, between Qumran Essenes and both Pharisees and Sadducees, and between Christians and all those other sects *within* Judaism under intense pressure from Greek cultural and Roman military imperialism. May I insist on one point before proceeding? I do not think that we are any less vicious about name-calling and story mongering in the late twentieth century than they were in the early first century. Polemics then and now look a lot alike to me.

The opponents of Jesus called him a glutton, a drunkard, a Samaritan, and a demoniac. The supporters of Jesus called the Pharisees legalists, nitpickers, hypocrites, and "whitewashed sepulchers." None of that is character analysis or job description, just standard antigroup nastiness. The supporters of Jesus said he was born of God without any human father. The opponents shot back immediately with (what else?): "Around here, we call that a bastard!" The supporters of Jesus said that God had raised him from the dead and left an empty tomb behind. The opponents shot back immediately with (what else?): "You guys stole the body and told a lie!" In his Gospel Matthew, for example, knows both those polemical antistories and handles name-calling in return as nastily as anyone else around (read his chapter 24).

Mary was not the paramour of a pagan, and Jesus was not the bastard of a soldier. That ancient accusation is but a defamatory antistory to Matthew's transcendental claims about Joseph, Mary, and Jesus. Such a slander is, of course, deeply offensive to Christian and especially Roman Catholic religious sensibility, just as Christian slanders against the Pharisees are deeply offensive to Jewish religious sensibility, and just as all such slanders should be deeply offensive to anyone with a sense of common decency or historical accuracy. But especially now as some Roman Catholics emphasize Mary as a co-redeemer alongside Jesus, I want to raise a different question, not about fornication or adultery, but about invasion and rape.

My parents grew up during Ireland's transition from colonial country to independent enclave, during a rebellion that led to a partition and a partition that led to a civil war. But neither of them were touched closely or deeply by Ireland's "troubles" of 1916 to 1922, even though they reached their young adulthood during those difficult years. I did not hear from them about the injustice of imperial oppression or national partition. My mother never mentioned anything I can recall. My father told stories about the "Black and Tans," British World War I ex-servicemen who were uniformed in black shirts and tan belts and shipped as police reinforcements to an Ireland under martial law during the Anglo-Irish war of 1919–1921. But they were anecdotal reminiscences rather than impassioned indictments. My own sense of political, institutional, structural, or systemic justice did not come from my parents, but from two other sources, powerfully instructive in the ambiguity of their combination.

One source was the ordinary and expected schooling in Irish history, which explained repeatedly how the British did awful things to Ireland. We against them, we always right and they always wrong, we always valiant and they always victorious. (We, of course, had clearly the better songs.) The other source was much more interesting and requires a little more background. As mentioned before, my mother's youngest sister, Ter, already in her mid-forties, had nursed her aging mother until she died in her mid-eighties. Nan, my father's youngest sister, had done the same for both her parents and for just about as long. When her mother died, Ter never married but took over the family business and bought a Jaguar. When her parents died, Nan married the first man who courted her and bought a lot of trouble. He owned a pub on the main street in Letterkenny but was unfortunately also an alcoholic. At times he was repentantly dry, but lots of other times he was, as we put it then, on a tear or on a skite. (Actually, as I think about it now, that Jaguar, whose engine could never be properly opened up on the narrow roads of County Sligo, was also a lot of trouble. It was often in a Dublin garage, just as Uncle Hughie was often in a back bedroom.)

My boarding-school diary regularly records: "Went up to my auntie's." That meant Sunday outings, with or without my visiting parents, to Auntie Nan's, whose belated married life had started in a new home a mile or so away on a hill behind the school (thank you, God). That meant meals and stories—meals from my aunt in the dining room, stories from my uncle in the bedroom. On such visits Uncle Hughie was often "indisposed" and banished from public participation. But that made it all the easier to get him by himself, and with a tongue loosed but not lost in liquor, he recited endlessly the IRA exploits of his youth. Always to this verbal conclusion, not about the British and the Irish, but about Eamon de Valera and Michael Collins. (They were once in agreement on opposing British rule in Ireland but later in disagreement on accepting partition as its proposed solution.) That grand finale came in one of two forms. The shorter and more prosaic one: "Dev's not fit to wipe Mick's arse." The longer and more poetic one: "Dev's a gobshite not fit to wipe Mick's royal Irish arse." And always to this visual climax. He produced, from a well-greased rag beneath his bed, a Luger used not in the fight for Irish independence of 1919–1921, but in the

Irish civil war of 1922, which immediately succeeded the acceptance of partition between the Irish Free State and Northern Ireland. The gun did not seem retired, just resting, waiting, hoping. A quarter of a century after the assassination of Michael Collins, he still stood absolutely on his side and resolutely against Eamon de Valera. This was much more complicated: not us against them, with us clearly right and them clearly wrong, but us against us, with right far more difficult to assess and thereby flickering doubts back on that other easy certitude. A simple lesson from the tradition at school, but a more complex one from a participant at home. I was learning, without as yet knowing it clearly or understanding it fully, about the differences between individual, personal, national injustice and structural, systemic, imperial injustice.

From that pedagogical ambiguity I took two truths with equal and fundamental certainty. One: the British did terrible things to the Irish. Two: the Irish, had they the power, would have done equally terrible things to the British (they did it to one another with the British gone). And so also for any other paired adversaries I could imagine. The difficulty, of course, is to hold on to both those truths with equal intensity, not let either one negate the other, and know when to emphasize one without forgetting the other. Our humanity is probably lost and gained in the necessary tension between them both. I hope, by the way, that I do not sound anti-British. It is impossible not to admire an empire that gave up all of India, but held on to part of Ireland, gave up Hong Kong, but held on to Belfast. That shows a truly Irish sense of humor.

Against that background, then, I wonder if Mary, especially with Joseph gone, had any influence on Jesus' sense of systemic evil? What would he have learned about political injustice not only from his own Jewish tradition, but also from his own Jewish mother? What had she herself experienced, and what would she have passed on to Jesus in his infancy?

At the dawn of the common era, the Roman Empire kept twenty-eight legionary armies of about six thousand men apiece along its threatened frontiers, along, for example, the Rhine to the west, the Danube to the north, and the Euphrates to the east. At that time there were no legions in the Jewish homeland, but four were stationed to its north in Syria. The first level of defense against resistance or revolt was the local auxiliary troops under a Jewish ruler like Herod the Great or a lower-level Roman governor like Pontius Pilate. The second level of defense was those Syrian legions under their upper-level governor based at Antioch on the Orontes. The third and final level of defense was all the legionary forces of Syria and Egypt, plus all the auxiliary troops of the local client-rulers, under one of Rome's best and specially appointed generals.

When Herod the Great died in 4 B.C.E., revolts broke out all over the Jewish homeland, and the second level of defense was swiftly invoked. Quintilius Varus, the Syrian governor, came south with one legion, left it in Jerusalem to control the city, and went back to Antioch but had to return immediately with two more legions and all the auxiliaries he could muster. His staging area was Ptolemais-Acco, due west of Galilee, and according to the Jewish historian Josephus, Varus sent part of his forces, led by his own son, against Sepphoris, capital of Galilee, captured it, reduced its inhabitants to slavery, and burned the city.

These are my questions. What happened to small satellite villages when legionary forces attacked their central city? What happened to Nazareth, about three and a half miles to the southeast, when Sepphoris was burned and its inhabitants enslaved? Josephus does not tell us, but I can imagine it from this parallel case. About seventy years later in the First Roman War, the third level of defense was necessary, and once again, Ptolemais-Acco was the staging area, as Vespasian and his son Titus gathered and organized their legions and auxiliaries. The first strike was against Gabara, due east of Ptolemais-Acco, due north of Sepphoris. Vespasian "slew all males who were of age, the Romans showing no mercy to old or young," according to Josephus, and "not content with setting fire to the city, Vespasian burnt all the villages and country towns in the neighborhood; some he found completely deserted, in the others he reduced the inhabitants to slavery." My question is this: How many women in and around

Sepphoris were raped by those legionary troops under Varus's son? I do not ask if Mary was raped, but was any woman not? One can only hope that Nazareth near Sepphoris was, like some of those villages near Gabara, "deserted" when the troops arrived, its inhabitants already in hiding and capable of staying there until the armies moved south toward Jerusalem.

Fire and slaughter, rape and enslavement, auxiliaries and legionaries, Mary and Jesus. Our best reconstruction dates his birth to the end of Herod the Great's reign, with all its attendant horrors of Jewish revolt and Roman reprisal from the enslavement of the population at Sepphoris to the crucifixion of two thousand rebels at Jerusalem. What would Mary have told Jesus about that background to his infancy? What could Mary *not* have told Jesus about that background to his infancy? Did she tell him about Varus's soldiers? Did she tell him what those pagan troops did to Jewish peasants? Did she tell him what those Roman legionaries did to Jewish women? Did she know enough to tell him, about a dozen years later, that Varus had led another three-legion army out against another rebellion, this time not in the hills of Galilee but in the forests of Germany, and this time not to triumph and vengeance but to destruction and suicide?

When the evangelist Luke described the meeting of Elizabeth, pregnant with John, and Mary, pregnant with Jesus, he placed on Mary's lips the beautiful poem known in Latin as the Magnificat. Mary praises God because "He has shown strength with his arm; he has scattered the proud in the thoughts of their hearts. He has brought down the powerful from their thrones, and lifted up the lowly; he has filled the hungry with good things, and sent the rich away empty." Within the standard protocols of Greco-Roman history and biography, it was quite acceptable to create speech-in-character and even action-in-character. Those were words or deeds that epitomized that specific protagonist's general character, speeches or events that articulated exactly what such a person would or should or could have said in such a situation. Tacitus gives a classic example as the British general Calgacus and the Roman general Agricola prepare for battle. Each is given a speech-in-character, a typical or representative address to his respective troops, and Tacitus is absolutely fair to each general's point of view. Calgacus says of the Romans that neither East nor West has glutted them, that they plunder, butcher, steal, and call it empire, that they make a desert and call it peace. Agricola says of the British that their best have long since fallen, that now only cowards and shirkers are left, and that they are not bravely making a final stand but are simply frozen to the ground in fear. Similarly, with those Lukan poem-speeches between Elizabeth and Mary. They are not historical records, but speeches-in-character. I accept them as such and think of Mary's character as formed not just by the general Jewish hope for God's justice on earth, but also by the specific experience of Varus's slaughter in Galilee.

Some Christians call Jesus redeemer, which means for me that he incarnated the Jewish God's attempt to reclaim the world from the violence of injustice and genocide by the nonviolence of resistance and martyrdom. Some Roman Catholics call Mary coredeemer, which means for me that Jesus first learned about the divine justice for which he later lived and died from his mother, Mary, who knew not only the general injustice that women have always suffered in a patriarchal world, but the particular injustice of military invasion and imperial retribution that she herself had experienced when Jesus was still an infant in her arms.

CHAPTER 3

And Above All Else Obedience

During interviews with journalists or discussions after public lectures, the question about entering the priesthood is usually accompanied by a tandem one about leaving. I find both questions of equal interest and the answers of equal importance. Since at sixteen I knew exactly what I was doing and did exactly what I intended, what changed by the time I was thirty-five? Did I change, did the Servites change, did we both change, or, with more subtlety and accuracy, did they change me? Did the adventure die from disappointment or relocate elsewhere under their orders?

I was moving, in 1950, from one institution to another, from boarding school to monastery. There was no homesickness, no painful nostalgia for lost family contacts. I realized only much later the advantages of spending adolescence away from home as a boarder. The school handled all the standard disciplinary problems of teenage rebellion and did so by peer control rather than professorial intervention. When we kids returned for holidays at Christmas and Easter and during the summer, we were so glad to be home that we were on our best behavior, and we did all sorts of fun things as a family. I came home, for example, on Good Friday, March 26, 1948, and the next three days we went off together east, south, and north out of Ballybofey. On Holy Saturday: "Went to Strabane in the car today. Had our tea there in Eliot's (I think). Good day." On Easter Sunday: "Over in Bundoran today. Day turned out rainy. Saw the new swimming pool and new tennis courts." On Easter Monday, always a bank holiday: "Went to Buncrana today. Had our dinner in the Bayview Hotel. Had our tea with us." Only much later did I appreciate the constitutive power of that combination: lots of family dependence during holidays, lots of family independence during the rest of the year. That started at eleven and was habit by sixteen.

There were differences in moving from an *Irish* boarding school to an *American* monastery (albeit on Irish soil), but all of them were clear improvements even in the most immediate externals. St. Eunan's College, with its four great walls and four great towers from the early 1900s, was a fortress, but Our Lady of Benburb Priory, with its warm red brick from the late 1880s, was a stately home. Ironic, that. I went to a boarding school in a medieval castle and to a medieval monastery in a magnificent mansion.

Benburb village took up one side of the road, and the mansion's demesne took up the other. The mansion became Ireland's first Servite priory in 1949, but Benburb itself was well known to me from Irish history for one of those famous Irish victories that became terrible in the aftermath of initial success. Owen Roe O'Neill's defeat of General Monro in 1646 brought over Oliver Cromwell and his avenging army in 1649. In 1949, as the mansion became a monastery, it stood high above the Blackwater River on the border of Northern Ireland's Tyrone and Armagh counties with a clear view to the spires of Armagh Cathedral eight miles away to its southeast. It was, in sheer appearance, a much more inviting building than my boarding school.

My room was no more austere in the monastery than in boarding school, and the food was very definitely much better. Even with Friday, Advent, and Lenten fasts, meals were much less monotonous, much better cooked, and much more plentiful. But that was not what struck me about them most forcibly. At school the priests ate in the same refectory as we did, but they had a separate table and were usually finishing as we started. We knew, in other words, that they had normal food while we had institutional monotony. I did not record that with any particular resentment. It was simply the way things were. In the monastery refectory, however, the three priests had a separate table, but everyone ate the same food. Had monastery been like school, I would not have thought anything of the continuity. But it was not, and I noticed that difference immediately.

Similarly with dress. A few weeks after our arrival came the official vestition and the start of a one-year novitiate. After that, everyone wore the same all-black, six-piece habit typical for early thirteenth-century monastic orders. I was used, since I was eight, to wearing a black floor-length soutane and white waist-length surplice as an altar boy. I was used, since I was eleven, to priest teachers wearing black floor-length soutanes and short elbow-length capes. Clerical or monastic habits did not surprise me. What struck me about Servite dress, as about Servite food, was that it was the same for everyone, from Father Prior himself to the youngest novice (which was probably myself). That I noticed, that I recorded, and that I remembered.

Those differences, small or great, minor or major, between boarding school and monastery were all emphatically for the better. What about difficulties? We spent hours each day in Latin prayer, but after five years of classical education, I was completely at home in that dead language, and in any case, liturgical Latin was unbelievably simple after Ciceronian prose. But there was one difficulty that followed me forever, and it never got any better, although it never got any worse either. Some said, unkindly but accurately, that it never could. No, it was not chastity. It was chant. Somewhere deep in my head was a mechanism that rendered pitch completely relative. I could never tell if I was on pitch, off pitch, or, more usually, sliding peacefully from one to the other. The heart of the problem was not that I hated chant, but that I loved it intensely, loved it loudly but inaccurately, and brought my whole side of the monastic choir down with me, which soon did the same for the opposing side as well. Put another way, the heart of the problem was that I could not see (better, hear) the problem.

During the seven years of preordination studies, one in spirituality, two in philosophy, and four in theology, our monastic community was arranged in church as facing choirs in front of the altar. With Mass, Office, and a half hour of meditation morning and evening, we spent between four and five hours there each day. On ordinary days Mass and the full Office was sung antiphonally in Gregorian chant on a high, fixed pitch. On Sundays or feast days, the Solemn High Mass and special Office used much more complicated forms of chant. My problem was not with those special days when I knew I was out of my depth and kept my voice inaudibly low. My problem was with those ordinary, everyday periods of high-pitched monotone chant as the daily Office traditionally sanctified the hours of monastic time from Matins and Lauds in the morning, through Prime, Terce, Sext, and None during the day, into Vespers at evening and Compline at night.

As far as I can diagnose my difficulty, I am not tune-deaf, but I am tone-deaf. If you hum a melody, I will certainly recognize it, and I can probably replicate it as far as *general* up and down go. But pitch (or key or tone, if those are synonyms) is a purely accidental phenomenon as far as I am concerned. I do not hear the differences if they are subtle, and I do not know when I have transgressed them. I was the bane of three successive choirmasters before I left the monastery and gave Gregorian chant a chance to recover. But by then, and through no fault of mine, it was too late for that magnificent tradition to survive.

My first choirmaster was also my novice master, and he had a touching faith in the pitch pipe. I had private sessions with him in which he blew it regularly in my ear and loudly in my face. All I had to do was learn to take and hold the official pitch for reciting the Office in plain chant. I could often *take* it correctly, of course, probably from pure statistical chance. But to *hold* it was always another matter, since I couldn't tell whether I was doing it or not.

Years later, my second choirmaster put up a notice mentioning recurrent problems with the choir: "(1) The epistle side is rushing the endings. (2) The gospel side is not coming in together. (3) Dominic. (4) Etc., etc." I got a number all to myself, and no explanation was needed. Finally, my last choirmaster put it most succinctly: "Your problem, Dominic, is that you cannot tell volume from pitch." That, I think, was absolutely correct. I loved the Office and chanted it loudly whether on pitch or not. If on, it was not conscious; if off, it was not deliberate. But as my pitch slid slowly downward, I took the whole choir down there with me. A postscript. That final choirmaster went later to a Servite parish in Perth, Australia. In a coincidence too unlikely for invention, I ran into him in Sydney one beautiful winter day in July 1999. We were strolling around Darling Harbor, and there was music all around us, but he never mentioned my toneless past. Maybe he had forgotten? More likely, he was trying not to remember.

In all of that, nobody, not even my most frustrated choirmaster, ever suggested I simply shut up. To be part of the community was to be part of the choir. Sometime in the mid-1950s we were on national television for a Sunday afternoon show from New York (it was then well known, but I have long since forgotten its name). Nobody suggested I stay silent, although I had every intention of lip-synching my way through the process. I do not know whether the producer in New York caught me during the initial practice for sound levels, but he relocated me from the outside into the middle of the choir. But, I repeat, nobody ever suggested silence or even a more subdued volume to cauterize my enthusiasm.

In summer 1957, right after ordination, I was singing a High Mass in a Servite parish at Gelsenkirchen-Buer in Germany's northern Rhineland. In the balcony at the back of the church was a lay choir conducted from the organ by its own choirmaster. At one part, as I was singing to them and they were responding antiphonally to me, the organ went abruptly quiet but the choir continued. I hardly missed it, of course, since I was serenely unaware that it was supposed to be giving me pitch cues. I learned afterward that the organist had thrown up his hands in despair, stopped playing, and stalked off the balcony. That was before the Second Vatican Council's changes had the priest facing congregation and choir, so, luckily for me, it all happened behind my back. And over my head.

No amount of personal incapacity could lessen, then or now, my love for Gregorian chant. I find it unspeakably beautiful in its integration of sacred word and sacred song as Christian faith, Latin poetry, and choral chant came together to create such hymns as the *Dies Irae* from the Mass for the Dead, the *Veni Sancte Spiritus* from the Mass of the Holy Spirit, or the *Tantum Ergo (Panis Angelicus)* from the Mass of the Blessed Sacrament. Latin and chant stand or fall together, and they fell together at the Second Vatican Council. It was surely wise to move the Latin Mass into everyone's vernacular, but was it equally wise to move Latin chant into careless oblivion? I think the council got it wrong: they should have halved the dogma and doubled the chant, maybe even removed the dogma and increased the chant.

If chant was always my beloved nemesis, everything else about the novitiate was exciting, exhilarating, and fascinating—I loved it wholeheartedly and passionately. As I look back now across half a century, I try not to let nostalgia or sentimentality infect my recollections. But that, as clearly as I can still see it, is the simple truth. Here, then, is my question. On a certain Sunday in that September of 1950, my life changed utterly, the past disappeared almost completely, and I never even noticed its departure or missed its presence. Is that only a distant and romantic delusion? And, if not, how was it possible? For example, that tiny red pocket diary from 1948 has three pages up front for memoranda. The first two pages are headed "Term: Easter. Books" and twenty-one titles follow for those five months. They are mostly murder mysteries about killers and detectives, historical novels about wars and escapes, adventure tales about pirates and treasures, cowboys and rustlers. The first two titles, for example, are *The Scarlet Pimpernel* and *The Four Feathers*. The last page is headed "Pictures in 1948" and seventeen titles follow. The categories are much the same as for the novels: *The Corsican Brothers, The Last of the Mohicans, The Spanish Main*.

Be that as it may, all novels and movies stopped abruptly and absolutely on Vestition Day that September. So did all that illegal reading with rearview mirror during study hall and bicycle lamp during lights-out. So did stamps, and I never saw my stamp collection again. So did everything else that had absorbed me up to that moment. But, as clearly, honestly, and accurately as I can reconstruct those moments at sixteen, I did not miss any of it. Neither did I miss any of it in the six years that followed before ordination to the priesthood. In all that time only approved novels were allowed during our seminary's annual two-week vacation together, and only approved movies were allowed on special occasions during those same years. How could I have left my earlier schoolboy life so easily or at least not missed it more fully?

I already knew about minor adventures *out there* in fields and woods and quarries. I had done that. I already knew about major adventures *out there* that you could read about and imagine in your mind. I had done that too. I was now learning, with utter fascination, that adventures took place inside yourself as well. There were adventures possible within your own heart, soul, spirit, and conscience, and those more than made up for anything lost outside. I did not miss the past because the present and future were much more exciting. I had entered monastic life for adventurous travel in a physical world and immediately encountered far more adventurous travel in a spiritual world. If I may misquote unpretentiously a famously pretentious sentence: I began to forge in the smithy of my soul the unformed conscience of myself. It was not, however, a lonely or individual project, but a disciplined journey within a worldwide history and an age-old tradition.

One simple example. The liturgical year was a complete cycle that went ordinary day by ordinary day, special feast by special feast, and ritual season by ritual season. It spanned time and place; it covered past, present, and future; it replaced the secular calendar with a sacred one; and it gave each day to a saint's life, a feast's remembrance, or a season's celebration. It created what was called the communion of saints, and it enveloped me more completely even than family or country. And I was living completely inside it rather than just praying about it from outside. It was a little like total linguistic and cultural immersion in a new language, except this language was as big as all the world. I woke up many mornings in the novitiate and studied that day's Mass and Office as explained in *The Liturgical Year* by the Benedictine monk, Dom Prosper Guéranger, O.S.B. I do not know if such early morning reading was legal or not, but the novice master never forbade it, possibly because he never imagined anyone doing it.

Much later, in the early 1990s, I was interviewed about my historical Jesus research on National Public Radio's *Fresh Air* and mentioned those long hours spent in monastic choir and Latin chant. It was description, not complaint. But a few weeks later a Lutheran pastor wrote to sympathize with me for those lost years and to empathize with my decision to leave monastery and priesthood. "How could one have a personal relationship with God in prayer," he asked, "when all was set and programmed, all was ritual, formal, and liturgical?" The letter left me a little speechless. It occasioned one of those precious revelations, beyond dogmatic declaration or traditional argument, when the divergence between Protestant and Roman Catholic religious sensibility shows itself most clearly. I have never, ever, thought that Latin chant opposes personal prayer. It is simply personal prayer as part of a *total* community at prayer. It helps you to distinguish, in prayer, between human echo and divine response, between your own will set to sound and the divine will that allegedly transcends it. And that distinction is as important for a young novice as it is for an elderly pope. As a simple everyday analogy: Does singing the national anthem communally enlarge or diminish personal and individual patriotism?

I loved, I repeat, everything about the novitiate as my introduction to monastic life and to the vows of poverty, chastity, and obedience I would take at the end of that preparatory year. I embraced it all with utter seriousness, but not, I think, without a certain sense of ironic self-observation as well. Still, in the twenty years between early 1950s and late 1960s, something obviously changed for me. During the process of dispensation from my priestly vows in 1969, an auxiliary bishop in Chicago sat down with me to fill out the required questionnaire. My date book tells me time and place. It was Wednesday, August 6, in Room 2142 of the Sheraton Hotel, Chicago, where the bishop was attending a conference. He had the grace to apologize for many of the questions he had to ask me.

The logic behind them was this: How did we miss the fact that you were a fake? How did we fail to recognize your insincerity? Was something wrong from the very beginning? When others were meditating and praying, were you just daydreaming and mumbling words? The questionnaire, but, to his credit, not the questioner, presumed the impossibility of change. Whatever was wrong now must have been wrong then, and if they could learn from my failure, they might be able to predict and prevent it in others. It was as if official authority wanted to annul the sacrament of priesthood (which it could not do) as easily as it was starting to annul the sacrament of marriage (which it should not do). Change is often sad, and divorce is always sadder. But it is sometimes also inevitable, between wife and husband, between monk and monastery, between priest and priesthood. It does not help to insist that nothing good or true was there even at the start. The bishop's second-to-last question was this: "Did you believe that entering the priesthood then was obeying the will of God?" His last question was this: "Do you believe that leaving the priesthood now is obeying the will of God?" To both questions I responded a simple yes. We both knew that something had changed between 1950 and 1969 and that the questionnaire sought to evade probing that change. It was safer to presume that I had been unchangingly lost for all that time. But, then and now, I knew there *was* a fairly radical change somewhere between profession of vows and dispensation from them. What that change was and how it happened is what interests me here.

In September 1950, twelve of us received the seven-hundred-year-old habit of the Servite order at a formal vestition ceremony. Beforehand we said good-bye to our families, whom we would not see again until the novitiate's concluding ceremony, the profession of simple vows, a year and a day later. Simple monastic vows do not mean easy as distinct from hard ones, but temporary as distinct from permanent ones. They are taken for three years, and after that time, one either leaves or takes solemn vows for life. Those vows are of poverty, chastity, and obedience. They are always given in that sequence, and for me, at least, that sequence represented the order of increasing difficulty. Where, then, within those three vows and across almost twenty years did the change take place, and why did it happen?

The vow of poverty is not about poverty, but about community. It does not mean personal destitution, but communal possession. It is, actually, a subdivision of the vow of obedience. As students, before ordination, we were given whatever clothes and books we needed, but we never had any money. As priests, after ordination, we also had use of community cars and were given ten dollars a month for incidentals. When I was in Rome's Servite monastery between 1959 and 1961 that monthly subsidy was called a "peculium," and it was only years later that I recognized its origins. In Roman slavery, a house slave could be given money (*peculium*) with which to conduct business, to share the profits with the master, and eventually to buy freedom from that master-as-patron. Its monastic usage in Rome was probably more an elegant joke than an equation of monk and slave.

I certainly never experienced the vow of poverty as particularly difficult, but I took it very seriously during the novitiate. The novice master explained that a vow of poverty meant no personal possessions, all things held in common. What you were given was for your use (*ad usum*) and not for your possession. Apart from some clothes, I had only three things of my own in 1950. One was a Parker pen-and-pencil set given to me by my parents after secondary-school graduation. (We had no American-style ceremony at boarding school. We just went home, and that was quite enough ceremony for most of us.) Another was an old-fashioned man's watch intended for a suit coat's upper left pocket with a chain to attach to the left lapel's buttonhole. (It was all on the left because, presumably, you took out the watch to check the time with your right hand.) That silver watch, whose chased face cover snapped open by pressing down on the winder, had belonged to my paternal grandfather, the John after whom I had been named. The final item, of course, was my stamp collection, but I had left it at home since it was clearly not part of the future program. On Vestition Day, when we had our last familial visits before the year of secluded novitiate began, I gave both the Parker set and the pocket watch back to my parents. I told Daniel the stamps were his, and he could keep or sell them as he wished. I did not attach any great difficulty or special virtue to these acts; it was just a simple case of playing by the rules of this fascinating new adventure.

It would have been difficult, on the contrary, to associate the normal understanding of poverty with my own experiences in the years 1950 and 1951. Benburb Priory was, as I said already, a beautiful late-nineteenth-century estate, and even if our rooms were austere, the buildings and grounds were magnificent. It was, however, a new priory, we were its second class, and the fervor of foundation was strong and sincere. The novitiate was "strict observance," which meant we could not interrupt it even for the funeral of a sibling or parent. We could interrupt it only to leave forever. We were, it was said, no longer "in the world." We were, it was said, "out of this world."

From those twelve novices who were vested in September 1950 only three were professed in September 1951. We were then ready for two years of philosophy and four years of theology, but they were to be at Stonebridge Priory outside Chicago. The American component of our class was already in session, the Cunard White Star Line was asked what it had available going westward most immediately, and it said second-class cabins on the *Queen Mary*. Southampton on a Saturday morning, crossing lazily to Cherbourg for more passengers, going to bed while they were still embarking, and waking later when the giant liner hit full steam and the open North Atlantic. The Statue of Liberty, New York Harbor, and the Hudson River docks by early Thursday morning. That, too, was out of this world. Finally, Stonebridge Priory was an early-twentieth-century estate whose buildings and grounds were, if anything, even more beautiful than Benburb Priory.

The large private rooms of the mansion, each with its own bathroom, were divided into three or four cubicles, and it was only in 1955 that the original building received a massive extension. The number of students was increasing each year, a million-dollar expansion to one hundred rooms was completed in 1956, and I spent my last year before ordination in those new quarters, which formed a hollow square with the 1916 mansion as one side. Unfortunately, student vocations peaked around fifty at exactly that same time. The complex, including what was once a magnificent choir chapel, was eventually sold and then refitted for its present use as an extremely elegant executive retreat center. The vow of poverty was not exactly difficult during those six years of preordination study either in that older mansion or its expanded reincarnation.

It was a little more difficult in the six years of postordination study. Between 1957 and 1959 I was at Maynooth College in County Kildare. My superiors thought it only courteous that the first Irish Servite taking a doctorate should do so back in Ireland. Maynooth College was founded in 1795 under British auspices to keep the Irish clergy out of continental seminaries and continental republicanism out of the Irish clergy. As Ireland's national seminary, it was also a Vatican-approved degree-granting institute and a component college of the National University of Ireland. By 1966 Maynooth College, like Stonebridge Priory, faced the same harsh realities of declining priestly vocations. It became a coeducational institution and a full university alongside the other ones under the umbrella rubric of the National University of Ireland. But when I went there in 1957 its large, double, hollow-square complex looked a lot like St. Eunan's College, somber, dark-stoned, equally male—but only much, much bigger. When I walked into my two rooms at Maynooth, I had to sit down and try hard not to cry. One room had a table (not a desk), a chair, and a hand basin. The other room had a bed, a wardrobe, and a hand basin. I was used to poverty-as-community, to rooms that were austerely functional, to rooms having whatever was necessary even if for use rather than ownership. These rooms were for diocesan priests who would have or could get their own furniture. I thought my rooms looked more like poverty-as-poverty than poverty-as-community. But, in any case, whatever Maynooth's

Dunboyne Institute lacked in furnishings, it more than made up for in the conversation and companionship of my fellow doctoral students.

Between 1959 and 1961 I went to the Pontifical Biblical Institute in Rome for a postdoctoral specialization in biblical studies. I was living once again in a Servite monastery, but now one with an undergraduate and graduate theological faculty. That was, once again, poverty-as-community, with a room that was monastic and functional, but quite adequate to live and work in. The Servites' Marianum College was located on a quiet street high up on the Janiculum Hill in the southwest quadrant of Rome. It was quiet enough because the street's horseshoe shape precluded city buses. It was high enough to walk on the flat parapet-protected roof at night and see across the glow of Rome to the lights of the Castelli Romani atop the distant Alban Hills. The vow of poverty was, once again, not that difficult to sustain.

I was reminded, if not about poverty as being very poor, then at least about poverty as being very cold between 1965 and 1967 in my last two years of postdoctoral specialization at the French Biblical and Archeological School in Jerusalem. It was founded in 1890 by Father Marie-Joseph Lagrange on the property of the French Dominican Monastery of St. Stephen, just north of the Damascus Gate. The student rooms were around an open-air courtyard, across which you walked to showers and toilets. When you came inside the school's thick, fortresslike walls in the summer heat, you felt as if you were inside an air-conditioned building. Unfortunately, you got exactly the same feeling in the winter cold. To work during the winter you needed gloves with the fingers cut out, your feet off the floor on a wooden rest, and your small stove as close to the other side of your table as possible without setting yourself on fire. All of those minor inconveniences were more than balanced by the privilege of living just outside the Damascus Gate of the Old City and walking its ancient streets every day.

It was also during my years at that school, on a very precise day and date, that I lost my romanticism forever. I took a study break most mid-afternoons, read a few pages of T. E. Lawrence's

The Seven Pillars of Wisdom, and brewed myself some Turkish coffee. Turkish coffee is made with about equal amounts of sugar and coffee and a very small amount of water in a long-handled minipot, and it produces a drink that can be taken out, bounced on the floor, and used as a handball. I thought how wonderful it might be, if I could get all the requisite permissions, to live for a few weeks in the deep desert with the Bedouin and find out what two thousand years ago was actually like. That romantic delusion died at Aqaba, on the Jordanian Red Sea coast. A colleague and I went there for a weekend with U.N. Irish friends. We all ate basically the same food, but I came down with dysentery. Within twenty-four hours I was almost too weak to get from bedroom to bathroom and back, I was obviously badly dehydrated (I had not known it was physiologically possible to dry-heave simultaneously at both ends), and we decided to make a run for Jerusalem. We had to stop regularly along the desert road north while I, clutching a toilet roll like a security blanket, got to know the conduits of the Hijaz railroad almost as well as the aforesaid Lawrence fifty years earlier, but, of course, for somewhat different reasons. Finally, it was Jerusalem, straight into the hospital, injections against infection, an intravenous drip of glucose-saline solution (Searle from America—I knew it, I was safe), a very long and well-drugged sleep, and, above all, the reassuring voices of the nursing nuns (Mercy Sisters from Ireland—I knew them, I was very safe). But never again would I dream of the deep desert or harbor romantic delusions, which were all very fine as long as a U.N. jeep was there to whisk you back to civilization if you got seriously ill.

In all of my twelve years of formal study, I never felt the Servites skimped on travel for education or even on travel as education. They never cited the "vow of poverty" to make what I considered then (or now) a foolish choice of educational institution or to refuse what I considered then (or now) a fair request for travel allowance. As I write this I am looking at the back page of my first passport, issued at Dublin, September 17, 1951, a time when Ireland had tight restrictions on taking currency out of the country and all such money had to be recorded officially on that document. It records: "Facilities £54—provided 29/6/1957 for travel to Germany." Underneath that is the date stamp and signature stamp of the Hibernian Bank Limited, Trim Branch, and its manager, Daniel Joseph Crossan, signed in my father's very distinctive hand. I was newly ordained, about to start my doctorate, and I had asked permission to spend the summer studying German as a priest in one of our Servite parishes there (and, as a side bonus, ruining that organist's Sundays). The answer was an immediate yes, and I took my first plane, Dublin to Amsterdam to Düsseldorf. I must have wanted to experience a first flight, but after that I avoided flying if at all possible. By air, all clouds look the same. By land, you can stop and see what is on the way.

Beneath that first official monetary record is another one, dated one year later, June 25, 1958, from Thomas Cook, Dublin. It is for £105 as a "Special Allowance" leaving the country. I had requested to continue studying German, but this year at the University of Vienna's lakeside campus near Strobl on the Wolfgangsee in the Austrian Salzkammergut. There were many other places to learn German and probably some much better, but I doubt if there were any more beautiful. I was in the middle of my doctorate in Ireland, and a Servite classmate, in the middle of his in Rome, was sent there with me, probably so that we could keep an eye on each other. The professors were Austrian, the students were American, and it was soon evident that they needed mediators, facilitators, umpires, referees, whatever might interpret one species to the other. My colleague and I found ourselves elected as official go-betweens and enjoyed ourselves thoroughly; thereafter the university offered two scholarships for Servites to come there each summer as chaplains, counselors, and general peacekeepers.

That summer of 1958 was a good example of travel on a vow of poverty (not that different from any student travel, actually). I was returning from Salzburg to Dublin by train and boat. I had my tickets, so that part was set and safe. I stopped for a couple of days at the priory for Servite students near the University of Louvain in Belgium, and their kind hospitality made possible a visit to the Brussels World Fair. But even the cheapest food available (a sandwich and beer at the German pavilion) was prohibitively expensive. By the time I left, I was completely broke. I did not eat for the next two days. I went from Brussels to Ostende and sat the rest of the day across the English Channel. I continued from Dover to London to Holyhead and sat the rest of the night across the Irish Sea. In a cold, wet dawn I made a reversed-charges call to Aileen and her husband, Tom, from the North Wall of the Liffey and asked them to pick me up, get me home, and have some breakfast on the table. But the vow of poverty was never used by the Servites to limit education, travel, or educational travel, and I never thought of it as oppressive. If I had to choose, in my twenties, between meal and museum or food and travel, my choice was easy. It was not the vow of poverty that eventually made monastic and priestly life impossible for me. That was not where the change occurred.

The vow of chastity is not about chastity, but about celibacy or, if you prefer, about chaste celibacy or celibate chastity. That means no sexual activity, no planning for or thinking about sexual activity, no imaging future or remembering past (if you had any past) sexual activity. It was more difficult for me than the vow of poverty, minimally so before ordination and maximally so afterward. As I said above, just about nothing changed between celibate life in an all-male Irish boarding school and celibate life in an all-male American monastery. I did not have that much trouble giving up a sexual life that had never existed.

The novice master talked about mortification of the flesh to protect the vow of chastity. The stories of saints we read and the lives of mystics we studied all made the same point. It sounded interesting so I tried it. I slept on the floor of my room for a couple of weeks. It was not that difficult. It just made your body stiff in the morning. I even tried out a hair shirt next to the skin for about the same length of time (it was, actually, some sacking from the basement). It was, once again, not that difficult. It just made you itchy-scratchy all the time. If, however, those maneuvers were supposed to keep your mind off sex, they only succeeded, at least for me, in keeping my mind on keeping my mind off sex. On which, left to itself, it was not spending much time in any case.

I have read the tales of other Irish schoolboys, from James Joyce (in *Portrait*) to Francis McCourt (in *Life* magazine), and I recognize from their accounts and recall from my own experiences the thunderings of Redemptorist retreats and Passionist sermons. Especially about sex. It was not that I was completely innocent, and there must surely have been more excusable wet dreams and more inexcusable masturbations than I can now remember. But what about youthful skepticism? What about the teenage ability to absorb a myriad of awful warnings, dreadful sanctions, and file them all somewhere beyond either belief or disbelief? As I came into and went out of the novitiate, the absence of sexual acts was not a primary concern, nor was the presence of sexual thoughts a major terror.

Some of that was probably personal, but certainly not unique. As a bleary-eyed, half-asleep altar boy of eight, I had helped enough equally bleary-eyed, equally half-asleep priests vest for six-thirty Mass. They were clearly human beings, to be respected but not feared, unless, of course, you were caught sword fighting with the candle lighters. As a boarder at eleven years of age I worried more about punishment for study-hall novel reading than about hell and damnation for masturbation. There seemed to me, even then, some presumption behind the sacrament of Penance that you might have something to confess. Be that as it may, in those six years of study prior to ordination three factors coalesced to make the vow of chastity relatively easy. One was isolation from girls, another was occupation of time, and last was concentration on studies.

Isolation. Stonebridge Priory was situated just across the border from Lake Forest into Lake Bluff and was, in the early 1950s, the northern end of the former's aristocratic estates along Greenbay Road. The buildings were set well back from the road and isolated amid 140 acres with one small lake in front (hence the stone bridge) and another at back. We were isolated not only by affluent place and opulent space, but also by monastic discipline. Family, relatives, or friends visited us on one Sunday afternoon a month and we visited them on Christmas Day or Easter Sunday. On other Sunday afternoons we went outside the grounds for a walk along Greenbay Road (no sidewalk in Lake Bluff, sidewalk in Lake Forest) and watched new-money cars watching old-money homes. We also went outside the monastery a few times every year for special events: to watch a high-school football game at the Servite St. Philip's home stadium on Chicago's West Side or the Catholic and public school play-offs at Soldier Field; to sing as the choir for the funeral Masses of fellow Servites or the local cemetery Mass on Memorial Day. (Death and football functioned as a privileged dyad because, I suppose, death and taxes did not apply since we were tax-exempt.) Apart from those periodic incursions and passing excursions, we lived in splendid isolation from the world. Even television required special permission and was restricted to Bishop Sheen, Notre Dame football, and *Hallmark Hall of Fame*. Such isolation made chastity much easier for me, but it also underlined the one major exception to its permanence.

Summers were the exact opposite. For six weeks we went daily by schoolbus to take courses at one of the two Roman Catholic universities in Chicago, either DePaul, run by the Vincentians, or Loyola, run by the Jesuits. (I think I remember U.S. 41 before the Edens Expressway.) We wore black suits and ties rather than the monastic habit, but sitting daily in coed classrooms was a startlingly new experience for me after boarding-school segregation and monastic isolation. Later each summer we went, for two weeks, to some lake in Wisconsin for vacation. Both those annual events balanced regular isolation with particular immersion and made it much more difficult for me as a late-teenage boy to forget the existence of late-teenage girls especially in summer-school shorts or lakeside bikinis. None of those distractions, however, made me consider leaving the monastery. Or, if they did then, I cannot recall it now. Maybe sex sent me to confession more often in those days, but I cannot recall that either and suggest it only out of abstract respect for my adolescent hormones.

Occupation. Every part of every day was controlled by either a normal-day or a feast-day horarium posted on the monastery bulletin board (*horarium* is Latin for hour-by-hour-ium). We were never doing "nothing" at any time. Apart from prayers, classes, and meals, we maintained by ourselves the mansion and estate, inside and out. Each of us had an allotted space to be swept or dusted for fifteen minutes each morning and waxed or buffed (in the old sense) for two to three hours each Saturday. Afternoons we alternated work and recreation for about two hours. Work meant keeping up the grounds; for example, we once completely reglassed a very large greenhouse. Recreation meant baseball, basketball, touch football, or ice hockey (remember those two lakes). Unlike my American classmates, I had never skated before but "learned" fast with a hockey stick as third skate. We did not have goalies—nobody wanted the job, and in any case, somebody might get hurt—but I was usually placed on defense in front of the open goal. The theory was that an attacker would have to go around me—body checks were out—and since I was liable to do anything (accidentally) with that stick, he had better swing very wide indeed. I was quite a potent defender just from the sheer unpredictability of my incompetence. All of that left little time for anything else, including girl thoughts.

Concentration. It was especially a concentration on study that neutralized any problems with sex as a major distraction, a serious temptation, or a terminal alternative to monastic celibacy. If I was more interested in stamps than sex as a boarder, I was similarly more interested in study than sex as a monk. The meaning of study had utterly changed for me from what it had been in boarding school, when I finished adequately but speedily to leave time for serious but illegal novel reading. My secondary-school grades, by the way, were adequate, but not at all brilliant. That 1948 diary records the Easter term exam results for my third year at secondary school. Those were a crucial last preparation for the Intermediate Certificate, the first of the two state-run national examinations for secondary-school graduation in Ireland. My average grade from nine exams was 65 percent. An average of 40 percent was Pass, an average of 60 percent was Honors, so I just made it. That was boarding-school study, but in the novitiate and scholasticate, study changed into something completely different.

I was not disappointed in the great adventure with God I expected to find in monastic and missionary life, and far from disappearing, in the one-year novitiate it was overlaid with a second layer, the adventure of spiritual and liturgical life. Then in the six-year scholasticate, those two earlier layers were overlaid with a third one, the intellectual and scholarly life. I see that much more clearly now than I did then, but I think I reconstruct accurately rather than invent creatively.

When I once described the Servites as a medieval order, a colleague took that term as critical disparagement. But by a medieval order I simply meant a thirteenth-century one, and I could never think of that century except with awe and admiration. It is the sixteenth and seventeenth centuries, during which Catholicism and Protestantism forced each other into opposite extremes (faith *or* works, Bible *or* tradition, individual *or* community, real *or* symbolic, etc. *or* etc.), that impress me negatively. In that separation within Christianity, Catholicism lost any internal but loyal opposition, any sternly self-critical voice from within. In that separation, Protestantism lost anything to protest against save itself and has continued to fracture into ever increasing diversity. In the thirteenth century, Roman Catholicism had not yet lost its nerve and had not yet allowed the iron to enter its soul.

My two years of philosophy and four of theology were heavily freighted toward the Scholasticism of the thirteenth century and the towering figure of Thomas Aquinas, who was, unfortunately, a Dominican and not a Servite. We did study history of philosophy, for example, but no history of theology, and certainly no history of nineteenth- and twentieth-century theology. I remain to this day ferociously ambivalent about that gap in my education. On the one hand, I wish I had read much more of those classic modern works and studied them at leisure and in depth. On the other, many who have done so seem trapped in that past history and unable to see the present or project the future. Be that as it may, what I recall most insistently from my own six-year preordination program were not those classes in canon law or learned apologetics (Latin theses proved from Scripture, tradition, and reason), but the tradition of the thirteenth century in general and of Aquinas in particular.

My two fundamental retentions from almost twenty years of monastic life are Gregorian chant and medieval Scholasticism. But I never took either the way I was supposed to. I never got either accurately. My career in chant was already discussed, and as you will recall, I got the *volume,* but not the *pitch.* Somewhat similarly, in studying Aquinas I got the *how,* but not the *what,* the *confidence,* but not the *content.* It was not that I disbelieved the content, and I certainly learned enough of it to pass my exams most satisfactorily. But what has stayed so deep that it will never leave me is *how* to think, the *what* being quite relative to that more important process. Here is what I mean by confidence rather than content.

Aquinas got up each morning, as it were, studied a pagan philosopher named Aristotle, and found his thought absolutely congenial and appropriate for creating and structuring Christian theology. Why was he never afraid of that conjunction? We did not spend much time, by the way, discussing tensions between Aquinas and ecclesiastical authorities or the advantages of being far away in Paris rather than close at home in Rome. That might have raised questions we were not supposed to see, let alone ask. But what I got then, loudly, clearly, and permanently, was this. However you name those twins—philosophy *and* theology, reason *and* revelation, history *and* faith—they can never be internally in contradiction. They are twin gifts of the same divine source, and we resolve *our* difficulties or contradictions between them without forgetting, abandoning, or privileging one too easily over the other. That stuck deep when so much of medieval theology is long gone. *What* went, but *how* stayed.

In the years of my scholasticate, from 1951 through 1957, that combination of isolation from women and concentration on studies made the vow of chastity relatively easy to maintain. But by the late 1950s and early 1960s that had begun to change completely, and more important, so had the church and the world all around me.

On the individual and personal level, there was no more isolation, but much more concentration. The balance shifted dramatically. In the twelve years between ordination to the priesthood in

1957 and dispensation from the priesthood in 1969, I spent six as a doctoral or postdoctoral student and six as a professor at a seminary, college, or university. As to isolation, six of those years were spent inside Servite monasteries in America and Italy, four more far away from them in Ireland and Jordan, and two in new multigroup monastic settings in the suburbs and city of Chicago. None of that, however, was as significant as this one fact: I returned to America in 1961 with a doctoral degree from Ireland's Maynooth College and a postdoctoral degree from Rome's Biblical Institute within a Roman Catholicism about to make liturgical changes long refused, raise dogmatic questions long avoided, and address disciplinary issues long suppressed. What it meant to be a monk and a priest was starting to change both in my own mind and in the minds of many around me.

On the corporate and ecclesiastical level, those were the years before, during, and immediately after the Second Vatican Council in the early 1960s. It was bliss in that dawn to be alive and heavenly to be young, have a brand-new doctorate, and, above all, be newly specialized in biblical studies. It was especially the Bible, with its texts seen now in their particular historical situations and specific literary intentions, that was helping and even forcing a fundamental review of the Roman Catholic tradition. But bliss for some was shock for others, and that created tensions within both monastery and priesthood. How, in the unchanging church, could ideas and actions absolutely forbidden yesterday become acceptable today and probably normative tomorrow?

Even as a student I had begun to ask questions, but more about dogma and liturgy than about ethics and discipline. I can still reproduce quite accurately, from my student days in the 1950s, the following interchange between myself and the monastery's Father Prior:

"Why do you read radical magazines like *America* and *Commonweal?*"

"I don't think they're radical except in trying to get down to the roots of things."

"Go down to the chapel and say a Rosary for answering me back."

"But I only said . . . "

"Say two Rosaries . . . "

"Yes, Father." Later, he came down to check on me, which I found beneath the dignity of everyone concerned.

Questions dismissed or forbidden in the 1950s were now openly discussed in the 1960s. A French theologian like Henri de Lubac, whose name I could not mention in our seminary, was now lionized at the council. An American theologian like John Courtney Murray, whose works on church and state I could not read in our library, was now on the cover of *Time* magazine. Everything I knew about Vatican politics from my two years in Rome was now public knowledge in Xavier Rynne's *New Yorker* articles. That was but the surface; the more serious issue was this. Calling a council to reform or update the church implicitly accuses those in charge of having failed in leadership, of having failed, in this case, by their very style of leadership. They had remained attached to an autocratic hierarchy commanding exclusively from the top down, a model bequeathed them by Europe's toppled monarchies and shattered empires, an image for the Catholic church transferred nostalgically from the Papal States of the past. The church, said its hierarchy, was not a democracy, but surely, I thought, it was not a curial oligarchy or a regal papacy either. It was a community of faith that had very ancient and traditional forms of leadership in flat contradiction with contemporary Roman procedures. It was, in other words, the very hierarchy itself that was under scrutiny.

At one point in the early 1960s I finished saying my own private Mass, walked into the monastic sacristy to unvest, and I apparently ignored while carefully overhearing a confrontation between that same Father Prior and another priest-professor, my classmate from that 1958 summer in Strobl. He had said Mass with his arms outstretched and hands facing forward in the classical prayer position from early Christian art (a posture like "hands up" in a robbery). He was told never to do that again, but to keep his arms within the width of his shoulders and his hands facing inward toward one another. Furthermore, said the Prior, he was placing him "under obedience" to do what was commanded (a phrase similar to "that's an order" in the military). I don't think I ever heard that ultimate monastic warning used before or after that morning. The issue was so tiny that its very triviality emphasized what was actually now at stake, namely, the traditional presumption of unquestioning obedience to ecclesiastical authority and monastic discipline.

Questions about liturgy and dogma, morality and discipline, tradition and custom were not just about those subjects, but more fundamentally about church hierarchy and ecclesial obedience. That brought up immediately the question of clerical celibacy. I had always understood that the vow of poverty was simply a subvow of obedience. When I was told to go from a monastery-mansion in Ireland to a monastery-mansion in America by second-class berth on the *Queen Mary,* I understood that the vow of poverty had nothing to do with destitution, but everything to do with obedience. Common property or money was distributed and used at your superior's command. You went where you were sent, when you were sent, as you were sent. But I had always thought of the vow of chastity as a quite separate and independent vow, not just a subvow of obedience. I had not even noticed before the early 1960s that although it was called a vow of chastity, it was actually a vow of celibacy. Chastity involves the humanly appropriate embodiment of one's sexuality and is incumbent upon all of us no matter how covert practices, overt actions, social customs, and cultural norms may differ among us. No matter how we stretch, break, or ignore the call to chastity, only a few of us publicly propose simultaneous or serial promiscuity as a breakthrough in human relations. Celibacy may, of course, be a free choice for anyone, but clerical celibacy, the law that priests must be celibate, no matter how venerable and ancient its tradition, was a matter of ecclesiastical hierarchy and church discipline. The vow of chastity-as-celibacy was a subvow of obedience, and when, in the early 1960s, ecclesial obedience came under debate, then so inevitably did clerical and even monastic celibacy.

For me that meant deliberate experimentation with female friendships and sexual relationships. Some of it was belated adolescent self-indulgence of which, despite its inevitability, I am not particularly proud. Some of it was trying to understand an option, test a possibility, and imagine a future I had never considered before. Most of it focused on this intractable problem: for me, by the 1960s, the monastic priesthood had become less important than biblical scholarship, and clerical celibacy had become much less important than female relationship. But I was also a priest-professor, and those twin facets seemed inextricably interlinked, indissolubly united. How, then, could I leave one without losing both? How could I possibly disentangle two roles so intimately intertwined? How could I cease being a monastic priest, but remain a biblical scholar? That was a more intricate and much scarier problem than whether I should leave the priesthood and get married. The latter was the easier question. It was the former that worried me by day and kept me awake at night. It was still there, in other words, that inaugural lure of adventure, but it was no longer centered on the priesthood but on scholarship. How, then, to retain it for the future?

When asked by journalists why I left I usually say, simply, in order to get married. That is true enough as far as it goes: I did leave, I did marry, and when I left I intended to get married. But today I've got additional questions about myself back then. If, in 1969, I could have stayed and gotten married, would I have done so? If the rules had changed to allow a married clergy, would I have accepted that alternative? My answer to that, even looking back some thirty years, is securely and absolutely negative. My priorities were very clear to me. First, I wanted to get married even if that meant I could no longer be a professor or even a scholar. Second, I wanted to remain a scholar and professor if that were at all possible. Third, I no longer wanted to be priest under any circumstances, even if I could remain one, still get married, and stay a scholar and professor (which, of course, I could not). But my problem, to repeat, as a priest-professor was how to stop being a priest and stay a professor.

I met Margaret Dagenais through a double coincidence in the early 1960s. She was teaching art at the Servite high-school seminary, and I was teaching Bible at the Servite college seminary. We met that way for the first time. She was also a professor at Loyola

University and, from a base in education, beginning to create its new fine arts department. We met there once again when I was a professor in the theology department. I was full-time at the seminary, with one class on Tuesdays and Thursdays, and full-time at the university with four classes on Mondays, Wednesdays, and Fridays (I must have had a lot of energy in those days). But even after we knew we had fallen in love, knew our relationship was irrevocably important for both of us and not negotiable for either of us, Margaret was not at all enthusiastic about my leaving the priesthood and our getting married. Her points were blunt and clear, because Margaret was always blunt and clear. (Once, coming home from a party for the university's history and political science departments, she was seated between two Jesuits in the backseat of the car. "Do you mind if I smoke?" asked one of them. "I think," she replied, "that smoking, like masturbation, is best done in private." That comment is from the mid-1970s, but I remember what she said to me in the mid-1960s just as well.)

First, she said, leaving the priesthood was my decision. It was not hers or even ours to make; it was mine alone. Even if it did work out, she didn't want to be responsible for it; if it didn't, she certainly didn't want to be responsible for it. Second, if I did leave, she was not at all sure how I'd move from monastery to monogamy. What about remedial adolescence? And, by the way, while she was on that subject, I was always to remember that there were lots of other women around, but none who would love me as she did. Third, I was her best friend, and she wouldn't consider marrying anyone except her best friend, but marriage is the surest way to lose your best friend. In summary, she was not pulling me out of the priesthood, she was not pushing me into marriage, and she was much surer of us as friends and lovers than she was of us as husband and wife.

I knew that was all brutally accurate. Margaret's mother had picked losers for husbands and had died in her early thirties after four failed marriages. Margaret, then still a young child, was reared by her maternal grandmother. She called her grandmother by her last name, Keane, and got into minor rows with other schoolchildren who said she was only "her grandmother" while

Margaret insisted she was uniquely "her Keane." Her grandmother opened a boarding house during the depression, kept enough food in the house for boarders, herself, and Margaret, celebrated anything and everything worth mentioning, and never let Margaret know how poor they were. One result was that a party for Margaret would always be a celebration of that triumph and a memory of her Keane. Another result was that, since Keane did not criticize her dead daughter, it was husbands who were not to be trusted too easily and marriages that were not to be entered too readily.

Even after I had left the priesthood in spring 1969 and we had decided to get married by that fall, Margaret was still not certain about it. What if it ruined everything? What if our marriage ruined our friendship? And maybe this unspoken one: she had been running her life by herself to this point (Keane was long dead), and she wasn't sure how I'd enter into that process and how she'd react to my involvement. My answers were simple. We love one another and want to live together; people call that marriage, so we should get married. If we find it's a disastrous mistake, we will get a divorce. We did not plan to have children. For one thing, Margaret was older than I was, and for another, we were both so set in academic lifestyles of study and travel that children would have demanded alterations we were not ready to accept. We judged it too late for us to make such a drastic change. A year or so later I had the following doctor-patient exchange before a minor surgery making that decision more or less absolute:

"I am curious," the doctor said. "How can you as a Catholic theologian undergo a vasectomy?"

"Because," I replied, "I am a bad Catholic, but a good theologian, and that makes a vast difference."

Margaret and I agreed on marriage but had set no exact date when I was called in for that episcopal questionnaire I talked about earlier. At its conclusion, taking me totally by surprise, the bishop said he would marry us in his church and asked when we would like the ceremony to take place. I think that was less an honor than a way of controlling any undue publicity. Caught completely off guard, I said one week from today at ten o'clock, and tried to figure out what date that would be. Then I called Loyola's downtown campus, where Margaret was teaching summer school, and invited her to lunch. "I have," I said, "something to tell you."

The vow of obedience means exactly what it says. You swear to obey your ecclesiastical superiors. The vows of poverty-as-community and chastity-as-celibacy are ultimately its subdivisions, but the vow of obedience is serenely and totally itself. I left monastery and priesthood, finally, not just because I refused future celibacy, but because I refused future obedience. I certainly did not leave primarily for sex. It was already quite clear by the late 1960s that heterosexuality (that's all I knew about) was quite available even or especially while one remained a monastic priest. Maybe anti-celibacy itself would have been enough of a reason, but that is not exactly how it happened for me. It also involved anti-obedience.

As I went through my own vocational crises in the 1960s, I knew others were going through similar decisions, but when I left in 1969 I did not know this statistic, which I only read thirty years later in a history of Roman Catholicism in America: the number of priestly resignations peaked at 750 in 1969 and declined annually thereafter. I knew many priests who wanted both to marry and to stay as priests but have no idea how many of that 750 did. I do know this: I wanted *both* to leave and to marry. I would not have married and stayed even if I could have done so; I would not have stayed even if marriage was never an option. That was part of my own particular history, not just with celibacy and marriage, but with authority and obedience.

In 1950 I thought obedience was about where to go and what to do. In the next decades I never had any trouble with that understanding, with obedience in terms of function and geography. I try carefully not to romanticize or idealize my memory, but as best I can recall, in almost twenty years I was never ordered to go anywhere or do anything I was not perfectly happy to accept. I doubt that the Servites were adjusting their plans to my desires, so I must presume that I readily adapted mine to theirs. Here is a fast tour of that vow of obedience from student to priest, from professor to scholar, from Ireland to America, from Rome to Jerusalem.

In the years of preordination study only summer school allowed for personal diversity; the rest of the year was standard college classes and uniform monastic life. I was part, as you will recall, of the third class at Benburb Priory. The second class, with over a dozen professed students, had studied philosophy in Ireland and went on to Rome for theology. Our superiors decided that most of that class would go into missionary work in Africa and that our class would supply high-school teachers needed for St. Philip's in Chicago. That was, for me, a surprise but not a problem. Furthermore, they needed science teachers, and I was to start an undergraduate degree in biology. There should be buried in the bowels of DePaul University's computers a grade for Brother Dominic M. Crossan, O.S.M., from that summer of 1952, for something like Biology 101 and presumably for other courses that I have long since forgotten.

In early June 1953 we finished our two years of philosophy, and three of us, two Americans and myself, were ordered to take our four years of theology at the Servite College in Rome. We would be going there immediately to learn Italian before school started in October. One week later the order was countermanded in my case. Father General in Rome informed Father Provincial in Chicago that, after that large class just ahead of me, they needed more Americans and less Irish at our international college. There was nothing unfair or prejudicial about that decision. The General wanted more American members of the financially powerful American province educated in Rome and stationed there permanently. The Provincial was reluctant to send too many students there since, in those early postwar years, they often came home sick or disabled for life. Those of us who had survived Irish winters in general or Irish boarding schools in particular found Italian monasteries simply more of the same and seldom got sick (maybe the Frascati helped). "Brother Dominic," said the Prior, "you will be going not to Rome, but to summer school."

I must surely have been first elated and then deflated by that rapid sequence, but cannot now dredge up even the faintest memory of my reaction. It may, of course, be totally blocked out by what happened next, because that rendered any Roman sojourn quite moot in any case. I got sick in late June. My temperature was pushing 104 by the time I got to the hospital in Waukegan, I was stiff all over, and in those pre-Salk summers, the expectation was obvious even to me. I remained there for a month, while they ran me through every test in the book and patiently waited for paralysis to confirm their initial diagnosis of polio. It did not do so.

I should have been terrified, but I never was. I was in isolation at the beginning, but fairly soon they put me in with another Servite, a newly ordained priest with American-Irish roots and hair to prove it. We called him Red, and he was the first Servite I had met on arrival in Chicago. He was in his last year before ordination when, on the morning of October 5, 1951, he was sent to pick up three Irish innocents off the overnight sleeper train from New York. He had borrowed his father's car for the day, intended to show us the Servite's establishment at Jackson and Kedzie, take us to his nearby home for dinner, and eventually get us back to Stonebridge Priory by nightfall. On what I later learned was Wabash Avenue, trying to slide between a parked car and the steel support for the El, he scraped the full left side of the car. We had been warned repeatedly by our American novice master in Ireland to keep our eyes open and our mouths shut for the first six months in our new country. "Everything will be different," he said, "but don't think, and especially don't say, that things are weird in America and that they do things correctly back in Ireland." So I said nothing out loud but thought to myself: Things *are* different here; in Ireland we usually go round posts like that. Later, watching Red grow progressively more apprehensive as the time for his father's return from work grew closer, I recognized that things were not that different in America after all.

Red was my roommate for most of that month in hospital, and his presence there underlined that Rome was finished for me even without the General's decision. He had a damaged heart (I only speak medically) with a badly scarred valve from rheumatic fever contracted at the Servite College in Rome. I had a rather marvelous time that summer even though I do not negate the temporary terrors of spinal taps (lumbar and suboccipital types) or bone-marrow taps. It is better, for the imagination, not to see the former's needle or the latter's corkscrew before insertion begins. What made it marvelous was Red's cheerfulness, companionship, and total lack of fear. He is dead now, I thank him always for July 1953, and, since Wabash is the street I took for twenty-six years to classes at downtown DePaul, I have repented quite often for that mental wisecrack about his driving. In March 1971, going through my father's personal effects after his death, I found in his wallet a folded, faded, and brittle-edged cablegram sent to my parents that same July 1953: "Polio virus clearing. No paralysis. Love, Dominic."

Summer 1954 was even better. "When I gave you Communion this morning," said the Prior, "your face looked very pale, and you're still a little too thin. You had better skip summer school this year and take a milk shake every day to improve your weight." The vow of obedience did have its moments. From about seven-thirty in the morning to three o'clock in the afternoon, five days a week for six weeks, I was on my own to read quietly in my room. I remember Dorothy Day's *The Long Loneliness,* Thomas Merton's *The Seven Storey Mountain,* and everything, everything, in the library by Jacques Maritain (*Art and Scholasticism,* for example). With Scholasticism it was always the confidence that counted for me more than the content, the lack of fear with which Christian faith confronted any current modernity, whether past, present, or future. That was then my attraction to Maritain, and when later he turned bitter, denounced the future, and lost confidence, he lost me as well.

By 1955 and 1956, the last two summers before ordination in May 1957, biology, which had hardly gotten started, was entirely forgotten. I was sent to take independent-study courses in advanced Greek at Loyola University. By then it was clear that our new biblical professor, Father Neal Flanagan, wanted me prepared for seminary teaching, but it was not at all clear that he would get what he wanted despite, or maybe even because of, the fact that *he* wanted it. Biblical scholarship was then seen as the problem child of Roman Catholic theology, and nobody then foresaw how easily it would be neutralized in the decades ahead. But, to summarize and repeat, in all those years from 1951 through 1957 I did what I was told, and as honestly as I can recall, I was perfectly happy with what I was told to do. Biology or theology, high school or seminary, Africa or America, any and all of that was fine with me, but I was not consulted about any of it and did not expect to be.

The postordination years were more of the same, although toward the end I had somewhat more say in my own future. Maynooth College in Kildare, Ireland, was chosen over Catholic University in Washington, D.C., for political reasons. Since the American province of the Servites was taking so many students out of Ireland, it was but courteous and prudent to send me, as the first Irish Servite doctoral student, back home to take my degree at the national seminary. My parents were living in Trim, County Meath, Aileen was married and living in Dublin's southern suburbs, and Maynooth is right in between, about forty minutes in either direction. After six years away from family, my two years at Maynooth were simply wonderful. I saw my parents every weekend and stayed with Aileen and Tom most Saturday nights. The pattern was always the same, a decision in which I had no say but whose result was better than I could ever have projected by myself. And more of the same followed.

I finished my doctorate in 1959 and expected an assignment as a professor at Stonebridge Priory, where I had once been a student. But Servite politics and some delicious irony intervened, and once again, I did what I was told. Our Father General had wanted to get and keep some Americans in Rome as part of the order's governing Curia, and as you will recall, he had chosen American classmates over my Irish self in 1953. One of them, my colleague at Strobl in 1958, finished his doctorate in Rome as I finished mine at Maynooth. The General told our Provincial he intended to keep that colleague in Rome and send him on to specialize in biblical studies. In the byzantine ways of such political maneuvers, the General would never simply tell the Provincial: "I have him, I want him, I'm keeping him. Do you have a problem with that?" Instead, retention was proposed as a necessity of further, ongoing education. A very bad mistake. The Provincial replied that it would be much better to send him Father Crossan instead. I had far more years of Greek, had been studying Hebrew for two years, had just done my doctorate on a biblical subject, and was also physically over there in Europe. So in 1959 I was sent from Maynooth to Rome, and the Provincial knew he'd get me back safely since I was totally useless for the General's curial plans. I did not know Italian and could not be properly romanized in just two years. My colleague and I met somewhere in Germany for a few beers, I got the full story, and we continued in our opposite directions, he to Stonebridge Priory as a professor and I to the Pontifical Biblical Institute as a student.

By 1961 I too was back at Stonebridge Priory as a seminary professor. That meant only one class on Tuesday and Thursday, so I asked and received permission to start a doctorate in Semitic languages at the University of Chicago's Oriental Institute for the academic year 1962–1963. I took courses there that year, but during the summer of 1963, the Norbertine Provincial mentioned to the Servite Provincial that they had nobody to teach biblical studies at St. Norbert's Abbey. "Our Father Crossan," said my Provincial, "has so much time on his hands that he's getting a second doctorate, and we'd be glad to send him up to you one day a week." Semitic languages stopped as abruptly as had the biological sciences a decade earlier, and in 1963–1964 I took a four-hour train trip from Lake Forest, Illinois, to DePere, Wisconsin, every Thursday afternoon, taught a three-hour class at the abbey the next morning, took a swim in its magnificent pool, had lunch, and took another four-hour train trip back home on Friday afternoon. I know, therefore, in any case, exactly where I was at one o'clock on Friday, November 22, 1963.

In all those years, preordination or postordination, I was never consulted on my hopes, fears, wishes, or desires. I never expected that to happen and never missed its absence. I was not asked, I was commanded, but no matter how hard I try now, I cannot reconstruct any disagreement, displeasure, or even disappointment with orders from my superiors. I doubt they always ordered what I wanted, so I must presume I always wanted what they ordered. But that was obedience in terms of where to go and what to do. There was also obedience in terms of how to think and what to say. That was, slowly but surely, where the problem arose and the crisis erupted. It happened between 1968 and 1969, but I had missed a warning sign from almost twenty years earlier, from my novitiate itself, from that novice master who was also my choirmaster. Earlier, not even a pitch pipe in my ear could make me hold a tune I did not get. Later, not even a vow of obedience could make me sing a song I did not hear. But that was, in 1950, my future's unrecognized metaphor.

CHAPTER 4

The Holy Is Not Just God

Leaving the priesthood is a form of divorce, but with no children to be damaged and no possessions to be divided. Apart from that, the trauma is quite similar. I was breaking with the only life I had known for almost twenty years. I was leaving the only life I had imagined as mine to the end. I knew even during my student days that certain thoughts should be left unspoken and certain theological views should not be voiced, and even with prudent silence, there were minor tensions between myself and my rather conservative prior. But, to the very end, there was no serious conflict between myself and my Servite superiors. That was not where the crisis occurred. We were what is technically called an *exempt* order; that is, we were not under the local bishop, but rather under a Father Prior for the individual house, a Father Provincial for the general area, and a Father General for the whole order. He, in turn, reported to the pope. So much for theory. In practice, however, the Servites had parishes and high schools in Chicago, which made them completely dependent on and functionally subordinate to the archbishop of Chicago. That was where the crisis occurred, but since a Latin tag demands we say nothing but good about the dead, I cannot say very much about Cardinal John Patrick Cody.

On a late August evening in 1968, two German friends I had met ten years earlier at the University of Vienna phoned from California. "Are you watching TV? Do you know what's going on? Is there a revolution starting in the streets of Chicago?" Feeling somewhat foolish, I admitted complete ignorance about the police riot at the Democratic Convention a few miles away, but mentioned a small "revolution" of my own then starting.

I had returned that day from vacation and found this letter, dated August 26, among two weeks of waiting mail:

Dear Dom,

Cardinal Cody wrote to ask for a "complete report" of your appearance on a TV program last Friday evening. This is to be given to him on Thursday, Aug. 29. Will you please drop in to see me on Wednesday, the 28th, 10:00 A.M.? I'll have to have some facts before seeing or writing to the Cardinal, and we haven't much time. From the tone of his letter I'd guess that he plans on having you removed from the Archdiocese. So: (a) explanation for him; and (b) some remote thoughts about plans for your future. What will your possible removal from the C.T.U. scene mean to the schedule for next year?

It was hand-signed "Oke," and Oke, first my professor and then my colleague at Stonebridge Priory, was as decent a human being as you could find. But he was now the Very Reverend Terence M. O'Connor, O.S.M., Prior Provincial of the Eastern Province of Servites, U.S.A. The letter was, despite its casual format, as official as could be, and it involved myself, the Servite Provincial, and Cardinal Cody in a serious confrontation. (C.T.U., by the way, was the Catholic Theological Union, a new multiorder seminary combining Franciscans, Passionists, and Servites, just about to start its first year near the University of Chicago.) What had happened?

On July 25, 1968, Pope Paul VI issued an encyclical entitled *Humanae Vitae* ("On Human Life") in which he had forbidden any form of artificial birth control. A few weeks later I was in my office at C.T.U. when WTTW, Chicago's PBS television station, called to invite me for a panel discussion on the encyclical. I said I would do it on two conditions. I would be in lay rather than clerical clothes (tie, not collar) and would be subtitled on the screen as "Catholic theologian" rather than "Catholic priest." I did not intend to deny I was a priest and did not mind how I was introduced or addressed, but it seemed to me a conflict of interest to criticize my clerical superior while wearing my clerical uniform. They said all of that was just fine, but Margaret, who was in the office waiting for me, listening to my end of the conversation and guessing what it was about, said, "This is it, isn't it?" I replied, "Probably."

Throughout the hour-long TV program (taped for later airing), on which I was paired for balance with a very conservative Oak Park physician, I repeatedly made a simple comparison. There were many Americans who deeply loved their country and respected their legitimate leaders but considered them totally, irresponsibly, and immorally wrong about Vietnam (and about much other foreign policy as well). There were similarly many Roman Catholics who deeply loved their church and respected their legitimate leaders, but considered them totally, irresponsibly, and immorally wrong about birth control (and about much other sexual theology as well). I had not gone looking for a fight, but neither had I declined, as I could have, the invitation to start one. I did what I thought a theologian should do, and the cardinal did what he thought a bishop should do. Hence my Provincial's postcard.

I met with Oke as requested, and a few days later I received a carbon copy of his response to the cardinal's "show cause" request. I have always kept it (and his earlier letter to me) in memory of the decency and courage of someone now dead. In four pages of small type, Oke defended my integrity as an individual, emphasized my ability as a theologian, and came dangerously close to accusing the cardinal's procedures of being the real problem. What he underlined again and again was, on the one hand, the illegitimacy of secret accusation and, on the other, the necessity of academic freedom:

The fact that his orthodoxy may be questioned, on only hearsay evidence, and without even being faced by those who accuse him, is very shocking to him. (As it is to me, too, Your Eminence.) . . . To be accused secretly, and not to be informed of the specific charges, is certainly opposed to academic freedom. . . . It was Father Crossan and a young Benedictine, who has since died, that Dean Jerry Brauer of the University of Chicago Divinity School first contacted concerning the possibility of some Catholic representation on or near the campus. If Father Crossan were simply removed from the faculty of C.T.U. at this time, it could well be construed as a censoring and restriction of academic freedom, and could seriously harm our image there as honest Catholic intellectuals seeking the truth. . . . Personally I have nothing but confidence in Father Crossan. We've trained him in scientific methods, and to punish or otherwise censure him without a fair hearing would be, in my humble estimation, a grave injustice to him and the training we've given him.

Far from throwing me to the wolves, Oke almost joined me out there among them. And then an extraordinary thing happened. Nothing happened. There was no reply from the cardinal, not to the Provincial and not to me, not a word, not ever. One explanation is that it had become clear very soon that my TV comments were but tiny wavelets in a vast sea of disagreement with *Humanae Vitae* and that it was more prudent to ignore than to emphasize them. Another explanation is that Cardinal Cody was an ecclesiastical bully who always backed down when anyone had, like Oke, the courage to confront him.

In any case, as the shock waves subsided and school started, I came to my own decision. Despite Oke's kind reassurance that I could always find a teaching job elsewhere, my life was already so intertwined with Margaret's that I was not at all ready for an easy exile from Chicago. I decided to leave the monastery and the priesthood as soon as I was ready, and my idea of getting ready was to find a teaching job outside and then announce my departure. I called Notre Dame University, which had invited me to come full-time when I was teaching one summer in the early 1960s at St. Mary's across the road. I said that it was still private but that I intended to request a dispensation, leave the monastic priesthood by the book, and get married in the Catholic church.

I asked if they were still interested in me. They said no. I also spoke to Loyola University in Chicago, where I had already been teaching full-time. Same private message, same definite negative response. Same elsewhere and everywhere within Roman Catholic university-level theological faculties. It was never a question of my competence, but only of my ex-priest status and/or my controversial orthodoxy.

Here, in contrast to Oke's letter, is another one I have also kept for thirty years. It is dated February 11, 1969, and was sent to me after it became publicly known I was leaving the priesthood. It is not important what priest or which university it is from, and I let it speak for itself without comment:

Some of my best friends have left the active ministry, and I certainly do not rule out the possibility in my own future. I find the present structures of the Church unreasonable, and often dehumanizing, and the attitudes against further change actually hardening in the Vatican and American hierarchy. The situation in the Church is not good, and I believe the present time is going to be difficult and painful. But . . . in the concrete circumstances of 1969 it is better not to have someone who is known to be waiting for his final papers of laicization on the staff. I hope things will be different by 1970, but only time will tell.

With best wishes,

In Christ, . . .

One afternoon late that fall of 1968, in the middle of a squash game with my Strobl colleague at the Y in Hyde Park, I came to a somewhat epiphanic realization. I was not doing things the honorable way. I should not get a job and leave; I should leave and get a job. I was almost making departure contingent on occupational replacement. I talked it over with Margaret, who was, as usual, refreshingly blunt. To leave or not to leave was still my decision, she said, but others might make it for me soon if I didn't make it for myself sooner. I should inform my superiors immediately rather than embarrassing them by having them hear a secondhand rumor or backstairs gossip. I should ask for a dispensation—it's only courteous, like giving notice. I brought up the possibility that they might refuse me or, more likely, just ignore me. Margaret suggested that giving them six months to reply was only fair after twenty years. I knew she was absolutely right and that that was what I had to do and do immediately, but neither of us admitted how scared we both were until long afterward.

I invited my Provincial for lunch, which was, I thought, a very 1960s way to do things. Oke did not seem surprised at my announcement. I told the president of C.T.U. and asked him to call a special faculty meeting, so I could inform everyone at the same time. "I have decided," I told the meeting, "to request dispensation from the monastic priesthood, to get married, to teach (I hope) at some Roman Catholic university. If it is acceptable to you, I'll finish out my classes here this winter quarter (this was already January of 1969) and leave at its end in March. I wanted you all to hear this directly from me and be able to ask me any questions you may have." I waited amid absolute and utter silence for a few minutes, then thanked everyone, and left the room. Later that night a handwritten note was slipped under my door from one of the senior Passionist priests: "Thank you for the way you did that and God be with you. In Christ, Barnabas." The next day we all went on with C.T.U.'s first year of classes, and even with an announced ex-priest-to-be teaching there, the heavens did not fall, the seminarians did not leave, and Cardinal Cody did not even intervene.

I know priests who were terribly hurt in leaving, hurt because they truly did not want to do so or hurt because of the way they had to do it. Many wanted to be married priests and were forced to make an agonizing choice. That was not my situation, and compared to many others, I had a very easy transition. There were really only three difficult months in the first quarter of 1969. I had one minor and one major fear. The minor one was that the cardinal would order me immediately removed from C.T.U. Margaret, once again: "I have a spare room used mostly for storage. We can redo it as your office anytime you want. If you get thrown out, thank His Eminence for the sabbatical, move in here, and get some work done." The major fear was more profound. I was a hybrid, priest and theologian, monk and scholar, and I had never thought of them as easily separable. Could I, and how could I, leave behind monk and priest, but retain theologian and scholar? What if I had to give up both?

This, by the way, is how the final departure took place. There were no farewell parties, no official good-byes for ex-priests in the late 1960s. There was no severance pay and no parachute of any kind. Yours was the failure, if not the disgrace, and no matter what was said in private between individuals, nothing at all took place publicly as far as institutions were concerned. I finished the quarter on a Friday, borrowed Margaret's car the next day, and, without seeing a single person, left the monastery forever. The car's trunk was more than enough room for some books, an IBM Selectric typewriter, and a very few clothes. Almost everything I had was black and stayed behind. The order had given me six years of doctoral and postdoctoral study. I had given them in return six years of seminary and university teaching. From my point of view, we broke even.

I had come up through the Roman Catholic academic tradition, in Ireland, Rome, and Jerusalem, rather than through any of the great American divinity schools. I was known (if at all) to the denominational Catholic Biblical Association rather than the nondenominational Society of Biblical Literature. Those who knew me might no longer want me; those who might want me did not know me. (That was not, if I may look slightly ahead, a case of simple paranoia. In the early 1970s I sent out articles on both fronts, to nondenominational periodicals such as *New Testament Studies,* the *Journal of Biblical Literature,* and the *Journal of Religion,* but also to the denominational *Catholic Biblical Quarterly.* The former all accepted them, but the latter was silent about my submission entitled "Mark and the Relatives of Jesus." I waited six months, then phoned the editor. He said he thought he had told me no and had sent me the outside readers' comments. He had not, but he now did. I found them very inadequate, for example, "I could not read my New Testament and imagine Mark attacking the family of Jesus." I changed envelopes and mailed the article untouched to *Novum Testamentum,* a major international journal. It was accepted without question.) There was a real possibility that, as both an ex-priest and a controversial theologian, I might always be unacceptable precisely where I wanted to go, that is, out of a Roman Catholic seminary and into a Roman Catholic college or university. It might be possible to become a biblical scholar in a Protestant seminary, but the potential conflict between orthodoxy and research in any seminary situation was exactly what I wanted to avoid from then on.

My two fears were still there, minor and major, but now somewhat more specified.

"What," I asked Margaret, "if I get a position in biblical studies far from Chicago?" Commuting back and forth across the country did not strike either of us as a good way to continue a relationship or start a marriage.

"You could," she said, "teach part-time or even just do research and write. Both of us can live on my salary. Would that bother your pride, or any of the other stuff, too much?"

That was an easy answer and hence only a minor fear. The major one I did not discuss with anyone, hardly even with myself. What if I cannot stay in theological education, religious studies, or biblical criticism, but have to start all over in some other academic field or even get out of scholarship into something completely different? In all those months I never considered that possibility consciously, but it was always there as subterranean fear.

In those months I was often uncertain when *no available position* meant just that and when it meant none for somebody like me. C.T.U., which was not yet accredited as a degree-granting institution, was in discussion with DePaul University, whose theology department was about to start a master's degree program. I would happily have moved from one institution directly to the other, but decided to test DePaul before getting my hopes too high. I knew the philosophy department's chair and asked him for an off-the-record policy statement from the president about whether an ex-priest could be hired in theology at DePaul. The reply was clear and unambiguous: "What happens between you and your bishop is your business. We hire in terms of our need and your competence, nothing else." The acting chair of theology asked me how many professors they needed in biblical studies for a master's program. I said three would be very good, two would be good, and one, as long as it was myself, would be quite acceptable. By March or April it was all settled. I was contracted as an associate professor to start in the fall of 1969 at DePaul. They said my résumé deserved that rank, but I would happily have accepted assistant status or anything else I was offered.

The combination of DePaul as both Catholic and university, Vincentian and educational, and Father John Richardson, C.M., as both priest and president kept me there for the rest of my teaching career. I never sent out a résumé anywhere, never considered moving elsewhere, and told search committees seeking me out that I would not waste their time and that I was not movable under any circumstances. It was not just a case of gratitude or of loyalty, although those were surely operative. It was simply respect for the university's integrity and for the support it always gave me. From beginning to end.

DePaul's motto is a quotation from the biblical book of Proverbs, in Latin, *Viam sapientiae monstrabo tibi* ("I will show you the way of wisdom"), and its highest honor is the Via Sapientiae Award, usually given for distinguished service to the university. Since nobody *must* get it, it is not obvious or explicit when somebody does not receive it. I was quite theologically controversial in the 1990s, especially within the archdiocese of Chicago, and it might have been safer not to have given me any such recognition when I took early retirement from DePaul in 1995. At the dinner for the recipients of that and other university honors, I sat next to a member of the upper administration, a priest, a professor, and a Vincentian. I told him that I appreciated the administration's courage and knew it would have been more prudent to have skipped me. "Yes, but it would have been wrong, Dominic," was the reply. That is what I mean by institutional integrity; that is what kept me at DePaul for twenty-six years.

I started out to be a monk and a missionary priest. I was ordered to become a scholar and a seminary professor. It was not originally my idea, but I was very happy to accept it. The best game around, the great adventure with God, had subtly shifted beneath my feet. But it was still there as powerful as ever, and its imperative was just as strong as before. Between August 1968 and August 1969 the delicate surgery of separating priesthood from scholarship while retaining the latter, of moving from seminary to university while staying in theology was complete. Six months after I requested dispensation from my monastic and priestly vows, I received a rescript from the Sacred Congregation for the Doctrine of the Faith. It was sent to the Servite Procurator General in Rome and thence down the chain of command to me. It was granted "die 4 Julii 1969." Somebody in Rome may have had a sense of humor, but I doubt it. In any case, it was a relatively speedy reply, and one of my Servite colleagues suggested that the Vatican had kept a signed dispensation waiting for years in the hope I might one day request it.

Even apart from any confrontation with Cardinal Cody, I may have left to get married in any case. About that I can never now be certain. But of this I am sure: if it had been possible in those days to have stayed as a priest-scholar and seminary professor, I would not have done so, even if that were the only way to have remained in biblical studies. There was by then a conflict of interest I could no longer endure. The only integrity that scholars have is to say honestly what they have learned and to say clearly what they have discovered. They should not trim their reports to what a leader expects or a people want. That is the conflict of interest I found in being a priest-scholar and a seminary professor. Others do not find it so, and maybe it is not always inevitable, but it was unacceptable for me then, and it still is. It is one thing to be a strategic consultant, another to be a press secretary. It is one thing to be an investigative scholar, another to be a defensive scholar; one thing to find an answer as you proceed, another to know the answer before you begin; one thing to do research, another to do apologetics. It is also necessary, I think, to declare which you are doing.

I do not speak here, emphatically do not speak here, about personal ethics, but about procedural ethics, not about the morality of intention, but about the morality of due process. It was, similarly, the due process of research scholarship that forbade for me any collusion with ecclesiastical censorship. It had nothing to do with thinking I was always right and the censor was always wrong. It had to do with accuracy and honesty, with refusing beforehand to decide what I could discover or afterward agreeing to change what I had found. To be specific, the *Imprimatur* or *Imprimi potest* (Latin for "it can be published") from Roman Catholic church authority may be quite appropriate on liturgical or pastoral books, but it has no place on the front pages of a research investigation or a historical study. Its presence represents a professional conflict of interest, a breach of scholarly due process, and should be named as such.

Maybe also, for me, beneath the procedural ethics of scholarly integrity and intellectual honesty there is something more profoundly imperative at work. It probably goes back again to that adventure thing. Where is the adventure in knowing what you must find before you begin searching, in programming the result before beginning the research? Biblical apologetics may be a valid defense of God, but I do not consider it an adventure with God. And that's where I was and still where I am.

I sometimes have to insist with interviewers that I left the Roman Catholic priesthood, *not* the Roman Catholic church. If I equated the hierarchy with the church, the leadership with the people, that is, the part with the whole, I might have done so. But the church is, for me, a community developing and adapting its multiform tradition across time and space. It cannot, as such, be identified with any set of leaders or even destroyed by a mode of leadership that is itself a structural abuse of power. There is also something deeper even than community and tradition or, better, the heart and conscience of them both. It is not found only in Roman Catholicism, but that is where I learned it (unless something Celtic got there first). It is a question of *sensibility,* a sacramental consciousness or embodied awareness that the holy appears through the profane if you can but see it, that the sacred calls through the secular if you can but hear it, and that the spiritual is only present to us in material clothing. That is what I mean by being a Roman Catholic. I could no more leave that incarnational sensibility than I could lose my brogue or shed my skin.

I wanted, on the other hand, a definite therapeutic distance between myself and the hierarchy, a deliberate strategic separation between myself and that institution. I did not want my research after 1969 to be controlled either positively *or negatively* by its agenda, neither done for it *nor against* it. If the danger, before 1969, was that the institutional hierarchy would censor me, the danger, after 1969, was that I would attack it. I would then be just as trapped by its agenda as before.

From all of that, I make this suggestion for the future of the church I love. It is a proposal that will not solve everything, but one without which we may not be able to solve anything. I imagine something like this. There is a Third Vatican Council. The pope convenes all the bishops of the entire world. Then, in a solemn public ceremony in St. Peter's Basilica, they all implore God to take back the gift of infallibility and grant them instead the gift of accuracy.

"Did you lose your faith when you left the priesthood?" Sometimes the interviewer presumes an affirmative answer rather than bothering to ask the question. I was a little stunned the first time, because that had never occurred to me even as a possibility. That transition had never shaken my faith in God or anything else, just confirmed my suspicion that we humans abuse whatever power we have unless we struggle against it consciously, concretely, and corporately. It happens in family and school, business and commerce, law and medicine, church and state. Managers do it and presidents do it, bishops do it and popes do it. Even more seriously, we usually project our own abuses onto God and thereby declare them justified. So what else is new? All I can do in response to that initial question is to repeat the parallel that got me into so much trouble with Cardinal Cody in 1969. I said just as there are many Americans who do not accept the option of *love it* (the war) or *leave it* (the country), so there are many Roman Catholics who do not accept the option of *obey him* (the pope) or *leave it* (the Church). But the transition from monastery to university forced me to think about both religion and God in ways I had never done before. The reason, however, was not loss of faith or even of innocence, but the difference between priest and professor, seminary and university.

In seminary teaching my subjects were always the Christian Bible in general and its New Testament in particular. But the majority of my classes at DePaul University were required courses in general education, that is, courses outside a student's specific major, courses described unforgettably by an adult student with this supreme compliment: "This is pretty good for a shitty-course" (think of that as a single word, a technical term for a non-major requirement). Each DePaul student took two courses in religion, and those classes moved necessarily far beyond Christianity or Roman Catholicism into Hinduism and Buddhism, Judaism and Islam, Confucianism and Taoism. Preparing those classes forced me to think about religion itself, maybe for the first time. I had spent almost twenty years "in religion" or "in religious life," expressions that implicitly claimed celibate asceticism and monastic discipline as the true ideal of religion. But I had never actually thought about religion in the sense of comparative religion, of the history of religion, of the theory of religion. That only happened at DePaul, teaching classes about *other* religions to students among whom there were growing numbers not only from outside Roman Catholicism, but also from outside Christianity.

Two convictions grew ever stronger as I taught those courses, and they continue with me to this day. One is about religion itself as a fundamental human experience across time and space. The other is about God or, better, the Holy, since God is but one name for the Holy. That first conviction is that religion is a fundamental necessity of the human spirit. There was, first, the fact that religion was so plural, multiple, and diverse across time and space and, second, the fact that its announced replacements, such as science or commerce, looked more and more like new religions. It did not seem that we humans could live without transcendent meaning. I think, in other words, that the Enlightenment got it wrong. I may be prejudiced in that judgment by the fact that

Ireland never had an Enlightenment (we did have the British, of course, and we found them most enlightening). The Enlightenment could have been correct that religion was but a scream against the darkness and newly irrelevant since we had just turned on the lights. It certainly had a case against religion's abuses and impertinences. But, now, after about two hundred years of experimentation with secularism, I do not think it was correct in proclaiming religion dead. All it did was create itself as an alternative one, thereby negating its own assertion.

Religious diversity struck me not as disproof, but rather as proof, of religion's validity. I saw religion and language as twin possibilities hardwired into our brains. But people don't have religion-as-such, they have this religion or that religion, just as people don't speak language-as-such, they speak this language or that language. Still, the necessity of language, whether it is Irish, Japanese, or whatever, like the necessity of religion, whether it is Judaism, Hinduism, or whatever, indicated some basic human response, and it was the necessity of that response that fascinated me.

As with religion, so with God. Before I started to teach comparative religion, God was always safely there within the confines of Christianity and Roman Catholicism. I took God for granted, in the best sense of that expression, the way children take parents for granted. But first a question about God and then a conviction about the Holy began to change that easy acceptance. What does God mean when some religions, like Judaism or Hinduism, have a god, gods, or goddesses and some others, like Buddhism or Confucianism, do not? That question arose not only from respect for the integrity of other religions in the world around me, but even more so for the dignity of other religions in the undergraduate seats before me.

To answer that question, I stopped speaking about God in the context of comparative religion courses. I spoke instead of the Holy, the Sacred, or the Divine. I did not speak of the Transcendent because undergraduates, although probably not too conscious of the difference between transcendence (God is out there somewhere) and immanence (God is in here everywhere), took the

Transcendent as meaning something distinct and distant, possibly even indifferent and uninterested. The Holy worked especially well as an umbrella term for the referent of religion, because it had a minimum amount of negative baggage for students. But this was never simply a device for slipping in God under a new name. It was an acknowledgment that the referent of Buddhism, for example, was not God but Nirvana and that both God and Nirvana could be included under the common rubric of the Holy. What happened inevitably, of course, was that my understanding of the Holy did not just remain as a special accommodation for Buddhism or Confucianism, but began to infiltrate and change my own understanding of God.

I thought of the Holy as the infinite mystery that surrounded, supported, scared, and fascinated us. That was not based on any logical arguments for its existence. Those arguments (for example, medieval proofs for the existence of God) always left me totally indifferent, since, if they worked, they would subsume the Holy under human logic. They would but prove the Holy as a subdivision of ourselves, and who needs that? What I find compelling is the empirical evidence that humans are meaning-seeking animals, that we pursue meaning the way heat-seeking missiles hunt exhaust. Whether we are *rational* animals seems to me quite debatable, but we do use reason or unreason with equal ferocity in our search for and defense of meaning. Reason seems negotiable for us humans; meaning does not. It is our drive for meaning that batters against that surrounding mystery. But because it is a mystery to be faced, not a question to be answered or a problem to be solved, the Holy receives multiple responses, some of which are obscenely destructive and some of which are magnificently creative, none of which is absolute (although each may claim it), and all of which together are truer than any one alone. Mystics, those who have been close enough to the fire to know that it can burn as well as warm, call that mystery the void of no-thing-ness or the abyss of meaning-less-ness. But it is precisely that chasm that lures our search for meaning, that keeps it ever restless and unsatisfied, that forces us to negotiate our discordant meanings with one another, that refuses ascendancy to any one final meaning, especially to that which denies and negates all the others.

No matter how much we discussed God, gods, or goddesses, talked about the Holy, the Sacred, or the Divine, no undergraduate student ever asked me in twenty-six years at DePaul how the Christian Trinity, faith in God as Three-in-One, touched upon or was touched by that religious diversity. Nobody ever asked if we Christians had a peculiar God, one, maybe, with multiple personality disorder or dysfunctional family syndrome. But that question was on my mind all the time. Surely, I thought, there must be something fundamentally and even universally true between the imagination of the universal Holy and the imagination of the specific Trinity, even if that Christian terminology of persons and natures was simply its once-upon-a-time Greek clothing. It did not seem adequate to respond that the Christian God appears to us as Creator, Redeemer, and Consoler, for example, since that made the threeness rather relative. It could be two, three, or more, so that those three were but some of the presumably far more multiple faces or masks of divinity, the divergent ways in which it appeared and was named by us. Yet the trinitarian or triadic structure of the Trinity did not seem to be as indeterminate as that. It was inviolable as three, no more, no less. It was a closed and interactive loop rather than an open and indeterminate list. That question finally brought the trinitarian God of Christianity and the universal Holy of world religion together for me in this very basic conviction. Trinity is not just the special or peculiar nature of the Christian God—it is the very structure of the Holy. I do not say the structure of the Holy *in itself*. Avoiding that terminology is not to privilege or protect it in any way. We do not know anything in itself, since in-itself-ness is always beyond us, even about ourselves to ourselves. I do not even speak of myself in itself, but only about myself as seen by me. Similarly, then, I speak of the structure of the Holy not in itself, but as seen by every religion I know and any religion I can imagine.

I came eventually, in those years and courses at DePaul, to equate the classical and somewhat concrete terms *Father, Son,* and *Spirit,* within Christianity alone, with more philosophical and abstract terms, *metaphoricity, locality,* and *particularity,* across the range of comparative religion. That was still adventure, but now of a much more internal kind, in faith and thought, than an external one, in place and travel. And here I remind you of the Latin roots of that word. *Advenire* means "to arrive" or "to come," but *adventurus* means "future arrival, postponed advent, deferred destination." Adventure is, therefore, an always future arrival. Here, then, is how I understand the Holy as Trinity, the triadic and interactive loop of the Sacred as perceived by humans across the vast diversity of world religions.

Metaphoricity. Think about Father. It is already a metaphor on three levels. God is seen first as person, then as parent, and finally as father, that is, for alternative examples, as person and not as power, as parent and not as king, as father and not as mother.

Metaphor is "seeing *as,*" *seeing* the clouds *as* ships and the sky *as* sea, and then saying that the clouds *sailed* across the sky. The Holy, the ultimate referent of religion, is always approached through some base metaphor, some absolutely fundamental "seeing as." But seeing as person-parent-father is but one metaphorical image. It is metaphoricity itself that is intractably necessary as an inevitable first moment in human relationship with the Divine. We do not just name it; we invoke it *as* this or *as* that. Metaphoricity is, in other words, a first element in the structure of the Holy.

I see clearly four major symbols, or base metaphors, produced by religion. There are probably others, but these are the ones I see most obviously: the Holy is imagined as power, order, state, or person. By *power* I mean something like birth or storm, for example, the Holy in most oral or primordial religions. By *order* I mean something like our road-traffic or air-control systems, but neither created nor controlled by us, nor, indeed, by any transcendent agent. It is simply there as the pattern of the universe, for example, the Holy as mandate of heaven in Confucianism. By *state* I mean something like peace or happiness, but not under human control or manipulation, for example, the Holy as Nirvana in Buddhism. By *person(s)* I mean Supreme Being(s), person(s) like us but infinitely superior, endowed not so much with hands or feet, sex or gender, as with infinite intelligence and omnipotent will. And here the word *God* is entirely appropriate, for it means precisely this, the Holy as person(s).

All of those fundamental metaphors speak truthfully about the Holy. Each metaphor creates its own set of social superstructures and cultural communities with attendant benefits and liabilities. None of those metaphors is totally and exclusively correct. All of those metaphors together are far more accurate than any one of them alone.

Locality. Think next of Son. That, too, is triply metaphorical, as person, child, son. It is, in cultural origins, intrinsically linked to father because, against a Jewish background, the firstborn son acquires a double share of the ancestral inheritance. The (firstborn) son is in a specially privileged but not exclusively unique relationship with the father and with all that the father is or has.

Apart, however, from that specific background, the first structural component, metaphoricity, always leads directly into a second one, which I term *locality* or *manifestation*. I use the wider term *locality,* because in comparative religion there is always some material phenomenon in which that inaugural metaphoricity is especially, particularly, or uniquely made evident on earth. It can be almost anything, although in every case the metaphor's locality seems spatially, ecologically, historically, or culturally inevitable. It can be some person, place, or thing, some individual or collectivity, some cave or shrine or temple, some clearing in the forest or tree in the desert where that ultimate referent is peculiarly met or specially experienced.

Christianity speaks of locality as incarnation. Jesus manifests in flesh the character of the Jewish God who resists injustice. He nonviolently resists imperial oppression, despite ultimate execution and unfortunate martyrdom.

Particularity. In classical Christianity Father and Son were always relatively easy to imagine. Even as metaphors, you could at least understand their content. But the Holy Spirit, also known as the Holy Ghost, was always ultramysterious. As metaphor it meant "breath" or "wind," something profoundly invisible, especially necessary, and powerfully effective. It came, said classical Christianity, from both Father and Son, and it alone bound believers to them. Without that Spirit there was no faith in God and no union with God. In comparative religion, that spirit is particularity.

A given metaphoricity and locality are always something experienced and accepted by believers, but not by nonbelievers. For example, beside our lakeside summer home in Indiana there was a giant cottonwood. It was over a hundred years old and over a hundred feet high. It was very beautiful and very dangerous. If a storm were to bring it down, the branches would take out our house and the roots our neighbor's, or vice versa. I could admire it, respect it, and fear it, but I could not see in it a manifestation of the Great Spirit as might a Native American. That was not my metaphoricity and my locality as a Christian. Put otherwise, that particularity did not work for me as a Christian.

That mystery of particularity closes the trinitarian loop, and here the best analogy to divine faith is human love. You must experience faith or love as if it could not be other, but simultaneously you must also acknowledge that of course it could be other. Imagine this. I wake up tomorrow morning next to my wife and say, "If I had not met you, fallen in love with you, and married you, I would probably have met someone else, fallen in love with her, married her, and be waking up next to her this morning." That would be a very imprudent way to start my day, yet it is probably true. It is also unspeakably crude in its denial of human particularity. Or imagine this. A young couple have just lost their firstborn child and I tell them, "Don't worry. You can always have another one." That, too, is unspeakably cruel in its denial of human particularity. So also, then, with your religion: you must experience it as if no alternative were even possible. But at the back of your mind, you must also recognize that alternatives are always present. Particularity is not relativity, not the belief that anything goes or that everything is the same, but the acceptance that our humanity, at its deepest moments and profoundest depths, is individual and specific.

For individuals, groups, and communities this metaphoricity and that locality, this seeing-as and that seeing-where, seem absolutely true, and all other possibilities seem but heresy, apostasy, infidelity—mistake at best and treason at worst. Whether through genetic or ethnic occasions, personal or cultural drives, psychological or social forces, *this* metaphoricity and *this* locality are experienced as choosing us rather than our choosing them. I do not say (although I know it is true): "I might have been a Muslim or a Hindu, but I was born in Ireland and so I'm a Roman Catholic Christian." *Particularity,* too, is part of the structure of the Holy, and it is only through it that *metaphoricity* and *locality* act upon us.

The greatest gift I received from teaching those undergraduate classes in comparative religion at DePaul was that understanding of the Holy as Trinity. It was not at all a way of slipping the Christian God into every other religion by the back door. Indeed, in the opposite direction, the Christian image of God-as-person was but one fundamental way of seeing-as, one perfectly valid example of metaphorical particularity. That understanding allowed me to accept my own religion with utter fidelity without having to negate the integrity of everyone else's. Particularity is not relativity. It is destiny.

Most of that never came up in class, and I never met a student who thought about it out loud for even a second. I usually started any discussions about God by asking this question: "How would your life change tomorrow if you became certain today that God did not exist?" Sometimes male students would respond that they could then do anything they wanted. Since classes were about evenly coed, female students would usually explain to them quite clearly that, no, they could not. Once we got past sex or reduced it at least to bad thoughts, and once it was recognized that law and police would take care of much else, there was only one final answer that always came up.

If there were no God, there would be no eternal life. It always came down to that. The purpose of divinity was our immortality. I neither debated that function nor disturbed that consensus, but I wondered silently if all of world religion came down to just that: a guarantee of one's own personal and individual immortality. Just that? Only that?

CHAPTER 5

A Villa on Ibiza

When Margaret and I left Ibiza in 1982, we did not know that it was for the last time. After a decade of glorious summers and impossible problems building a house on that beautiful Mediterranean island and living there for three months each year, we did not know that by 1983 all those problems would be solved, Margaret would be dead, and I would never get back to Villa Aisling again. In retrospect, the most intractable of those insistent difficulties were but pale metaphors for and phantom warnings of that permanent loss, that final separation.

I have read best-sellers about spending a year in Provence or living under the Tuscan sun and wonder if Jennie and Peter in France or Frances and Ed in Italy were much smarter or just much luckier than Margaret and Dominic in Spain. I recognize the beauty of climate, serenity of vista, ecstasy of environment, and eccentricity of population that they describe. I recognize their frustration with foreign locations, but each obstacle is eventually removed and is amusing in the retrospect of fictional story, if not of factual memory. But never in those books does frustration slowly climax into fury, so that instead of smiling indulgently if condescendingly at native peculiarities, the authors want to scream and throttle the lawyer, the architect, the builder, the plumber, the electrician, and many more besides. Fury, by the way, precludes condescension.

Why was our experience so different? France and Italy were not Spain, the Mediterranean mainland was not a Mediterranean island, the 1980s and 1990s were not the 1970s. Does that explain it? Those others bought older houses and refurbished them from itch; we built from scratch. Does that explain it? Maybe it was simply the random fate of time and place that forced us to final fury despite the beguiling scenery and seductive climate all around us. Maybe we broke some law of real estate (cosmic, foreign, Spanish, Mediterranean, insular, or all of the preceding?) by falling in love with an empty site rather than one with a fully or even partially finished house on top of it. Of this I am sure: we were not deluded romantics imagining languid summer idylls to be achieved without problems, struggles, or difficulties. But we did expect them to be diverse, successive, and soluble rather than specific, systemic, and insoluble. We were not romantics about Ibiza because our guidebook was Elliot Paul's 1937 memoir, *The Life and Death of a Spanish Town*. I have it beside me now, the cover a little ragged, the pages a little brown, and the smell a little musty. The inside cover has our stamped address: Villa Aisling, Cala Llonga (S. Eulalia del Rio), Ibiza, Baleares, Spain. Cala Llonga is mostly a tourist phenomenon, and its official town is nearby Santa Eulalia del Rio, the titular town of Paul's elegy for a traditional past lost to modern brutality.

Santa Eulalia is slightly to the north of Cala Llonga along the coast as the seagull flies, but farther away by an inland road skirting the intervening hills. Sometime in 1936, before that road was there, Elliot Paul came over those hills and looked down from the northern cliffs at the narrow bay of Cala Llonga. "One mounts, the vista shifts and changes, and then on the other side of the divide one looks far down into a narrow sheltered cove, converging cliffs joined by perfect crescent beach, green-yellow depths of water over sand, impenetrable blue." It was a "secluded cove, remote and beautiful" in 1936. We stood on that same spot in 1972, and although it was no longer either secluded or remote, it was still incredibly beautiful. The small bay opened widely to the Mediterranean at its eastern end, narrowed as the encasing cliffs came together at the beach, and then opened widely again to a deep, western valley. In 1936 the bay was empty, but as Paul continued, "at the foot of the steep ascent are a house and several sheds."

In 1972 there were hotels and restaurants on either side of the beach, but in the northwestern corner and west of the hotel you could still see ruins of those buildings once owned by the bay's only inhabitant, sixty-year-old Mousson the potter. He had the strange idea of dividing everything he made between himself, his wife, and his two helpers. "In each *peseta,* four *reals.* One worker, one real. Where Mousson got his ideas, it is impossible to say. They were dangerously simple and will cost him his life. The neighbors called him a communist. Mousson read a little, learned as much as he could of what a communist might be, and accepted the designation." The Spanish Civil War began, and its waves of atrocity washed over Ibiza: pro-Franco planes killed fifty anti-Franco civilians, anti-Franco anarchists slaughtered a hundred pro-Franco prisoners, pro-Franco troops machine-gunned four hundred anti-Franco republicans. Mousson died, for the wrong name but the right attitude, and all the beauty of Cala Llonga could not obliterate that tragedy. Spain was a miniature of what Europe would be, and Ibiza was a miniature of what Spain already was.

When Margaret and I visited the Greek island of Corfu we took as our guidebook *My Family and Other Animals* by Gerald Durrell. When we went to the Spanish island of Ibiza we took as our guide a very different author, a very different book. Two writers, two Mediterranean islands, Ibiza from the first half of the 1930s, Corfu from the second half of the 1930s, but only the latter would induce romantic delusions. I stop as I type this and look up amazon.com. The Corfu book is alive and well; it "usually ships within 24 hours." The Ibiza book "is currently not available," and its author has become Paul Elliott. I would not wish Durrell out of print, but Paul back in. He entitled his threnody on the young women of Santa Eulalia to whom he had taught English *"Les Jeunes Filles en Fleur,"* and he concluded with their names as "wounds incurable, hopes in cinders, and beneath their white feet a dead land and the shadows of vultures wheeling!" We were neither lost romantics nor innocents abroad when we first saw Cala Llonga, but we had more to learn than we ever imagined.

Margaret had no family, so mine was now ours, and we decided to visit Ireland for a week each summer. But as long as we were already in Europe, where could we spend the rest of the summer? We had both traveled extensively, if separately, all over Europe and did not want to keep doing that each summer. Margaret wanted us to go together to two particular places: to visit the Cotswolds together, stay at the Bay Tree Inn in Burford, and have old Stilton with older port after dinner, and to visit Torcello in the Venetian lagoon, spend a day with its ancient mosaics, and have a martini at Harry's Bar. We got to Burford twice in the early 1970s, but as our Spanish adventure began, Venice was postponed again and again. We finally decided to go there from Ibiza in the summer of 1983. My date book is crossed out and hard to read, but Margaret's is not. We were to be on Torcello in the Venetian lagoon the last three days of that June. Where else to go, however, apart from those two special locations initially agreed upon? We both loved the islands of the Mediterranean, but apart from Capri we had been mostly on those in Greece, from Delos and Myconos to Crete and Rhodes. Neither of us had ever been to Spain's Balearic Islands, and so, in June 1971, we stood where Paul had stood about forty years earlier, fell totally under the spell of that beguiling view, and put down a deposit on Plot 149, Urbanization Cala Llonga, SA.

Ibiza, by the way, is an island with several unbearably honky-tonky overbuilt coastal sites, but many other ones retain an unchanged Bronze Age landscape of stone terraces, of oleander and bougainvillea, of wild thyme and wild rosemary, of apricot, olive and fig, of azure sky and glistening sea. The other Balearic Islands are Majorca, Minorca, and Formentera. James Joyce describes them in *Finnegans Wake* like this: "therenow theystood, the sycomores, all four of them, in their quartan agues, the majorchy, the minorchy, the everso and the fermentarian with their ballyhooric blowreaper." I first read the *Wake* on Ibiza/Everso, an environment that made the book seem quite sane, and took the name of our newly built Villa Aisling from its pages: "an aisling vision more gorgeous than the one before t.i.t.s., a roseschelle cottage by the sea for nothing for ever." Aisling is the Irish word for "dream," but the dream was not for nothing, not forever, and touched at times by nightmare.

During those years on Ibiza I learned the hard way about two very different types of society. One type is a *universal* or *functional* society. You have, at least in theory, equal access to properly due goods and services irrespective of who you are or whom you know. I go to get my driver's license, for example, and presuming the set fees are paid and the test passed, I should get it. I do not have to know somebody who knows somebody who is related to the examiner's second cousin once removed. If that sort of process intervenes, universal or functional societies call it corruption, bribery, nepotism, influence peddling, or old-school-tieism. But almost all of the past world and some (much? most?) of the present world consider it none of the above, just normal procedure, just business as usual.

Another type is a *patronal* or *influential* society. Your access even to appropriate goods and services depends inevitably on whom you know and whom that person knows. You are a client appealing directly upward to a patron or a client appealing indirectly upward to a patron via a broker. And, of course, as with clients, brokers, patrons upward, so with patrons, brokers, clients downward. Each must get something in a relationship obviously asymmetrical with regard to power, money, and influence, but curiously symmetrical with regard to need, service, and response. In ancient Rome, for example, clients waited outside rich villas to "greet" the emerging master every morning, to accompany him to the baths through the crowded streets, and to receive in return a *sportula,* either money for a meal or invitation to a meal. (Pliny the Younger once insisted that such client/patron meals should have the same food and drink for all alike, that no inequality or discrimination should be allowed. "But how," asked his friend, "do you not go broke with that morality?" "Oh," said Pliny, "when we eat together, I eat as they do normally—they do not eat as I do normally.")

When I was working on *The Historical Jesus* in the late 1980s, I read a lot of historical and anthropological studies about clients, brokers, and patrons within the patronage system as an ancient and even modern Mediterranean phenomenon. To emphasize its pervasive importance in the first century, I entitled my book's three parts: "Brokered Empire," "Embattled Brokerage," and "Brokerless Kingdom." The question I asked was this: Granted that humans related to one another patronally in that ancient world, how else but patronally could they relate to the Divine? Was religion, with its priests or prophets, its teachers or mystics, its temples, sacrifices, and prayers, an unavoidable broker or intermediary between the human and Divine? Was this or that religion or this or that way within the same religion the only way to the Holy? No broker, no access? Or was religion a way of bringing the community and the Holy into as unmediated a confrontation as possible? If Jesus was the only way to God, did that mean he was, on the one hand, a broker of power or, on the other, a model of holiness? Did he control access to the Jewish God of justice *or* incarnate fully the Jewish God of justice? Was Christianity, to stay with that religion as an example, a matter of finding some appropriate saint who had access to Mary who had access to Jesus who had access to God? Was it client to broker to patron, up and down that heavenly ladder? There is a huge difference between a private access to holiness and a public example of holiness. There is a huge difference between a mediator-as-broker who bars or controls the way and a mediator-as-model who exemplifies and opens up the way.

I read and used that brokerage material in the late 1980s and early 1990s, but I first encountered it, in the unrecognized flesh, in the late 1950s and early 1960s. At the Servite college in Rome, an American priest-colleague working on his doctorate (the client) knew the papal master of ceremonies (the broker). The master of ceremonies was not a cleric in charge of liturgical ceremonies, as one might think, but the layman who handled social audiences. He could get you not private interviews, of course, but good front seats at more general meetings with the pope (the patron). Whenever my colleague or I (he was broker for me) requested audience tickets for visiting American friends, we got very good ones without any difficulty. At Christmas, Easter, his birthday, and his name day, we went to see our broker and brought a small gift (never, never, never money). I learned Italian, off a secure base in Latin, by hearing and speaking it rather than studying and writing it, so I recall by ear, not sight. The visit was to *porge auguri* (spelling doubtful), that is, to offer our congratulations and pay our respects. It was very important to him that his house be crowded, so that he made a *bella figura,* looked important within the community, on such occasions. It is the same scene that opens *The Godfather,* Part I, and its formal process, but not its criminal content, is an example of standard Mediterranean patronage operations.

I did not realize then what was involved in such processes, but I ran into it again, head on, in Ibiza in the 1970s. I am *not,* repeat *not,* talking about bribes. I often wished it were as simple as that and even asked, when I got desperate enough, whether we were supposed to be bribing somebody. It was not that at all. It was simply a society, a bureaucracy, still poised somewhere between an older patronal and a newer universal model of operation. I was not in the least interested in criticizing that model—I just wanted to understand the system, get with it, and have a villa built.

Urbanization Cala Llonga had bought out the entire northern cliff of the bay. They blasted out, surfaced fully, and balustraded securely a very fine road along its base, took it around the outside tip of the bay, and stopped in a nice, circular dead end. They then blasted out a second road parallel to the first one halfway up the cliff and covered it with dirt and loose stones, leaving from its open edge a 45-degree drop down the hillside. It was that second "road" we climbed in an old Citroen for the view that sold us on Cala Llonga in mid-June 1972. Our plot was sited below and accessed down from that upper road just as it started its curve around the hill above the open sea. We told the company that we were buying a plot not for an investment, but for a villa, and that we would return in 1973 to start the process. They said there was no problem, that was what they were there for, and that by the next summer, maybe, the upper road would be surfaced and completed. It was not done by 1973, or by 1983, when I stopped caring about it.

On my desk as I write is a file of correspondence about two inches thick. It records in excruciating detail our repeated failures to get that villa built in 1973, 1974, and 1975. I spare you the details, but one letter is too perfect to omit. We had written to the Madrid conglomerate of which the local company was a minor subsidiary requesting (actually, demanding) help in building our villa on the site they had sold us for that purpose. They replied:

Although we intend setting up a "Works Management" service to place at our customers' disposal, the fact is that it is not yet sufficiently organized to be able to offer it to you and to make ourselves responsible for the results. In all events, we are at your disposal to help you with the greatest impartiality and in a disinterested way. But for the moment we cannot commit ourselves at all in this matter. We have no hesitation in recommending FISA, it being the Island's most important firm and its reliability being unquestionable. We doubt, however, that they will undertake the execution of a chalet, it being a work of little importance.

That letter put us beautifully in our place ("of little importance"), and we particularly liked that term "execution." It seemed most appropriate. By summer 1975 we decided to quit. Only the projected price, not the expected villa, seemed to rise successfully. That, unlike the building, had gone up 35 percent between 1972 and 1975. It was simply time, however, to learn about Mediterranean patrons, brokers, and clients, 1970s-style.

After lunch in a restaurant on a hillside back of the beach in early summer 1975, its expatriate British owner asked us how our villa project was coming along. We admitted that we were giving up, selling the site, and accepting defeat. We were wrong, he told us, to work directly with those big building companies the way we did. That wasn't how it was done around there. We should have obtained a "facilitator" (his word), a resident, multilingual individual whose job was handling villa construction for absent, foreign owners. He would get us a lawyer, architect, and contractor, get us the permits and do the paperwork, all for a flat 12 percent of the construction price. After he left our table, we sat there talking for hours, eased by gin and tonic for Margaret and Campari and soda for me. We decided to try one more time and finally drove over to see George Jensen, the "facilitator" he had suggested. That term was totally inadequate to the situation. A facilitator helps or assists in doing what might still be done without him, but with less speed and more difficulty. Our "facilitator" was a cosmopolitan expatriate Dane, but also an on-the-spot Mediterranean-style broker without whom we would never have gotten anything done.

Our method of payment was hilariously simple, and two years earlier we would never have dreamed of doing it. The contract for our two-level stepped-down-the-cliff villa had six payment stages: 10 percent on signing, 25 percent on lower-level completion, 20 percent on upper-level completion, 20 percent on inside completion, 20 percent on outside completion, and 5 percent after six months of occupancy. Construction was to start in September and be finished in May of 1976. We gave our facilitator-broker a camera and four rolls of film, we sent him $10,000 or so every time he sent us a roll confirming next-stage completion, and we first saw the finished villa as our flight from London's Gatwick Airport descended the eastern side of the island in early June 1976.

During the two years we were attempting to get the villa started, construction wages had changed dramatically in Spain. It was long overdue. But so had the zoning regulations, also long overdue. When we first stood atop the northern Cala Llonga cliffs in 1972 and looked at the southern ones across the bay, they showed a zigzag scar among the pines. A road had been blasted out for a hotel at the top. The group went bankrupt, and the hillside was declared a green zone, but the road scar would remain for at least a hundred years. To our right, beyond the beach, beyond the valley, beyond the golf-course development of Roca

Llisa, a haze of smoke rose incessantly against the magnificent Mediterranean sky. It was a giant, open, permanently burning garbage site among the hills. Years later as we sat on our terrace at cocktail time and watched the flocks of seagulls winging seaward down the valley, we tried to forget that they had just spent a hard day at the dump. There were rumors, apocryphal I presume, that the hotels below just ran their sewage pipes out to sea and that you could meet in the bay at noon what you had left in your toilet at dawn. Be that as it may, by the early 1970s, zoning regulations, developmental controls, and planning laws were badly needed on Ibiza and the other Balearic islands.

There was to be no more building until a comprehensive plan was drawn up locally, regionally, and Balearically. The whole had to await each component's proposal, and each component's proposal had to await the whole's approval. That was ideal, sensible law, but it would totally dislocate local business and ensure that construction workers, with their new and improved wages, would have no work. The legally unacceptable but politically necessary compromise was that, yes, there would be building projects, but, no, there would be no building licenses. Not for us and not for anyone else. The local authorities knew all about the villa, our lawyer reassured us, knew there was a construction crew with a nine-month job up there, knew it had no building permit, but had no intention of stopping the job. The villa was completed, and then the trap snapped shut.

There were no electricity poles on the upper road, and electric power was supplied for construction by a hookup to one of the lamp poles on the lower road. That was, in effect, a 150-yard, 220-watt extension cord snaking up the 45-degree hillside over the rocks and around the pines to our site. That was also how we got our electricity those first summers after the villa's completion. It was weird, but it worked, and since the whole complex of lower and upper roads belonged to Cala Llonga SA, everyone seemed satisfied. It was also quite illegal and quite public, rather like building without a permit, so we tried, in our lawyer's favorite phrase, "not to worry." We didn't worry, and this is what happened.

When we arrived at the villa for the summer of 1978, we found inside a small and antiquated gas refrigerator, a large package of candles, and a report that the inspector had declared the electric hookup illegal (which it was), dangerous (which it was), and about to be severely fined unless removed (which it immediately was). We contemplated a summer with lots of visitors and no electricity. My brother, his wife, and their three boys, for example, were coming in July for two weeks. We tried not to imagine keeping food for seven in that tiny, antique refrigerator instead of our regular full-sized electric one. So we opened some duty-free liquor and made emergency plans. By ten o'clock the next morning we had gathered all the usual suspects in the director's offices of Gas y Electricida SA in Ibiza town. Besides ourselves we had George Jensen for us, Paco Perez for Cala Llonga SA, and even our lawyer on the phone from Palma. Yes, they all agreed, it was a quite illegal hookup, and Cala Llonga SA should not have done it, but here were the Crossans who had come all the way from America for three months and surely GESA would not leave them without electricity. It was now a personal and human problem, not an impersonal and legal one. The director relented and told the inspector to ignore the hookup for that summer, but warned us that it all better be regularized as soon as possible. That had been solved in good Ibicencan fashion. But then, and only then, did we learn of the fatal problem, the ultimate catch-22.

This was the series of legal documents required for Villa Aisling. First, a special military permit from the Ministry of Defense, since we were foreigners building in a coastal zone. Second, a building permit from the Santa Eulalia municipality. Third, after the construction was completed, a dwelling permit from the Ministry of Housing, a certificate that the house was fit and safe to be occupied. Finally, an electricity contract with GESA, the subministry for gas and electricity. You could not get the electricity contract without the dwelling permit. You could not get the dwelling permit without the building permit. You could not get the building permit without the military permit. All of that made eminent legal and bureaucratic sense, but we were now trapped. We had neither military nor building permit and had been assured that that did not constitute a problem. That was quite correct, apparently, for getting a house built, but not for getting it supplied with electricity.

A word about our lawyer. When we sat in his impressively paneled offices in Palma, we always felt he could do anything, get anything done. We imagined his heraldic coat of arms as a lion *rampant* with the motto "Not to worry" below it. He came over to Ibiza that summer of 1978 in an attempt to sort out the electricity impasse. We went together to the small, white-walled room for permits and certificates in Santa Eulalia's town hall.

"I have," said our lawyer, "a villa in Cala Llonga constructed without a building permit, and now I cannot get a dwelling permit for the electricity contract."

"You should," said the clerk, "have thought about that before you constructed the villa, shouldn't you have?"

That was just about the content of the conversation, and as our lawyer flew back to Majorca, we changed his escutcheon to a kitten *couchant* with the motto "Worry, worry a lot."

The solution, once again, came through major local brokerage, and I emphasize that bribery was never in question. A complex of vacation apartments in the style of a Spanish village was being built in the early and mid-1970s just below that restaurant whose owner had first sent us in search of a facilitator. He himself was involved in the project, and so was that facilitator. We had come, in other words, full circle. They had obtained dwelling permits for more apartments than were actually constructed. "What," our facilitator asked GESA's managing director, "if I give you one of those unused certificates and you use it to grant the Crossans their electricity contract? It is, after all, in the same bay." There was no deceit, everybody knew what was happening, but everybody wanted the problem solved. The certificate, beside me as I write, is clearly for Urbanization Pueblo Esparragos, not Urbanization Cala Llonga, but is dated about the right time for our villa, July 28, 1976. It worked. It was accepted. I have also beside me a GESA contract dated August 10, 1981, and in the upper left corner under "Dwelling Permit" is the date July 28, 1976.

Our facilitator was the perfect broker in dealing with lawyers, architects, and builders. But we soon realized he was not effective with plumbers, electricians, or carpenters. Initially we presumed his influence with those latter who had worked on our villa. We were wrong there, but it took us a long time to learn. One part of the trouble was that nobody said no on Ibiza. I never heard anyone reply, "This we will not do" or "That we cannot do." If we asked a plumber, even one from the company that had put in the toilet, to come and fix it now that it was leaking, he would make a precise appointment for a day and time, get detailed instructions on how to find us, and never come. Again and again, over and over. Always a new excuse, always a new promise. In our first years with a finished villa, we found it impossible to get plumbers, electricians, or carpenters near the place.

There was only one other villa on the upper road, but several ones, mostly French-owned, just below it on the lower road. We talked to the Parisian couple on our road, and once again, we learned belatedly how it was done on Ibiza. They all had a common caretaker who looked after their villas during the winter and prepared them for occupancy before they arrived for a month each summer. He was also their facilitator or broker for all villa maintenance jobs. He got, and could unfailingly get, any plumber or electrician, mason or gardener, carpenter or painter who was needed.

He made an appointment to see us and discuss becoming our caretaker as well. He and his wife came together and brought us a watermelon as a gift. We sat together and had a drink, they looked over the villa, we finally got round to the subject at hand, and they proposed $1,000 a year. That fee theoretically involved regular visits and security checks as well as arrival preparation and cleaning. But, unlike all our neighbors who were there for only one month each summer, we were there for three months. We knew that Francisco did not visit those other villas "regularly" or, in fact, at all. What actually happened was that for two days, the Thursday and Friday before somebody was to arrive, he, his wife, and their only child worked furiously to get the house ready. When we asked him if he would come up to our villa every week when we were gone, he replied that he could not promise anything as specific as that since the road was often impassable in the winter rains. That was beautiful, really beautiful, unanswerable, uncontrollable, impossible to check up on. We appreciated that fact, reached for our checkbook, and never again had any problems getting maintenance help for the villa. We simply asked our caretaker, and somebody always came.

And there were a lot of summer villas around. When we first saw Francisco, he was riding a Vespa-type motorcycle. When we last saw him he was driving a Renault 4. By then he also had a telephone (we never got one), and his daughter was in a convent school on Majorca. We were very glad to have him and pay him whatever he wanted, and we had absorbed another lesson in basic Mediterranean brokerage. You need more than one broker to function adequately. There are major facilitators, and there are minor facilitators. That classification does not judge their worth, but simply describes the level of problem they solve.

By 1981, after five years of struggle, we had finally solved the electricity problem. We still did not have either a military permit or a building permit for the villa, but at least their absence was not causing any immediate difficulties. They were also about to become completely irrelevant.

A couple of years later in Chicago, we returned from a party on Saturday, April 30, 1983, and Margaret complained of chest pains but dismissed it as indigestion. On Sunday evening they returned, and I called the doctor. Was she relaxed or doing something strenuous? Was it just in her chest or in an arm as well? No, she was lying on the couch watching *Masterpiece Theater,* and, yes, the pain was in her arm as well. He sent us straight to the emergency room at Northwestern Memorial Hospital, about five minutes away. Margaret disappeared behind closed doors, and I was told to stay in the waiting room where I would be "more comfortable."

After about an hour and a half, the resident, in phone consultation with our doctor, was deciding whether to send Margaret home or keep her that night for observation. In the middle of that process Margaret had a heart attack. I did not see her for another hour or so until after she was stabilized and being moved to an intensive care unit. It was all terribly unreal. Margaret looked exactly the same, nothing in her face indicated what she had been through, and I had seen nothing for myself. After she was sedated for the night, the intensive-care physician warned me that the next twenty-four hours would be critical and that I should be ready for anything.

The next morning was equally unreal. Margaret went through her date book and gave me a long list of people to inform, appointments to cancel, and jobs to do. She seemed her old and unchanged self or, if anything, more energetic than ever. (I did not know then how to calculate the effects of sedations and tranquilizers.) She was soon moved to an ordinary room, was allowed visitors, took a stress test, wore a heart monitor for twenty-four hours, and was sent home in two weeks. We both thought all had gone well and that she was home to recover.

We told ourselves that her case was more like my brother's than like my father's, more transient problem than permanent damage, more fortunate warning than serious restriction. After my father's heart attack in 1963, his activity was severely restricted and his life limited to eight more years and a second heart attack. After Daniel's heart attack in 1979, his doctor only limited his activity by shifting him from squash to tennis. (He must never have seen him play tennis.) We thought, therefore, that my brother's heart had not been damaged as badly as my father's. We did not know then that he too had only eight years to live from first to fatal attack. We told one another that this was not like Dad's heart attack, but like Daniel's. We even wondered if we could get to Ibiza (and that side trip to Venice) if not in June, then at least later in the summer.

Margaret was still spending most of the day in bed. We lived at Harbor Point, a high-rise on Chicago's lakefront, and she was to walk around the hall of our floor once each day. But her legs hurt when she did it, and not recognizing a damaged heart throwing off small blood clots, we thought it was weakened muscles from too much time in bed. On Thursday, May 19, at almost the same time as that first Sunday, we were lying on the bed watching TV. Margaret suddenly thrashed around with her right arm and leg and tried to speak from the right side of her mouth. She had been given all sorts of pills to be taken every so many hours and had decided, rather than wake up many times at night, to lump them together a little into only two or three wakeups. I knew what she was trying to say: "I've overdosed on those damn pills, I've overdosed on those damn pills." But her whole left side was completely paralyzed.

I held her on the bed with my left arm as she kept trying to get up and dialed 911 from the telephone on her side of the bed. I told the dispatcher about the heart attack and said my wife was having a stroke. Margaret kept shaking her head and saying it was the pills. The fire ambulance arrived within five minutes, reassured me that it did not look like a stroke, and kept me in the front with the driver because I would be "more comfortable" there. It was, indeed, not a stroke, but a transient ischemic attack, a passing blockage of blood flow to the brain resulting in a temporary paralysis. Margaret, however, was back first in intensive care and then in an ordinary room. We never saw the implications of leg pain or ischemia, and her cardiologist, if he knew, never told us anything. He usually talked in medical jargon, and when he was gone, we tried to find a nurse willing to translate for us.

One day I was in Margaret's room when her monitor went crazy. Within about ten minutes the room was filled with staff— the cardiologist, residents, interns, nurses, a large group of medical personnel. They asked me to step outside to the waiting room where I would be "more comfortable." I retreated instead to an empty room across the hall and stood in its doorway. I could not see Margaret, but only the foot of her bed, as the room was L-shaped, with the narrow entrance and bathroom to the right and the bed hidden back at a right angle to that entrance. They must have been in her room for over half an hour and came out in hierarchical procession. The cardiologist looked straight at me, said nothing, and started down the hall past me to the right. I hurried past the entourage, caught up, and asked him what had happened. He said, "She certainly cannot afford to lose any more pumping action." That was it, that was all, and I stood there, gasping for breath, torn between wanting to keep up with him and learn more and going back immediately to Margaret. I let him go and went back.

I usually talked to Margaret first thing in the morning, and we discussed the best time for me to come over in keeping with medical plans for her day. On Saturday, June 4, we talked around eight o'clock, and she said to wait until the Sunday *Chicago Tribune* was available and then come over with it. An hour later the call came from the intensive-care station.

"Please get over here immediately."

"What's wrong?"

"Get over here immediately, please."

"Is Margaret all right?"

"They are doing resuscitation right now. Please get over here immediately."

The message was quite clear, and the nurse's face, as she was running down the hall to stop me before I reached Margaret's room, confirmed it. I took a while to say good-bye, alone in the room with Margaret, her face turned toward me on the pillow, serene and peaceful but gone forever.

The cardiologist was still waiting for me at the nurses' station. I asked him what had happened at the end, and he said that he could do an autopsy that afternoon if I wanted it and let me know by evening. I was not interested in clinical details and knew enough already. Margaret's heart had been far more terribly damaged by that first heart attack than even my father's. I thought that she was slowly recovering, but she had been slowly dying. I knew it then, and the problem was not information but survival. I told him there would be no autopsy. Margaret had no family in the world, and I had none in America. How was I to do what had to be done, to bury my heart in a wooden box? I thanked everyone, asked to use the telephone, and called a close friend, a Jesuit priest at Loyola who had known Margaret since her Chicago Art Institute days. The first and most important thing to do, he said, was to call a funeral home. They would take over and tell me what else to do, and, yes, he would be sad but honored to say her funeral Mass.

I crossed Michigan Avenue from the hospital to the funeral home, a few blocks from east to west. They took me through all the decisions I had to make and concluded with this: "Come back as soon as possible and bring a dress in which you think Margaret would want to be buried." With details of wake, funeral Mass, and burial all settled, I went home and started telephoning our friends and colleagues. When I called Ireland, Daniel said he would come over immediately to represent the family, went upstairs to pack, and started smoking again.

Friends came that afternoon and again on Sunday, staying with me until Daniel arrived that evening. Their support was precious beyond words. Sister Marion Joseph, sister of Aileen's husband Tom, a Mercy Sister and surgical nurse at the Mater Hospital in Dublin, was in Chicago taking a course on pastoral counseling. Her support and Daniel's were also precious beyond words. They got me through the wake on Monday evening and the funeral on Tuesday morning. I was not able to eat much, save for toast and tea, until a lunch set by friends that Tuesday afternoon. Daniel stayed for a week and helped me with all sorts of legal and financial details. When he left he invited me to come back with him to Ireland for the summer, but I decided against it. That was the first of several purely instinctive, but instinctively correct, decisions I would make in the next three months.

During the five weeks Margaret was in hospital, I taught my assigned courses at DePaul. Everything was suspended during class, and then, when I left the room, it was waiting there for me at the door. When you only get, say, three days to bury a beloved person and then go back to a full working schedule, it must be almost impossible to mourn properly; it must be almost inevitable that you shelve the full implications of your loss, postpone the full reckoning with your new status. Margaret had died the first weekend of June, the same weekend we left every year, and would have left that year, for a visit to Dublin and a summer on Ibiza.

I now had three months in Chicago with nothing to do but mourn. DePaul kindly offered me something to do for the summer, but I declined, as I had done with Daniel's invitation. I did not particularly know why I refused, and I certainly never thought to myself that I needed a summer to mourn. My reaction was instinctive, immediate, definite. We sometimes talk, in such situations, about moving on, getting on with life, but that is not what happens at all. It is a changed person who moves on and gets on with life. It is your consciousness of life that is changed when you get that close to death. Everything looks exactly the same, but everything is changed utterly forever. Mourning is accepting the loss of one person, but also accepting the difference in your own person as well.

I know now that I had been given the terrible luxury of a three-month mourning and that I had been lucky enough not to throw it away. I realized it only slowly that summer. I had on my desk the final proofs of *In Fragments,* a very complicated book about the aphorisms of Jesus, about sayings like "Blessed are the poor" or "Let the dead bury their dead." Checking them required great concentration and absolutely no creativity. It was all I was capable of, and it kept some continuity where some was desperately needed, but it made me wonder if I could ever do enthusiastic scholarship again.

I stayed close to home and spent days of almost ritual regularity. Margaret's closet was full of her clothes, a case full of her jewelry. In a second bedroom, used only as her studio, everything was hers—easel, canvas, stretchers, oils, paints, works already finished, and one in process for a show at Loyola that fall. I spent a couple of hours every afternoon taking that all apart, slowly, deliberately, tenderly. I took down the clothes, closed them in boxes, and prepared them for the Salvation Army. I gathered together everything in her studio, organized the items in categories, and gave them to various local artists and art departments.

Friends had offered to come in and do that all for me, especially with Margaret's clothes. Once again, I had declined without particularly knowing why. But I noticed that after spending a few hours taking down her dresses, some unremembered but some charged with memories of time and place, and folding them carefully, I felt not as I would have expected, much worse, but much better. I finally understood what was happening. I had only three days to bury Margaret and to do it all in public. Now I had the luxury of three months to bury Margaret slowly and privately. I had been forced to say good-bye in an inhuman hurry; I now had more than enough time to do it humanly and slowly.

By the end of the summer Margaret's studio was repainted and recarpeted. I gave the works from that show-in-process to our closest friends except for three I kept for myself. But unlike the rest of our condominium, there were no pictures for the walls of that ex-studio. Aileen, Tom, and some of their children had planned to stay with us that July on Ibiza. They stayed instead in a hotel, went to Villa Aisling, took from their frames about a dozen prints which then ended up, full circle, on the walls of that redone room.

I also knew by the end of the summer that I was ready to go back to Ireland, that it was no longer flight but visit, and that it would be a good test to do once more, but alone, what Margaret and I had done together for a decade of summers. Aileen and Tom had a vacation house near Gorey on a small promontory above the sea along Wexford's mid-eastern coast. Their eldest son, John, was to be married to Michelle that late August, but he made time beforehand to go windsurfing with me from the beach below that summer home. I had learned to windsurf on Ibiza and could more or less handle winds up to force 5, around 21 knots or 24 miles per hour. Off Ibiza even strong breezes and high waves were usually on-shore, and it was hard to be scared when the sun was hot, the wind warm, and the dress minimal. But the Irish Sea is not exactly like the Mediterranean. The on-shore wind sliced southward in the wide straits between Ireland and Wales, the sea, despite good weather that summer, was never the beguiling blue of the Med, and the panoply of full wetsuit, weatherproof jacket, and life preserver made everything much more serious. The coastline alternated between long beaches and rocky intersections jutting out into the sea. You roared out to sea from the beach. That was the easy part. Then you turned around to come back, preferably without falling off and preferably on the same line. There was no particular danger in falling off, as a windsurfer stops immediately when you drop its sail. But each time you attempted to pull up the sail, the wind pushed you down the coast a little, and if you could not get back on that outgoing line, you would come in toward the rocks or at some beach beyond them. The choice was success, disaster, or ignominy, having to carry a heavy board and furled sail back home atop the headland. John was younger, stronger, bigger, and better than I was, so I was pushing myself all the time. I did all right, but at times I could not tell if I was scared stiff or frozen stiff. Aileen got used to telling her youngest son on my every return, "Get your Uncle Dom a brandy, Padraig." I recommend raw terror as excellent therapy, and afterward I knew (almost for sure) that I was going to be all right.

I was more sure after the first anniversary. An editor I had known for many years was moving to a new publisher. He took me out to dinner, said he wanted my name on his first list, and asked if I had a set of essays that could be combined into an instant book. I did not have a set of essays for an instant book, but I had a lot of sources left over from *In Fragments*. I called him the next morning and suggested *Four Other Gospels,* a study of some major extracanonical gospels, ones not included in the official New Testament. I wanted to write it in two months, June and July 1984, to see if I could still work in a sustained burst of creativity. I could, I did, and that little book will always be very special to me. After it, I knew that I was going to be all right—but that I was still different than before.

We did not know that 1982 was our last summer on Ibiza, that Margaret would be dead by 1983, that I would never return, and that the villa, put up for sale immediately, would be bought three years later. I said that above and repeat it here, but I have some doubts about Margaret. She was funny about doctors, funny amusing and funny weird. "Don't tell them anything," she said. "If they're so smart, let them tell you what's wrong." That attitude, derived from watching her closest friend die of cancer the year before I met her, did not make any sense, and well she knew it. If challenged, she would just laugh it off as if it were a joke. But I always wondered what she actually told her doctor in the privacy of routine visits. Two details from that summer of 1982 make me wonder if she knew or half knew more than she told herself, me, or any doctor.

I woke up one night an hour or so after falling asleep. The full moon spread a swath of light across the sea, straight down the bay, over the covered terrace, and through the fully opened French doors into our bedroom. It was bright as day, and Margaret was sitting straight up in bed. No, she had not been asleep, no, it was not her heart, no, she did not want to go to the hospital that night or a doctor the next day. It was only indigestion. She was sorry she woke me. Yes, when we got back home she might have it checked. Looking back now I realize that, in medical matters, I never knew what Margaret may have half sensed and never told, right to the very end.

That same 1982 summer she was experimenting with calligraphic art for a course at Loyola. She taught calligraphy courses regularly, and they involved relentless practice with many different alphabets and styles. But this was somewhat different in that the calligraphy itself twisted and turned to form shapes appropriate to what it said. I had with me a book by Roberto Juarroz with his poems on one page and translations by W. S. Merwin opposite them. I was still working on the manuscript of *In Fragments* and planning to quote a verse from one poem as the epigraph for the Prologue. It spoke about the "empty space" that Jesus left "in each word / and even in your own tomb / to build the future." Margaret read the book but chose a very different poem and experimented with it most of that summer. I still have the final, finished draft, about eighteen by twenty-four inches, on parchment. The writing, in Spanish and English, is sometimes so tiny as to be illegible and at other times normal size, sometimes horizontal and sometimes vertical, sometimes superimposed in heavy script on lighter script so that the latter shows brokenly behind it.

The poem's refrain is "if we knew the point where . . ." and what follows are phrases such as "where something is going to break" or "where the thread of kisses will be cut." But the only consolation for such prior knowledge is "we could unwind that point like a streamer / or at least sing it 'til we died" or "we could put another point on that point / or at least go with it to its breaking." Down at the bottom left of Margaret's page, on the last line, is one final example: "if we knew the point where my death will come closer to yours . . ." That might just be coincidence or retrojected imagination on my part. Even if it is not, Margaret may have been thinking of her mother, her grandmother, her best friend, and not about herself. But, in any case, we did not know the point, even right up to the very end.

CHAPTER 6

Calling It Story Is Not Enough

When I first heard the words *Epistle* and *Gospel* they were not parts of a book, but sides of an altar. I begin there not to prove a point, but to establish a setting. I did not know them as parts of the New Testament or the Bible, cannot even remember those latter terms coming up, and never saw either of them as a book until long after I entered the seminary. What I knew, knew very well, knew eventually by heart were the Rosary, the Stations of the Cross, the ecclesiastical missal, and the monastic breviary. Biblical story came to me first as prayer in worship, and nobody spent any time insisting on its factuality, its inerrancy, or its literal truth. But back, for a moment, to the Gospel and the Epistle, parts of a church, at eight years of age.

In the era before the Second Vatican Council, the priest celebrated Mass at an altar on a platform raised three steps or so above the floor of the sanctuary. We altar boys knelt on the bottom step, our backs to the people behind us. As we faced the altar, the priest read first the Epistle section for that day to our right and then the Gospel section for that day to our left. In between those readings the missal book had to be transferred from the right to the left side of the altar. That was where I came in. I was eight, I was small, I was scared. The big open missal sat on top of a big metal stand. Both were heavy, and together they were very heavy. The stand was not the rectangular wooden fold-up type you could grab each side of securely and balance equally. It had a flat round base, a single columnlike upright, and a sloped top no wider than the open missal atop it. After the first reading the priest moved from the right side of the altar and stood waiting in the center, waiting for me to move the missal from right to left.

I moved into the center at the bottom of the steps behind him, genuflected, and with hands joined ascended the steps toward the Epistle side. Early in the altar-boy game I had learned the slight smooth kick that allowed you to walk up steps without tripping over your black, floor-length soutane. No problem there. But then came the problem. I had to stretch up and grasp the column of the stand with both hands, lift the stand and its missal clear of the altar, walk back down the steps to the center, genuflect, walk up the steps again without being able to look or see down (kick, kick, kick), and relocate missal and stand in their new place on the Gospel side of the altar.

It was always scary but, of course, no more so than coming backward down a tree tall as a mast. When I think of Advent, to this very day I do not think immediately of the coming of Jesus. I think first of how Advent readings were from the very start of the missal, how that unbalanced it dangerously so that you had only a few pages open to left and all the rest closed to the right on the stand, and how the odds went way up that it would land with a resounding crash somewhere on step or floor between Epistle side and Gospel side. I loved it, the scary part especially, and I never dropped the missal. That was just one more part of the altar-boy challenge, and I record it only to emphasize place and context. Before I ever knew the term *historical Jesus,* he was wrapped in a cocoon of prayer and liturgy, of popular and official piety in which nobody ever insisted that all was literal or that all was metaphorical, but only that all was prayer. That left later questions open for a later time.

We did not say the Rosary every night in our family, but apart from school or church, I remember it on visits to both grandmothers (both grandfathers were already dead). For my paternal grandmother it was a regular, pre-bed, family ritual, with the cottage's cold, hard, flagstones beneath your knees as you leaned into a chair's seat before the kitchen fire. My maternal grandmother was very different. She died at eighty-four in 1948 and was bedridden in a very comfortable room above the shop in all the visits I can recall. You could hear her say the Rosary to herself if you stood outside her door. Initially we children tried to time our entrance toward the end of a sequence since we knew we would be invited to join her in prayer. Eventually we gave up as we learned that the Rosary went on all the time, over and over and over, again and again and again, all day, all the time, whenever she was awake. I knew those stories first as prayer. The Annunciation, Visitation, Birth, Presentation, and Finding in the Temple. The Agony, Scourging, Crowning, Cross-carrying, and Crucifixion on the Cross. The Resurrection, Ascension, Pentecost, Assumption, and Coronation of Mary. They were not called stories but mysteries, and although they were distinguished as, respectively, the Joyful, the Sorrowful, and the Glorious Mysteries, any one was presumably as mysterious as another. Nobody insisted they were literal; nobody suggested they were not. That neither hardened my heart nor closed my mind ahead of time.

Same for the Stations of the Cross, for the passion of Jesus from condemnation to entombment. The five Sorrowful Mysteries were expanded, as it were, into fourteen more detailed moments and spread around the inside walls of church or chapel. You knelt for the Rosary, you walked and stood for the Stations. The biblical Simon of Cyrene was there to carry Jesus' cross in the Fifth Station. The legendary Veronica was there to wipe Jesus' face in the Sixth Station. No difference was made between those stories, no questions were asked about them, but neither were any claims made concerning them. Simon received the cross on his shoulder. Veronica received the image on her handkerchief. Each was as true as the other in prayer, and future discriminations were not foreclosed.

All of that early experience and much more that followed in hours of daily Gregorian chant and daily monastic breviary reading left me with a capacity to go easily and happily in either of two directions. I could ask historical questions and answer them as strictly as necessary: No, I do not think this or that was intended or should be taken as a literal story. Such a conclusion was

never the end for me, was never more than a first step in understanding. If the story had been created, and especially when it
had, that only pressed the question: What was its purpose, message, meaning? If it was history, that might be explanation
enough. If it was parable, the explanation was only beginning.

That word *parable* introduces something constitutive for all my
work on the historical Jesus and earliest Christianity. It is also
something that media interviewers find particularly difficult to
understand, or at least remember and record. The *Chicago Tribune*
put me on the cover of its magazine section for Sunday, July 17,
1994. My face was in the bottom right quadrant under a large
statue of Jesus as the Sacred Heart, and the caption read:
"Searching for Jesus: Can this man change what Christians
believe? John Dominic Crossan of DePaul University." (One of my
colleagues said she had never seen my face look so unhappy, and
I replied that she had never seen my face after three hours of
being photographed outside while staring straight into bright
sunlight.) The writer summarized me as saying that "Jesus was a
mortal man in the fullest sense of the term. He was conceived and
born in the conventional way (no Virgin Birth), did not perform
miracles (no Lazarus, no loaves and fishes, no lepers), did not
undergo resurrection (no Easter) and after his execution, was
probably eaten by wild dogs (no joke)." No mistake in that, but
no sense of parable either.

In the interview I emphasized, as I usually do, that to say a
story is not history may be accurate, but it is also not enough. You
have to ask, first, if it was intended as fact or fiction and, if as fiction, what its purpose was—was it a pure entertainment or a
teaching device? It was never enough to say this or that was not
a historical story. It was never enough to keep pounding the negative (no x, no y, no z). It was necessary, thereafter, to ask if the
nonhistorical, that is, the fictional story was intended as pedagogical challenge. Was it, for example, a parable, that is, a fictional story with a theological punch, a made-up tale that kicked
you in the rear when you weren't looking? I had used the example of misreading Aesop to explain the vacuity of hearing an

ancient story as historical when it was never intended as such. That got lost, as it often does, in interviews, and only the negative was left. This or that in the Gospel was not history. Of course not, but that's only the negative. It was never intended as history, but as parable. That's the positive. And then the work of understanding the parable's point begins.

My own term for reading a piece of recorded past as history when it was intended as parable is the *Aesopic fallacy,* and here, to make my point as clearly as possible, is my explanation of that mistake. But since my subject is parable, I give it now as a parable, that is, a fictional story with a theological punch.

The Aesopians are an ancient and venerable religious community going back in time over two and a half millennia. Their religion was founded by a Greek slave named Aesop, and his book *The Fables* is accepted by all Aesopians as their inspired text of sacred scripture. They have recently been embroiled in a nasty public dispute, which ended up in a very high-profile legal battle.

It began when a group called Scientists Against Mythology described the Aesopians as a bunch of half-witted weirdos. The Aesopians immediately sued them under the new federal law forbidding hate-mockery of individuals for peculiarities of race, creed, color, ethnic origin, or physical challenge. (It was passed in central Florida after somebody called Mickey Mouse an impotent rodent.) The obvious choice as lead prosecutor was Johnny Cockroach, but he was already involved as counsel for Bart Simpson before the House Committee on Un-American Family Activities (and besides, as he told the press, he did not have a word that rhymed with *genre*). The Aesopians reluctantly took as their second choice a Boston-Irish lawyer named Póg Mahóney. He was brilliant, he was ruthless, he was devastating.

The first expert for the defense was a Pulitzer Prize–winning historian from Harvard. She was shredded on the stand as Mahóney insisted and the judge agreed that she must answer a simple yes or no to the questions put to her.

"Were you alive in ancient Greece at the time of Aesop?"

"No."

"Have you read all the extant documents from ancient Greece?"

"Yes."

"Do you think that those represent all there ever were from that time?"

"No."

"Then, Madam, since you do not know everything that happened in ancient Greece, is not your assertion that animal linguisticality did not occur there simply a personal historical bias?"

The second expert was a Nobel Prize–winning biologist from Stanford, but he too went down in flames.

"Are there changes in animal evolution so that earlier capabilities are later lost?"

"Yes." (A whole series of forcibly admitted examples followed, with much debate about nonflying chickens.)

"Do you know, or does science know, every single species of presently living animal?"

"No."

"Could there be some animals even now, in the canopies of the rain forest or the depths of the sea, about which we know nothing, not even of their existence?"

"Yes."

"Then, Sir, since you do not know all past or even all contemporary animals, is it not fair to say that your assertion of their nonlinguisticality is simply an individual prejudice?"

The jury took only half an hour to find for the prosecution and to assess both compensatory and punitive damages amounting to $14 million. Both legal teams were mobbed by the media on the courtyard steps.

"What will you do next?" the defense was asked.

"We are going all the way to the U.S. Supreme Court."

"What will you do next?" the prosecution was asked.

"We are going all the way to Walt Disney World."

I presume your agreement that, if Aesopic literalists existed, they would be weird and, since there are none around, it is quite politically correct to say that out loud. But, if they were, none of us could disprove them any more, of course, than they could prove their belief. But, reduced to anger in face of their intransigence, we would end up shouting: "It's a genre of speech, a special type of story, dummy. It was never intended as history. It's a fiction with a message. It's a parable." That term, by the way, is used in both a narrower and a wider sense. If message-carrying fictional stories have animal characters, we call them fables; if human characters, we call them parables (narrow sense); if superhuman or divine characters, we call them myths. But we can also use *parables* in a wider sense for all such stories, especially since subhumans, normal humans, and superhumans may interact in the same made-up tale. In any case, they are all heavy-message music for those with ears to hear.

Imagine, finally, what we would think of a listener who had just heard Jesus' parable about the sower, gone home, and announced this: "I got some very good advice this morning on proper sowing techniques to improve the cereal yields in Lower Galilee." We would surely say: "It's a genre, dummy. Whatever he was talking about, it was not about sowing. It's a parable, friend. Now what's the hidden punch line?"

Scholars have always thought that earliest Christianity did not create many parables *by* Jesus, that most of those we have in the Gospels are probably original. I have always agreed, but my suspicion is that the early followers of Jesus were too busy creating parables *about* him to have time for making up ones *by* him. That, as I discuss in the next chapter, was my foundational intuition for thirty years of research and publication: Is that intuition true, and would it hold up to detailed study? But there is first an even more basic question: Why did I think about that so early and pursue it so long? What arguments persuade me that this or that tale is fiction, not fact, parable, not history? When do we have character-in-incident (Jesus actually, factually, historically did this or that) and when do we have incident-in-character (Jesus could have, would have, should have done this or that)? And why am I ready to accept such arguments and instances when other scholars clearly are not? Have I presuppositions about story that are deep down in there from early experiences as Irish or Catholic or both together? And lest this become too abstract, I use as my prime example the virginal and divine conception of Jesus (do not, by the way, call it the immaculate conception; that is something completely different), the story about the angel's annunciation, Joseph's doubt, and Jesus' origins.

I knew, already in the 1970s, that there was an ethical problem with that story. Jesus was born of a virginal conception, a divine action that made him wiser than the Temple priests at twelve years of age, according to Luke 1–2. But, as you will recall, I was teaching comparative religion at DePaul in that decade, so what about a similar story concerning the Buddha? He, in fact, was hands down better than our Jesus—he came out of a virginal womb walking, talking, teaching, and preaching. Did I tell the class that the Christian story was history, the Buddhist story parable, the Christian one fact, the other fiction, ours the truth and theirs a myth or lie? I said that both were parables, the fictionally wondrous birth of a factually wondrous person.

By the 1980s, that position was getting much clearer in my mind. I had never thought of it as a theological argument about what God could or could not do, but as a historical argument about what God had or had not done. I spoke about divine consistency, about a general trust that the laws of physics or gravity will not change when we are at 37,000 feet over the Atlantic in a 747. But none of that, said a critic on a Chicago TV religious broadcast, indicated that God had not done with Mary exactly what the Gospels said, had done it only once in a special and unique situation. Once and for all forever. That sharpened the question. It was still a historical one: What did those first Christians who told that story wish to communicate? But the historical one was merging with a literary one: What type of story was that about the virginal conception of Jesus?

In the second half of the second century Christian and pagan intellectuals started to debate such questions with one another. Before that point pagan criticisms of Christianity were mostly general slurs, religious ("They are god rejecters!"), social ("They are people haters!"), or cultural ("They are baby eaters!"). But around 150 C.E. Justin Martyr, a highly educated and widely traveled

Christian, insisted in his *First Apology* that the virginal and divine conception of Jesus was no more implausible than all such other tales in Greek and Roman history: "When we say also that the Word, who is the first-birth of God, was produced without sexual union . . . we propound nothing different from what you believe regarding those whom you esteem sons of Jupiter. For you know how many sons your esteemed writers ascribed to Jupiter." He then gives a whole list of such Sons (and one Daughter) of God: Mercury, Aesculapius, Bacchus, Hercules, the sons of Leda, the Dioscuri, Perseus, Bellerophon, and Ariadne. Justin was, of course, quite ready to argue that the Christian story was much, much more significant in its antecedent prophecies and in its consequent results than those other stories. "We will now prove [Jesus] superior—or rather have already proved him to be so—for the superior is revealed by his actions." But he never suggested that the Jesus case was unique in all the world, just that he was far better than all the other Sons of God. He did not and he could not do otherwise, since virginal conception and divine impregnation at the start of a life and risen apparition and heavenly ascension at the end of a life were accepted possibilities of his cultural environment.

If a Christian apologist could not and did not claim uniqueness, a pagan polemicist could not and did not claim impossibility. About twenty-five years later, Celsus wrote *On the True [Pagan] Doctrine,* a work known from later quotations in a Christian rebuttal, and he can only say this:

Are we to think that the high God would have fallen in love with a woman of no breeding? . . . After all, the old myths of the Greeks that attribute a divine birth to Perseus, Amphion, Aeacus and Minos are equally good evidence of their wondrous works on behalf of mankind—and are certainly no less lacking in plausibility than the stories of your followers. What have you done [Jesus] by word or deed that is quite so wonderful as those heroes of old?

Neither Christian defender nor pagan opposer ever dream of discussing Jesus' conception as uniquely possible or generally impossible. The pagan criticism was dangerously and necessarily open-ended: What has Jesus ever done for the world that makes his divine-birth explanation credible? And there, of course, in terms of comparative cosmic benefits, was exactly the place a Justin would have made his stand for Jesus. In the ancient world, the pagan cannot say your story is impossible, the Christian cannot say our story is unique. In the modern world, when each claims precisely that, they are both equally wrong. Impossibility and uniqueness are, once again, but twin extremes of nineteenth-century rationalism, like the twin halves of the sinking *Titanic,* whose tragedy was that century's result and symbol of too much certitude.

It was, above all else, the following parallel that showed me how to read that Jesus story as its first writers wanted it to be understood. Suetonius was a second-century Roman historian, a younger contemporary of Tacitus, but better than him on imperial gossip. He recounted the full life and great achievements of Augustus Caesar, who had finished off the Roman civil war by victory and the Roman republic by cunning. He was savior of his people, peace-bringer to the world, and divine in three different ways. His adopted Julian clan was descended from the goddess Aphrodite-Venus and the human Anchises at the time of the Trojan War, a thousand years before. His adopted father was the deified Julius Caesar, which made him, as his coins proclaimed, *divi filius,* "son of god." And, finally, after his own death, he was deified by the Senate in his own right. But, in case that was not enough, Suetonius adds this fourth index of divinity. He adds it, incidentally, only after telling you the wonderful life of Augustus. At his death there were many supernatural portents, says Suetonius, and, by the way, this is how he was conceived:

When Atia had come in the middle of the night to the solemn service of Apollo, she had her litter set down in the temple and fell asleep, while the rest of the matrons also slept. On a sudden a serpent glided up to her and shortly went away. When she awoke, she purified herself, as if after the embraces of her husband, and at once there appeared on her body a mark in colors like a serpent, and she could never get rid of it; so that presently she ceased ever to go to the public baths. In the tenth month after that Augustus was born and was therefore regarded as the son of Apollo.

You will notice, by the way, that, unlike the pagan God, the Jewish God invited the woman's consent before proceeding.

At this point, I think I finally get it. Both those stories, that of Suetonius and that of Matthew-Luke, are parables, but they are absolutely competing parables, and the second dares to challenge the first one directly and explicitly. Augustus Caesar is divine, is Son of God, and his coming was prophetically foretold a thousand years before, as Virgil's *Aeneid* assures us in magnificent poetry. He is, in fact, the incarnation of the Roman God of power, seated on the Palatine, backed by the legions. But Jesus is the incarnation of the Jewish God of justice, a peasant child born far from home in somebody else's outhouse. But he too is prophetically foretold, in Isaiah 7:14 ("the virgin is with child and shall bear a son"), creatively misread by both Matthew 1:22–23 and Luke 1:27–31 to mean that the virgin remained a virgin while conceiving, rather than that she was one before, so that, in other words, this was her firstborn child.

It is so much easier and safer to discuss whether God exists or not, whether Jesus is Son of God or not, whether mother Mary is a virgin or not. One could even be agnostic about all of that. But those competing parables present a far more dangerous choice: Does God exist as justice or as power, is that Justice God incarnate in Jesus or that Power God incarnate in Augustus, and is the responding Mary or the sleeping Atia a typical example of how justice and power operate in this world? It is so much more dangerously relevant to accept those stories for what they were and still are: a challenge to choose justice or power as the basis of one's world. At least so far, those competing parables seem permanently valid, seem permanent options precluding neutrality and demanding choice. Which side are you on, who are you with, where do you stand? Power or justice?

The question comes back to me immediately and inevitably. Undergraduates asked it, and audiences still ask it: "Yes, but are you saying everyone knew they were *only* parable back then, or that they thought they were history back then, but you think they are parable right now?" I try not to show pain at that slipped-in word *only,* and I used to answer something like this. Ancient peoples could hear those stories and not ask that question about literal truth. If they believed them, they were true. If not, not. I do not speak like that anymore. It was a condescending answer because, more and more, I find those ancients just like us and us moderns just like them. In matters of vital importance, moderns and ancients alike accept or reject stories far more on an ideological than an evidentiary basis. We too, Enlightenment or not, ask far too seldom: "Yes, but is that literally true?"

My change in answer started when, for a whole weekend, I was mesmerized by the accusation and counteraccusation between Clarence Thomas and Anita Hill. As I listened afterward to people debating those discordant stories, I heard primarily ideology rather than evidence in argument. On one side: men do that sort of thing all the time (therefore). On the other side: women are being socialized into victimhood (therefore). In the trial of O. J. Simpson, a similar situation developed. On one side: the police in general, L.A. police in particular, and one special cop railroad innocent black defendants all the time (therefore). On the other: athletic superstars, pampered by fan adulation and media attention, think they can get away with violence and even murder (therefore). Those competing stories seemed much less actual, factual accounts to be tested against evidence (beyond a reasonable doubt) and much more metaphorical narratives true or false according to one's ideology, theology, philosophy, or vision of the world.

My DePaul undergraduate class starts at eight-thirty in the morning, and I am in the room around eight-fifteen. There is a heated argument among a small group of early arrivals over Oliver Stone's then-recent movie *JFK*. On one side: "That's the sort of conspiracy thing the government does all the time." On the other: "Our government would never do such a thing." I listen until time for class to begin. Both sides are definite, articulate, and unyield-ing. Neither side ever mentions a single shred of evidence either way. The story of *JFK* is true or false depending on the hearer's ide-ology. It is accepted or rejected as a metaphorical summary and symbolic condensation of one's vision of reality.

Stories are dangerous stuff. Some are literally true, and it is always necessary to know which claim that status. But literal sto-ries fill our newspapers each morning and our garbage cans each evening. Others are only metaphorically true, and it is necessary to know which claim that status. It is by them we live and for them we die. They are *only* metaphor as around us is *only* air— try doing without it. Many of my academic colleagues would agree with that preceding analysis, even with that explanation of the virginal conception of Jesus, and yet they seem stuck in neg-ativity, in the last century's debate between the village atheist and the pious pastor. "No, it could not happen (ever)." "Yes, it did happen (once)." The future, however, belongs to another ques-tion. What did those people intend to communicate by creating those stories as parables about Jesus? This pushes me backward to wonder why all of that seems so obvious and inevitable to me. It sends me back to where I first heard most of those stories—in prayer, a context in which, happily, nobody argued for or argued against questions of historicity. That just did not come up, neither with biblical history in prayer nor, for that matter, with Irish his-tory in song.

In the early afternoon of September 29, 1965, I was standing at the starboard rail of a ferry heading for the straits south of the Sea of Marmara in Turkey. The boat had left the docks near the Galata Bridge at the confluence of the Bosphorus and the Golden Horn that morning and was due into Çanakkale by early evening. As we steamed through the straits I was thinking Hellespont rather than Dardanelles, studying the distance from shore to shore, and trying to estimate the pull of the current between the Black and Aegean Seas. I was imagining, against my classical schooling, the legendary Leander's nightly swim from Abydos, on the eastern bank, to his lover Hero, the priestess of Aphrodite, at Sestos on the western one. In those days I was more impressed by the nightly swim than the nightly love and did not know anything about the Dardanelles campaign in World War I.

I eventually started talking to another passenger who seemed just as glued to the starboard railing. He was a retired army officer intending to cross over from Çanakkale on an official visit to the Gallipoli Peninsula for the British War Graves Commission. We talked the rest of the way, or rather he talked and I was very glad to listen. That beautiful afternoon, under a beautiful sky and over a beautiful sea, I learned everything I still know about that terrible campaign (apart from the Australian film *Gallipoli* and the British book *Hell's Foundations,* much, much later). I still think, because my that-day companion did, that Churchill's strategy could have prevailed, that a little more navy audacity and a little less army stupidity could have forced the straits, and that British naval guns pointed at the heart of the Ottoman Empire could have broken the stalemate of slaughter on the Western Front. So many coulds that never happened. Still, he was knowledgeable, impressive, and persuasive. I listened very carefully, but all the time something strange was happening at the back of my mind.

He explained in clear detail both the strategy and tactics of the campaign and spoke about landings at Sud-el-Bahr and Suvla Bay. Half my mind and attention stayed with him, and the other half went off on its own. I knew pretty much by heart an Irish patriotic ballad about the 1916 rebellion called "The Foggy Dew" (that's with one "Foggy," not the older folk song with two). It contrasted Irish soldiers in the British army who had died and been buried far from home with those who had died in the Easter Rising and were buried near home in Dublin's Glasnevin Cemetery. "'Twas better to die / 'neath an Irish sky / than at Suvla or Sud-el-Bahr." So now, for the first time, I knew where those places were. They were across that narrow space of water and over that narrow peak of land on the seaward side of the Gallipoli Peninsula. But what, then, about those other equally remembered lines from later in the song: "Their lonely graves / are by Suvla's waves / on the fringe of the grey North Sea"?

I was still listening, because my companion's voice was quiet and very persuasive. I do not know if he himself had been there in 1915. Maybe he told me, and I still did not know enough history to be impressed. Maybe he did not, and I was too immature to ask. Maybe those words from a past song distracted me too much from a present voice. But that phrase, humming to an insistent musical rhythm that my head could hear much more accurately than my voice repeat, kept interfering with concentration. If those places were on the Gallipoli Peninsula, they were in the Aegean, they were on the fringe of the wine-dark sea, not on the fringe of the grey North Sea? Did I get it wrong? But I had learned it so early, and that stuff usually stuck hard. Did the ballad get it wrong? But how could a popular song make a mistake like that? The problem stayed with me the next day at Troy, whose ancient war, after the day before, seemed more blood and guts than honor and glory. My memory was clearly wrong—it should surely be "or" not "on." It must have been "by Suvla's waves / or the fringe of the grey North Sea." But whether the balladist wrote it wrong (unlikely) or I heard it wrong (likely), that incident emphasized for me how I got and kept whatever I have of Irish history.

As I said earlier, I first learned the Jesus story in prayer rather than in the gospel, in church rather than in the Bible, and nobody raised questions of literal or figurative meaning, factual or fictional content, history or parable as genre. I think something similar happened with regard to Irish history. I learned it in schoolroom classes, got the appropriate grades, and passed the official state exams to prove I knew all about it. But if I met biblical history in prayer, I met Irish history in song. Let me be more accurate: that is the way I enjoyed it then, that is the way I remembered it afterward, and that is the way I know it now. Even when I did not know what I was learning, learning unknown European places through Irish patriotic lenses, it was as story in ballad form that it got in there early and firm.

Sarah and I have a favorite tape copied for us on a visit home to Ireland in 1986. We were in Patricia and Daniel's home, I admired a tape called *Classic Tranquillity*, and they made a copy for us. A suite of all the classic Irish melodies of my youth, it is completely orchestral—it has no voices, no words. We keep it for ritual occasions. It was once the tape we played leaving Chicago for our weekend home, Innisfree, on Bass Lake in northwestern Indiana. It is now the tape we play trailering our boat from mid-Florida to either the Gulf or Atlantic coast. We have already worn out the original copy, but expecting that, we had made extra copies. Sarah listens to the orchestra, admires the melody, and hears only music. I hear words to every melody and know most of them by heart from long ago. Some are love songs or emigrant nostalgias, but most are Irish history, the sad record of rebel hopes, betrayed comrades, and lost causes.

I do not know when I learned all those songs, but it must have been very early because I still know them fairly well. It was at least as early, or earlier, than I learned official schoolroom Irish history. Once again, as with biblical history in prayer, so with Irish history in song. Nobody insisted that all was literal, and nobody distinguished fact from fiction. I was allowed to absorb them profoundly as story, further discrimination was never mentioned, and such could be done much later when and if it were necessary. I did not ask whether it was fact or fiction that "young Roddy McCorley goes to die / On the bridge of Toome today." I did not ask whether it was fact or fiction that "just before he faced the hangman in his dreary prison cell / British soldiers tortured [Kevin] Barry / Just because he would not tell." I knew then about the disastrous French-assisted (the word is used loosely) rebellion of 1798 from songs, and half a century later, their content is still all I know or remember about it. From "Boulavogue," from "Kelly the Boy from Killane," from "The West's Awake." At one end of the country it was this: "The ships we were wearily waiting sailed into Kilalla's broad bay." At the other, this: "Poor Wexford stripped naked hung high on a cross / Her heart pierced by traitors and slaves." I can walk across the recent centuries through Irish history in songs of rebellion and, today if not then, celebrate resistance as always necessary without accepting "blood for blood, without remorse" as ever advisable. My memory and knowledge of Irish history are held by songs sung, rather than lessons learned. I know, by the way, no songs from the 1840s.

The advantage of not having someone insist, early and explicitly, that one's stories, whether they are biblical or national, are literally fact and inerrantly true, is that you are left free, at least later, to do two things. The first is to recognize ideology, whether it is theirs ("We are only trying to civilize you natives and convert you savages") or ours ("They are only trying to enslave our people and loot our resources"). The second is to distinguish, within an accepted or rejected ideology, when the story is parable and when the story is history. Otherwise, you may become trapped forever, able only to insist on factuality and historicity or, conversely, able only to insist on unfactuality and inhistoricity. It is truly sad when all you can say about Christmas is that there is no Santa Claus.

Story is a beautiful word and our mind's best gift. *Story* is also a weasel word and the coward's best call. It does not say parable, it does not say history. It does not assert fiction, it does not claim fact. Many biblical scholars prefer to use it in discussing their narratives and thereby avoid conflict by denying historicity for some or most of those tales. If you do not raise the issue, you need not answer the question. Recall, for example, such stories as the walking on the waters, the stilling of the storm, or the miraculous catch of fishes. Those stories were intended, to my mind, as parables, as warnings that when the disciples or the Twelve, that is, the leadership of the church, take off without Jesus, they will get nowhere and catch nothing.

If I took all of those stories literally and historically, rather than parabolically and figuratively, my reaction would not be "I do not believe them," but "I do not care about them." I admire acrobatics and love the *Cirque de Soleil,* especially in its permanent home, half an hour from where Sarah and I now live. If God or Jesus was interested in circus tricks, that's nice, I suppose, but I just don't care—not, I don't believe. They are not important enough for disbelief (the way that racism, sexism, or homophobia must be positively disbelieved). They are only worthy of unconcern. To those who take everything literally in the Bible, especially the New Testament, and most especially the Gospels, I now prefer to be polite rather than nasty. When a fundamentalist said to me in the past, "I believe everything in the Bible is literally true," I used to respond, "If Jesus was the Lamb of God, does that mean that Mary had a little lamb?" That was the nasty version. The polite response, which I now prefer, to "I believe everything in the Bible is literally true," is, "If Jesus walked on the water, how nice for Jesus."

Sarah and I stand in line at the supermarket check-out counter and read the covers of those informative magazines, the *Star Magazine,* the *Globe,* and the *National Enquirer* (or is it the *National Review?* I get them confused sometimes). Diet and gossip, sex and scandal, marriage and divorce, miracle and prophecy, angels and aliens. "My wife was taken up into a spacecraft, impregnated by an alien, and has just delivered its baby." What should you say if you met such a person? Surely this: "How nice for you, I hope mother and child are well, and do have a great life." Not harsh disbelief, but polite unconcern.

Here is another question on that same subject, linking back to the difficulty in deciding if ancient writers and readers took their own parables as straight history. We see people pick up those magazines and drop them among their groceries. How would you decide, *for sure,* whether they believe or disbelieve what they have just bought?

"Excuse me, you here. Do you really believe that stuff?"

"No, of course not. I just buy it for fun."

"Excuse me, you over there. Do you really believe that stuff?"

"Yes, I do. You have a problem with that?"

Maybe ancients were just like moderns, just like us. We all, most of the time, too much of the time, cruise carelessly between fact and fiction, history and parable, and let ideology replace evidence.

Many reasons prevent me from avoiding the issue of historicity by talking simply and serenely about story while avoiding any further distinction between parable and history. Here are five of them.

A first reason is historical. Once the issue was raised during the Enlightenment, it cannot be ignored. I do not think the

Enlightenment was an unmitigated blessing. For all the marvelous gains in reason and experiment, science and technology, there were heavy losses for the human spirit as well. We began to think that ancient peoples ("other" peoples) told dumb, literal stories that we were now smart enough to recognize as such. Not quite. Those ancient people told smart, metaphorical stories that we were now dumb enough to take literally. Enlightenment, yes, but Endarkenment also.

A second reason is legal. It comes from recent experience in this country. Our legal system is based on a jury's ability to reconstruct history and not just to admire story. In the Simpson trial both sides had wonderful stories to tell, complete with dramatic interludes, rhymed couplets, and confrontational pyrotechnics. One story said that the defendant was a confirmed murderer. The other story said the defendant was a framed innocent. Both sides had story, but only one side had history. Even if we will never know which had fact and which fiction, only one of those twin options was correct. When Simpson left the court, he was either a freed murderer or a framed innocent. Not both, but one *or* the other. History matters, especially history reconstructed beyond a reasonable doubt. Or, again, when young children accuse parents, guardians, or caregivers of sexual abuse, satanic ritual, and even cultic murder, the stories are lurid, detailed, and obscene. They are certainly stories, but are they true? Sometimes? Always? Never? Which ones are true and which delusional? Ruined lives, destroyed families, and traumatized communities, from Salem to the twentieth century's end, warn us that "story" is not enough. All history may be story, but not all story is history. It is necessary to call things by their proper name, in the Bible, in the courtroom, and in life itself.

A third reason is ethical, and I have touched on it earlier with regard to stories about Jesus' birth and the Buddha's birth. It is, as I said before, an ethical imperative that we not claim our story is fact and true, theirs is myth and lie, if both are powerful and particular parables. For centuries, we Christians have declared our Jesus story is history in a way unique for all the world. Our

Jesus did, in an actual, factual, historical sense, such things as no one else has ever done or ever will do. It is not just a perfectly valid case of faith expressing itself by parable, in Christianity as in any other religion; it is that all others have parable (or myth), and we alone have history. It is necessary, once again, to call things by their proper name, and to apologize not for two thousand years of legitimate particularity, but for two thousand years of illegitimate superiority.

The fourth reason is theological. We Christians find in Jesus the incarnation of Yahweh, the Jewish God seen as justice itself. This, we believe, is how that God became flesh and lived and died in the unjust normalcy of our everyday world. But if all politics is local, all incarnation is very local. It is about enfleshment in time and place. It is, in other words, about history. All four of our canonical Gospels insist on this historical rootedness. They update Jesus, of course, Mark to the 70s, Matthew and Luke to the 80s, and John to the 90s. But they always update the historical Jesus of the 20s. He is always both dated in there-and-then, amid all the usual suspects (Caiaphas and Annas, Herod and Pilate), and also updated to here-and-now for new times and new places, new needs and new communities.

The final reason is cultural. There has always been a deep fissure between body and soul, flesh and spirit, within Western sensibility. It stems from long before Jesus, from a Platonic dualism in which the real person is spirit-soul temporarily stuck in body-flesh. No matter whether that dwelling is seen as a distracting palace, a nomadic tent, a fleabag motel, or a prison cell, it is accidental, temporary, and transient. If Jesus is human, in that Platonic acceptance his body-flesh is of minor import, and how then can history be of great importance? Further, and worse, if Jesus is divine, then his body-flesh must be like those random bodies-for-a-day that pagan gods and goddesses assumed for earthly transactions here below. Jesus must have had a "seeming" body (the technical term is *docetic*) just as they had. Against all of this, earliest Christianity strove sometimes successfully, mostly unsuccessfully, to retain its Jewish roots untouched by Platonic and pagan dualism of body-flesh against and inferior to spirit-soul. Today that fissure still haunts our contemporary sensibility as we keep those components separate, not like two sides of a single coin, but more like a gift in a wrapping. The result is that we sensationalize the body, sentimentalize the spirit, commercialize them both, and brutalize the human person in that process. History matters, not because it is sure or certain, not because it removes doubts or differences, but because we are enfleshed spirits or spiritual flesh and we are only fully human in that conjunction. For all those reasons, crowding in on me and interacting with one another, I cannot say "story" in order to avoid the necessary distinction between fact and fiction, parable and history.

"You are not reconstructing history," I am told, as I mentioned earlier. "You are only seeing your face at the bottom of a deep well." It is usually a cheap crack, not so much in theory as in practice. In theory it raises very interesting questions. In practice it speaks of others, but not of oneself; it dismisses them without offering any reciprocal self-criticism of one's own work. The original author of that comment was an Irish Catholic, and I think it may well have been, in its inaugural statement, both accurate and fair. In 1909 George Tyrell said, in his *Christianity at the Cross-Roads,* that "The Christ that Harnack sees, looking back through nineteen centuries of Catholic darkness, is only the reflection of a liberal Protestant face, seen at the bottom of a deep well." That was about the German theologian Adolf Harnack's book of 1900, translated later as *What Is Christianity?* But, whether it is correct or not, it was an individual judgment rather than a general criticism. Today it reappears as both. Reconstructing the historical Jesus is only well gazing.

On the wider level, that criticism negates any reconstruction of the historical Jesus, or of any significant historical figure, or, indeed, of any history at all. On the narrower level it invalidates my own interpretation of Jesus as a first-century Galilean peasant resisting Roman imperial injustice in the name of Jewish tradition.

That, my critics suggest, is only a covert sympathy for nineteenth-century Irish peasants resisting British imperial injustice in the name of Catholic (or Celtic) tradition. I see, in other words, not a Jewish face from long ago, but only my own Irish face projected backward. There is, behind the strategy of dismissal, a valid question. Can we, any of us, ever do historical reconstruction, or are we always superimposing our own current prejudices on past events? That is, of course, not just a historical or methodological question, but an ethical and moral one. I imagine, in response, three options in any historical study.

One option is narcissism. You see only your own face and do not even recognize it as such. You think you see the past, but see only your own retrojected present. Then, like Narcissus in Greek mythology, you fall in love with "the other," who is simply your unrecognized self. There is, by the way, a marvelous parable about Narcissus written by Oscar Wilde (I cite from memory):

> The waters wept for Narcissus after his death.
> "No wonder you did," the author-persona says, "he was so beautiful."
> "Was he?" the waters reply. "We never noticed. But we miss seeing the beauty of ourselves mirrored in the clarity of his eyes."

Narcissism, I recognize, is always a practical option, but it is not always an inevitable one. It is possible but not always necessary that historical reconstruction be but narcissistic worship of our selves.

Another option is positivism, and, if narcissism is an illusion, positivism is a delusion. It tells us that we can see the past exactly and precisely as it was, unchanged, untouched, uncontaminated by our own viewing process. It tells us that we can look in a mirror (or a well) and see our face without seeing our own eyes seeing. (Try that sometime.) Positivism or historicism is always a theoretical option, but it is not always an inevitable one.

A final option is interactivism, the attempt to create as honest a dialectic as possible between the past and the present, between the viewed and the viewer. It acknowledges that each will change the other and that only in such a mutual dance is historical reconstruction possible. But it firmly denies that narcissism or positivism are the only and inevitable fates awaiting historical study. In thirty years and half as many books on the historical Jesus, it has been method (how I do it) and methodology (why I do it that way rather than some other) that kept interaction as honest and mutual and balanced as I could make it.

I tried recently to look down a deep well on a lecture visit to Bath in Maine. It was not actually very deep, and the owner assured me that I would see nothing at all if I found one that was. I could see my own face in this one and found, of course, exactly what I expected. In that exchange the water was disturbed by my face, and my face was distorted as a reflection. Each had changed the other. Of course. Even more recently I was on United flight 2261 out of Portland, which was late into San Francisco because of bad weather. A cabin attendant warned us about opening those overhead bins as we prepared for landing because, she said, to prolonged applause, "Shift happens." Of course. As with packed overhead bins, so with interactive historical reconstruction, shift happens. But who shifts whom? Did I shift Jesus into me, he me into him, or each into the other?

Between story and history lurks memory. It speaks like story, but claims like history. If it is privately mine, nobody can rebut it. If it is privately ours, we may have a duel of recollection, mine against yours, and it may be at best a draw. If it is publicly mine, I better be careful—I can be checked, there may be documents, and they may even be accurate. But sometimes a document, no matter how official, is only as good as somebody's word, and that is only as good as somebody's memory.

I talked earlier about Michael, my mother's favorite brother and preceding sibling. According to his baptismal record, Michael Farry (Jr.) was born October 16, 1896. According to the 1901 Census of Ireland, recording the occupants of every house in the country for the night of Sunday, March 31, Michael Farry (Jr.) was then four years of age. So far so good. But according to his tombstone in Carrownanty Graveyard, he "died 24th May 1935 aged 34 years." That should be thirty-eight years of age, and the mistake is only a tiny detail, but it is a warning about the accuracy even of things carved in stone.

The apostle Paul wrote his letters twenty years after the death of Jesus, and sources used in the Gospels stem from that same time or even before it. But the Gospels themselves were written between forty and sixty-five years after the death of Jesus. Many of my scholarly colleagues fill those yawning chasms by claiming oral tradition and especially preliterate memory. I agree, of course, that both exist, but I am much more skeptical about its retentive accuracy or even whether it is a good general explanation for the ongoing Jesus tradition.

My mother was, as I mentioned earlier, a housekeeping perfectionist, and very little of any importance got thrown away. If it was once significant, and if it ever might be so again, it was wrapped, boxed, and stored away in a closet. That was how I found my five-month diary from early 1948 after her death in March 1983. It is so small, so very small, and so annoying, so very annoying. It fits in the palm of my hand, and its red leather cover (from the days before everything was made out of plastic) stares at me always from somewhere on my desk. It is a warning and a reminder about memory.

When I first discovered it, I thought, "Oh, that's right, I kept a diary one year at boarding school." But I am almost sure that if the subject of diaries had come up in conversation a week before I found it, I would have said nothing; I would not have remembered ever having kept one. And now I cannot tell which is early memory and which is later knowledge. That ambiguity bedevils much that I now find within its pages. I read some incidents about which my memory is fairly certain. I can add details to them not in the diary, and I think they are accurate. I can even add images, as I did earlier in this book, in thinking about Auntie Mary's funeral or all those stamp-collecting activities. I read the nicknames of professors and can put full names or faces to one or two. I read the nicknames of school fellows but can put full names or faces to none of them save my four-year special friend and a member of our "bus" who had a brace on his leg. What is most dismaying is not how few details I remember or how many details I have forgotten. It is my inability to distinguish, having read it, between what I recall from memory and what I "remember" from reading.

There are several references, some I cited already, about driving with my father. My mother always sat in the back to be farther away from the expected accident, the awaited crash, the inevitable disaster. I got to sit in front next to my father. I remember that, I envisage that, I see the picture in my mind quite clearly. I am always to his right, he is always to my left. But that is the positioning in an American car, not, of course, in a British car, not in a Vauxhall, not in our car. But no matter how much I try to correct my image, I cannot do so. That earlier picture is not hidden away somewhere waiting to pop up correctly once reality admonishes its mistake. It refuses to reappear. Later experience in America has completely eradicated and utterly replaced the earlier Irish image, the actual reality of him to my right and me to his left.

I think a lot about that experience and several other memory lessons learned from reading that diary. They have made me skeptical about memory tradition linking later Gospel to earlier Jesus as a simple and fully adequate explanation of that continuity. They have also made me very receptive to recent discoveries in the psychology of remembering, the neurobiology of memory, the fallibility of eyewitness identification, and the fallacy of recovered-memory accusations.

One example. A robbed person has a general impression of a face and picks someone from a mug book. That picked face is then selected from a lineup. In the courtroom the jury hears utter and complete certainty as the defendant is pointed out by the witness on the stand. How can it not convict? Why should the accuser lie? But think about those exterminating overlays as each identification erases any previous one until eyewitness testimony convicts even against a defendant's alibi. It is not a question of certainty, but of accuracy, and no amount of personal certainty can replace factual accuracy.

Another example. We all claim to know exactly where we were on hearing about certain national tragedies. So much for certainty, but what about accuracy? Who challenges you on your memory? Who checks you on it, or how do you check yourself? A psychological experiment was begun at Emory University the day after the *Challenger* explosion. A group of first-year students recorded in detail how they had learned of the tragedy, and their reports were then sealed. In their fourth and final undergraduate year they wrote answers to the same original question about how they learned of the launch disaster. Both accounts were then compared. First, many never remembered making the earlier record. Second, all had a somewhat different, and some had an utterly different, second record. Third, and more alarming, that second record was asserted as correct; the first one was explained as mistaken. In other words, and once again, the later memory had completely eradicated the earlier one. Students did not even attempt to fake it and say, quite understandably, "That's right, the former one is correct, the latter one is wrong." Fourth, and most disconcerting of all, there was no positive correlation, but often a heavy negative correlation, between certainty and accuracy. A student, for example, who got all the details of her first record wrong in her second one, scoring 0 out of a possible 5 for accuracy, had scored her own certainty as 5 out of a possible 5.

From all of that, I make very careful claims for memory in this memoir. Almost nothing is a "new" memory, recollected, reconstructed, or created for this book. They are, at least, ones that have been around for a long time. I have checked with Sarah repeatedly: "Did I tell you about this before now?" So, at least, I am not creating it today. I have checked others with Aileen in Ireland. I have been able to check some against documents. I have eight passports, starting from 1951, from the days when visas were regular and entrance and exit stamps were necessary. But all of that generates honesty rather than accuracy. I have spent thirty years reconstructing the historical Jesus. I have done so self-consciously and self-critically and have tried to do the same on reconstructing myself. But what justifies this memoir is how my own personal experience, from Ireland to America, from priest to professor, from monastery to university, and, above all, from celibacy to marriage, may have influenced that reconstruction. Where has it helped me see what others have not, and where has it made invisible to me what others find obvious?

CHAPTER 7

The Limits of a Talking Head

In 1993 DePaul University hosted a conference arranged by the departments of religious studies and university ministry under the title of "Jesus and Faith: Theologians in Conversation with the Work of John Dominic Crossan." One criticism, made in similar language by two separate scholars, forced me finally to ponder the question that ended the last chapter: How and to what extent did my own life influence my reconstruction of the historical Jesus, a project in which I was spending my entire professional career?

One participant commented:

[Crossan] is not as self-conscious as he might be about how his own roots in a colonized Ireland and his own experience of oppression by the Roman Church have influenced that portrait. . . . [He] never spells out explicitly where he is coming from theologically, and he seems less aware than he might be about how his own religious/spiritual situation cannot help but shape and influence both how he investigates the truth about Jesus of Nazareth and what his reconstructed portrait actually looks like.

Another participant noted that I did not "perform any ritual of social location" and that I ignored the obligation of "situating oneself in context." But she also admitted that "this matter of self-contextualization still strikes me as elusive, indeed as less concretizing than we like to imagine, given the vast generic emptiness of categories such as 'race,' 'class,' and 'gender' until they are painstakingly filled, and as sometimes provocative of mere confession."

I recognized the validity of those criticisms, but also the difficulty articulated so accurately in that final comment. It is not enough to locate myself theologically by saying simply that I am Roman Catholic. It is not enough to locate myself socially by saying simply that I am white, European, and male. Those are generalities, and we live in particularities: I am not just Roman Catholic, I am an ex-monk and an ex-priest, and, moreover, I am one who, if he had to do that all over again, would do it all over again. I am not just European, I am Irish European, I am from a European colony within Europe, and I am of the first postcolonial generation of that fractured country. I said, as a reply in 1993, that I feared, if I talked too much about myself, the "depth and breadth of those particularities (even without introducing Freud) would fill the space available for any other subject, would invite dismissal because of them or concentration exclusively on them, and, as all becomes autobiography, nothing would ever change in a world of inequality and injustice" and such change was the challenge of Jesus' Kingdom of God.

In the years that followed I noticed one recurrent feature of journalistic interviews and lecture questions. Although the subject was the *historical* Jesus, the questions were as often theological as historical, and although the subject was the historical *Jesus,* the questions were as often biographically about me as biographically about him. I have, on the one hand, severe doubts about that process. It seems part of our contemporary inclination to talk about the speaker, not the subject, the actor, not the film, the author, not the book, the politician, not the program. It seems just part of our current voyeuristic individualism, part of our pervasive chatter (saying something about nothing) and blather (saying nothing about something), part of our talk-show display of comparative hemorrhoids. But, on the other hand, I understand *all* historical reconstruction as a dialectic between the viewer and the viewed in which each changes the other, an interaction between the present and the past in which each interprets the other. In that situation, questions about my own experiences, biases, and prejudices seem fair to ask, and I have always answered them as clearly and honestly as I can.

I also began to answer in books written after 1993, but slowly and carefully lest the focus shift too easily or primarily from the historical Jesus to the historical me, that is, from the sublime to the ridiculous. Reactions by critics and reviewers reminded me of the double bind involved in such revelations. For every one who acknowledged the validity of their presence, there was another who found them irrelevant. When I mentioned my theological conclusions, they were sometimes taken as theological principles. I was doing history only to justify a position of faith already in place at the very start. I was seeking and therefore finding a Jesus who was simply the reflection of my own personal likes and dislikes. I describe Jesus as a "Mediterranean Jewish peasant" under Roman oppression, I am told, because of sympathy for the past sufferings of Irish peasants under British oppression. Despite all that and whatever the risks, I write this present book to face fully the relationship between, on the one hand, my own life and faith and, on the other, my study of the historical Jesus and earliest Christianity. My own understanding, by the way, is that a thirty-year research project has forced the historical me to change rather than the historical Jesus not to do so. That is what I explore in this chapter: How, within the necessary dialectic of any valid historical reconstruction, the seeker and the sought change each other mutually, steadily, inevitably.

A question asked as often as the one about why I became a priest is why I decided to study the historical Jesus. I wish I could invoke a vision or a revelation, something photogenic and sexy for media consumption. Jesus appeared to me in a dream: "Dominic, tell my story. Tell it straight and true. Dominic, tell my story. I leave it up to you." That would put the rap back in rapture, but it is unfortunately pure fiction. The question, however, is a very good one and a much more searching one than the questioner usually knows. When I started my lifetime research on the historical Jesus in the late 1960s, there were only about three other scholars in the whole world who were focusing that exclusively on him. You could not count the number of experts working on Paul or on this or that Gospel, but the historical Jesus was the abandoned child of scholarly research. As I write now, in the late 1990s, I am not sure that number has changed very much. There are currently lots of books on the historical Jesus, but few scholars working exclusively on that subject. Most write a Jesus book and then move on to more important topics, like Paul.

Most of my research up to 1969, when I left the monastic priesthood and became a professor at DePaul University, was on matters of interest within the order or the church after the Second Vatican Council of the early 1960s. Typical articles were on Mary in the New Testament or divorce and remarriage in that same New Testament. When I moved to a university setting, I had to decide on a long-term research project, rather than on discrete subjects of immediate relevance to a changing church. In the late 1960s, both at Mundelein Seminary and at the Catholic Theological Union, I had taught graduate classes on two rather separate subjects. One was on the parables of the earthly Jesus; the other, on the apparitions of the resurrected Jesus. The former course concerned stories *by* Jesus. The latter course concerned stories *about* Jesus. I could have taught anything from the entire New Testament, but I had chosen the Gospels over the Epistles, and specifically those two sets of stories within the Gospels.

It was a free, deliberate choice and not an imposition by curriculum constraints. I try now not to retroject later interpretations into earlier decisions, but I am fairly certain of two points. First, on a surface level, I was fascinated back then by that dualism of *story by* or *story about* Jesus, and I wanted to let them interact dynamically within my own imagination. Second, on a deeper level, I was fascinated by story itself, by the types and possibilities of narrative. Think of it as a triangle, with *story by* and *story about* as the bottom points and story itself as the apex. I did not, of course, see all the future implications of that triangular dynamism, but its exploration has sustained a lifetime of both creative scholarship, personal meaning, and Christian faith.

In the following sections of this chapter, I will reconstruct that exploration as best I can, but first, and appropriately, two personal narratives framing it, two stories about stories about Jesus.

In summer 1960 I was a student at Rome's Pontifical Biblical Institute. That year the city promised not only hot skies, but crowded streets as the games of the XVIIth Olympiad spanned the city from the northern Stadio Olimpico to the southern Palazzo dello Sport. By early June I had only one concern: how to get out of that city before the heat intensified and the crowds arrived for those Olympic weeks in late August and early September. My Father Provincial wrote from Chicago appointing me chaplain for a Servite-sponsored month-long tour/pilgrimage arriving in Lisbon, proceeding to Rome, and leaving from Paris. My being already in Europe saved the tour the price of a transatlantic ticket. I never had, as you will recall, any difficulties with my vow of obedience as it related to where to go and what to do. And certainly not that time.

One stop on that tour was at Oberammergau amid the Bavarian Alps. For over three hundred years, the villagers have performed a passion play in thanksgiving for protection from a plague at the start of the seventeenth century. It is now played in its own theater with around one hundred performances during the summer of each decade's turning. I remember two things very clearly from that visit. I was very cold all the time. The other pilgrimage stops were in far warmer climes, Fátima in Portugal and Lourdes in Spain (for Mary), Monte Carlo in Monaco (for Grace Kelly) and Rome (for Pope John XXIII), so I did not have very warm clothing with me. The passion play theater, which seats about five thousand people, is covered above the stage and the auditorium, but it is open to the sky in between. I had one of those small fold-up raincoats and wore it the entire performance over a short-sleeved shirt. I spent all of that day shivering.

I have no particular recollection of what Caiaphas, Pilate, Peter, Judas, Mary, or Jesus looked like, but one scene has always stuck in my memory. It is the crowd scene before Pilate in which everyone demands that Barabbas be released and Jesus be crucified. That scene allowed dozens of people to appear on stage and gave everyone in the village, at least on rotating days, a chance to be in the play. The big roles were set, but the crowd scenes were open for each performance. The result, however, was a stage filled to capacity with a shouting mob composed mostly of women and children. That allowed the children a chance to perform, and they must have enjoyed the license to shout aloud before a public audience. But what they were shouting was: "Crucify him! Crucify him!"

After I returned from Rome to teach at Stonebridge Priory, the first scholarly article I published was in a 1965 issue of *Theological Studies* entitled "Anti-Semitism and the Gospels." I still had a lot to learn, but after Oberammergau, I knew there was something terribly wrong with those Gospel stories about the execution of Jesus. I did not know very clearly what was wrong, but something had rung terribly false as they were enacted as public performance rather than read as private text. I was cold in Oberammergau and spent most of the play shivering, but I was shivering for the wrong reason.

That is one story, from late September 1960. The following one is from early April 1995. In the weeks before Easter I was on a promotional tour for *Who Killed Jesus?* a book whose subtitle was *Exposing the Roots of Anti-Semitism in the Gospel Story of the Death of Jesus*. On a Wednesday evening I spoke and autographed books for the Barnes & Noble store in midtown Manhattan at 6th Avenue and 22nd Street. Such events usually took place in an isolated bay where about thirty chairs could encircle the speaker closely and no microphone was necessary. But in this case, I was on microphone and loudspeakers throughout the entire store at seven-thirty in the evening. I did not like that process since it forced everyone, whatever their interests, to listen to twenty minutes on the historical Jesus. At the end there were about thirty seated listeners who had come to hear the talk and another thirty listeners who had arrived during it. I thought some of them might be annoyed, and the first question someone asked me confirmed my expectations.

"You said that the Barabbas story was created by Mark because, as he saw it, the Jerusalem crowd had picked the brigand rebels as their wrong saviors in the war against Rome that started in 66 C.E.?"

"Yes."

"Mark himself made it up? The choice of Barabbas over Jesus never happened? It's not true?"

"Yes."

"Then why can't you just call it what it is—a lie?"

I cannot remember what I said, but it was probably defensive because I had never thought of the problem that way before. Why did I not call that incident or the many others created, in my view, by the traditions or the evangelists lies? They were not true, so were they not lies? I knew I was not afraid to call things, even Gospel things, by their proper names. If I thought *lie* was the proper term, I would have used it. So why had I not used it? What had always prevented me from doing so?

Those two autobiographical stories are separated by thirty-five years. I keep them in tandem to emphasize two abiding concerns of my own research. First, that I do nothing as a Christian to brutalize the Jewish people. Second, that I do nothing as a scholar to brutalize the Gospel writers. That first concern does not derive from ecumenical sensitivity or post-Holocaust repentance. That second concern does not derive from scholarly fear or Christian complacency. Both concerns derive from my attempt to understand what certain stories meant to the people who first told them, to reconstruct as securely as possible what actually happened long, long ago, and to establish simple historical accuracy.

The dynamic interaction of Gospel parables as stories *by* Jesus and resurrection visions as stories *about* Jesus was the matrix that generated thirty years of research. They were like electrical polarities creating a force field between them. I do not hint for a moment that I saw the later implications of that dialectical tension. I had not the faintest idea where I was going, but I did know I was going somewhere. I recognized certain points from teaching those twin courses in the late 1960s.

First, when Jesus spoke about the Kingdom of God, he did so especially in parables, in fictional stories created for that very purpose. Those narratives came straight from the fabric of humanity and yet were somehow adequate to the contour of divinity. The good Samaritan story in Luke, for example, told of an ordinary mugging on the dangerous desert road from Jerusalem down to Jericho. It told of a priest and a Levite who did not stop to help and of a third traveler who did more than anyone might have expected: bound up the sufferer's wounds, carried him to safety, paid for his convalescence, did everything, in fact, but give him his own donkey. Yet he was a Samaritan, not kin but a stranger, an ethnic opposite at best and an ancient enemy at worst. That story must have left behind it a very unhappy audience, challenged not just to sympathize with the mugged individual, but to identify with a *Samaritan* who had helped a *Jew* in distress. Parable was a fictional story with a theological punch, a story created precisely for that theological or, better, religio-political punch. It did not ask you if you believed in the facts of the story, if you thought, for example, that you could check them out in the police archives of West Jericho. It asked if you believed in a God who demanded assistance for opposites or even enemies in terminal need and what you thought, not just about your helping them (which might make you feel superior), but of their helping you (which would make you feel inferior).

Second, when the evangelists spoke about the resurrection of Jesus, they told stories about apparitions or visions. People have visions, all religions describe them, and some new religions have started from them. There is nothing impossible in that. They are historical events, they can be located in time and place, and, however they are explained, they are real happenings. So are dreams, for that matter. Both are simply altered states of consciousness, possibilities hardwired into our brains. But were those postresurrection stories accounts of historical visions or apparitions? What sort of narratives were they? Were they histories or parables?

Take, for example, the race to the empty tomb between Peter and the Beloved Disciple in John 20. The Beloved Disciple gets there first, looks in first, and believes first (or alone?), and Peter gets nothing except to go in first. I did not think that story was ever intended as a historical event, intended to describe something that first Easter morning. It always looked to me like a calculated and deliberate parable intended to exalt the authority of the Beloved Disciple over that of Peter. So, from that time on, this question pressed in on me: Were there other stories in the final chapters of the four Gospels intended not as histories, but as parables? And, if parables, parables of what?

If Jesus had a special preference for parables about God, did the evangelists have a special preference for parables about Jesus? That basic, abiding, and underlying question seemed easy to understand even if its implications and conclusions were controversial. Yet as time progressed I found journalistic reporters (and scholarly critics also) unable to record it fairly and accurately. I seldom attempted to rebut media misinterpretation on that subject. Sometimes it came from a need for sensation or confrontation, sometimes from a writer's own prejudice against me (if fundamentalist) or against my subject (if secularist). Only once did I make a major demand for retraction and correction. I hated to do that and normally did not do it since it always sounded like whining "I said, you said." I probably made a mistake on this issue, and let newspapers and magazines get away with far too much. But this was a particularly egregious instance of inaccuracy.

The article itself was carefully, intelligently, and accurately written in the religion section of the *Toronto Star* for Saturday, April 8, 1995. The writer had interviewed me one other time about a year previously and understood what we were discussing. He contrasted my book *Who Killed Jesus?* with an opposing volume entitled *Jesus Under Fire*. He cited that latter book's summary of me as follows: "[Crossan] denies the deity of Christ, declares that Jesus' pedigree—including his virgin birth in Bethlehem—is myth-making by the writers of the Gospels, and concludes that the stories of Jesus' death, burial, and resurrection were latter-day wishful thinking of the early church." That, in proper quotation marks, was from *Jesus Under Fire* (Jesus, of course, was never under fire from me, just some other people's interpretations of him). As a summary of my position that quotation is somewhere between a mistake and a lie depending on whether its authors are considered fools or knaves. But the *Toronto Star's* reporter was perfectly accurate in citing it as their opinion, not necessarily mine and not necessarily his. He also reported, quite accurately, that "for Crossan, empty tomb stories are parables of resurrection, not the Resurrection itself." But between writing and publishing, a strange transformation happened.

Journalists do not choose the pictures, captions, and headlines for their articles. The anonymous (at least to me) person responsible for that part of the process superimposed my picture on that of Thomas touching the wounds of the risen Jesus in John 20. It was a very clever combination, as both of us have our hands and fingers raised in similar position; the large boldface title was "Doubting Thomases." Fair enough, at least as editorial comment. But the subheading in smaller bold type reads: "The Resurrection is merely a parable for John Dominic Crossan, a leader among biblical scholars challenging traditional Christian beliefs." Under the juxtaposed pictures was this caption: "Faith? Picture shows Doubting Thomas, who didn't believe Christ rose from the dead. Author John Crossan calls the Resurrection story 'wishful thinking of the early church.'"

I faxed my protest to the paper's ombudsman, he consulted with the writer, and the following retraction appeared prominently bolded in the religion section three weeks after the original report: "Correction. Author's views were misstated. Contrary to a photo caption and headline printed on April 8, author John Dominic Crossan does not hold that the Resurrection is merely a parable or that the Resurrection story is wishful thinking of the early church. The *Star* regrets the errors." That happened twenty-five years after my original intuition about parables and apparitions, about stories by and stories about Jesus as parable rather than history, but I have always found a strong stench of burning straw whenever it was discussed. It was always easier to caricature and ridicule it than to explain it clearly and then debate it honestly. And it always struck me as a strange reaction. Jesus created parables to speak about God, and nobody said: "Those are merely parables" or "He is saying God does not exist." But when I suggested that the early Christians did exactly the same for Jesus, created, for example, parables about the resurrection (and much else besides), people said, "Those are merely parables. You are denying the resurrection."

Finally, where else in Gospel stories about Jesus were there parables *we have misread* as histories? And, if parables, parables of what? When I looked at the so-called nature miracles of Jesus I noticed that, while healings and exorcisms were usually performed for outsiders, those nature miracles were usually performed for insiders, for his companions, for the disciples, for the Twelve. Recall those I touched on in the last chapter. They rowed all night without Jesus and got nowhere, they fought the storm with Jesus asleep and almost drowned, they fished all night without Jesus and caught nothing. Those stories screamed parable at me, not history, not miracle, but parable. They shouted at me: "It's a parable, dummy." They were never intended to be about a miraculous walking on the water, a miraculous stilling of the storm, or a miraculous catch of fishes. They were not historical stories about Jesus' power over natural forces, but parabolical stories about Jesus' power over community leaders. With him they could do anything and get anywhere; without him they could do nothing and get nowhere. What could be simpler or more obvious? They were not about a divine circus, but a divine church. I find it very interesting, by the way, that within a generation of Jesus' death evangelists had to warn church leadership about operating without Jesus, about sailing off alone or fishing out there alone without Jesus aboard.

Try another example, an even more obvious and important one. We say that Jesus multiplied loaves and fishes to feed five thousand people. And we immediately rush in to believe or disbelieve, to assert impossibility or to claim uniqueness. Delay the Aesopic fallacy for a moment and read, actually read, the story. Read it line by line as told in the twin versions of Mark 6:35–44 and John 6:5–13. Read *all* of it as you do any story to get its meaning. Notice two key elements. Jesus does not turn stones into bread or bring down manna from heaven as in the desert model of the Old Testament Exodus from Egypt. He takes what is present, what is already there, the ordinary loaves and everyday fishes already contained within the crowd. That is what he multiplies. Furthermore, the disciples are forced, kicking and screaming as it were, to be intermediaries at every stage of the process. At the very start their solution for the hungry crowds is to send them away to buy their own provisions. When Jesus tells them it's their job to supply food, they almost jeer at him. Listen:

When it grew late, his disciples came to him and said, "This is a deserted place, and the hour is now very late; send them away so that they may go into the surrounding country and villages and buy something for themselves to eat." But he answered them, "You give them something to eat." They said to him, "Are we to go and buy two hundred denarii worth of bread, and give it to them to eat?"

Thereafter, it is never Jesus who deals directly with the crowds, but Jesus who commands the disciples on behalf of the crowds. They organize the people, distribute the food, and take up the leftovers. Once again, I see not just miracle, but miracle-in-parable. It is the duty of the disciples, the Twelve, the church to make sure that food is distributed fairly and equitably to all. And the church is very reluctant to accept that responsibility ("You give them something to eat"). Reluctant then, reluctant now. This is a parable not about charity, but about justice, about the just distribution of the material bases of life, about the sharing of that which is available equitably among all. There is more than enough for all when Justice multiplies and distributes what is already available. "What would Jesus do?" WWJD asks. "What would justice demand?" Jesus asks.

When Jesus wanted to say something very important about God he went into parable; when the early church wanted to say something very important about Jesus they too went into parable. It seemed to me terribly obvious: the more important the subject, the more necessary the parable. It seemed to me terribly simple: the parabler had become parabled. Yet it always seemed terribly hard for journalists to understand. It was as if they could not get past the negative question or conclusion, "So it never really happened?" Or worse, "So the story is untrue, false, a lie?"

Sarah and I were on a lecture tour of the major New Zealand cities for about three weeks in July 1999. It involved a series of seminars organized by the religious studies and continuing education departments at Victoria University of Wellington. For general publicity I was to be interviewed on television along with a more conservative colleague from the country's oldest institution of higher learning, Otago University. The host was Paul Holmes of the *Holmes Show,* which airs nightly after the evening news on TV 1 and is watched by about a quarter of the country's population (for format, think of *Larry King Live* running *Dateline*). We were all in different studios, Auckland, Christchurch, and Dunedin. In other words, it was talking-head time. And each of us had about three minutes on the air. An assistant producer and camera crew came to the hotel in the late afternoon to prep the host's questions and to get a thirty-second teaser for airing during the newscast. We talked for about half an hour, and I emphasized that transition from parables *by* to parables *about* Jesus just discussed. That was the one and only point I wanted to make in my three minutes of immortality. She mentioned that her six-year-old daughter was already asking if those Gospel stories were really true. I joked that she was just reaching the age of reason but would soon get over it. At the interview's conclusion, that very intelligent journalist summed up my message with this: "So the Gospel stories are just fictions?" It was still all negative. There was still no grasp of the positive power of parable.

Fictions and parables are both made-up stories, but although fictions are for entertainment, parables are for message. As a good example of fictions, read parts of the *Infancy Gospel of Thomas* from the second century. A boy bumps into Jesus accidentally, and Jesus kills him. His parents complain to Joseph, and Jesus blinds them. Another boy is killed by accidentally falling off a roof. Jesus is blamed but raises him from the dead to vindicate his innocence. And so on. It is Jesus the Christ as Dennis the Menace. It is as if God went in search of the Inner Child and found him to be Superbrat. I would not dignify those made-up tales with the term *parables;* they are simply fictions,

stories, and, in terms of the character of Jesus, less than fortunate inventions.

As a scholar I have always been equally interested in materials and
in methods, in what texts need to be studied and in how one goes
about that process. The *materials* for Jesus' parables involved
divergent Gospel versions as evangelists adopted and adapted
them for their own purposes. The *methods* involved the use of contemporary literary criticism to unleash the full metaphorical and
poetical power of those parables. In the very early 1970s I organized several already published articles into a book entitled *In
Parables* and went in search of a publisher. I did not want a
denominational or a religious publishing house, even one as excellent as Fortress Press. I wanted a secular one, because I hoped the
book would interest both religious readers, because of Jesus, and
nonreligious ones, because of parables. That double focus, by the
way, would remain a constant for the next thirty years.

I knew a very eminent biblical scholar who was an editor for
Doubleday, so I sent him a prospectus for the book. He told me
not to bother with Doubleday right now, because unless it was
about the devil, they wouldn't be interested. I should send it to
Harper & Row, because they were more serious about religious
publishing. I have no idea what he meant by that devil crack or
what made him temporarily so annoyed at Doubleday, but I sent
the proposal to Harper & Row (later HarperCollins), they accepted it, and so began a thirty-year collaboration. Aside from books
specially invited by others, I have always published with them,
and my respect for their integrity has grown steadily across the
decades. That calls for one comment, because many scholars
have denigrated publishers who attempt to combine scholarly
work *and* popular audience. I have never been asked to cut a single line in all those years. I have been asked to explain this section better, to expand on that section somewhat, to clarify what
an editor finds obscure, but never to cut out content, abbreviate
length, or dumb down thought.

That first book, *In Parables,* appeared in 1973, and it had two
very important effects. I was, as you will recall, in danger of falling

between two stools. As a student, I had been educated in the Roman Catholic and European academic tradition (Ireland, Rome, Jerusalem), and as a scholar, I was known, if at all, within the Catholic Biblical Association. In those days that was still something of a clerical club; I had left the club and was rather unsure of my continued welcome there. I was not known, either as student or scholar, within the major divinity schools or the Society of Biblical Literature in the interdenominational and American tradition. I had never been part of that club. But two professors who were deeply involved in that latter tradition telephoned me because of my work on Jesus' parables. Each in his own way said something like this: "I really like what you're doing, and by the way, who the hell are you?" Each in his own way made certain that I became known within the Society of Biblical Literature and the wider world of American scholarship. Both promoted me although I was not their student, promoted me simply because they accepted the value of publications over institutions, ideas over pedigrees.

Norman Perrin, of the University of Chicago, a New Testament professor and scholar of the historical Jesus, called me one evening in 1972 after my article on parables had appeared in the international journal *New Testament Studies*. He said he had given it to the members of his doctoral seminar that morning and invited them to tear it apart, but they thought I might be right. Later he invited me to sit in on an interdisciplinary seminar led by the philosopher Paul Ricoeur, the theologian David Tracy, and himself. I sent them a prepublication manuscript of *In Parables*, we discussed it together, and the general audience reaction was this: "We love your parables stuff, but skip that historical Jesus stuff. Literature yes, history no." I listened and responded, but never considered changing the book's subtitle, which was and remained *The Challenge of the Historical Jesus*. I already knew by then where I was going. It was not just after the *parables* of Jesus, but after the parables of *Jesus*. Perrin also proposed that I lead a five-year Parables Seminar within the annual conventions of the Society of Biblical Literature between 1972 and 1976. He was its president in 1973, and it was very nice to have him on my side.

Robert Funk, of the University of Montana, was then executive secretary of the Society of Biblical Literature, which he was bringing, willy-nilly, into the twentieth century. He was also, like Perrin, a scholar of the historical Jesus. In 1973, he finished his five years as executive secretary and proposed a new journal to be issued by the society starting in 1974. The society's regular publication, the *Journal of Biblical Literature,* was primarily philological, exegetical, and canonical. It neither discussed anything of great human interest nor any longer represented the wide spectrum of interests evident in the annual meeting, but it was very useful in holding together a membership embracing everything from atheism to fundamentalism. Funk proposed a second journal called *Semeia* and subtitled *An Experimental Journal for Biblical Criticism.* Its function was to do everything that should be done and that the flagship *Journal of Biblical Literature* was not doing, to investigate new theories, new methods, and new materials. He invited me to become an associate editor for the new journal's first six years, and then I followed him as general editor for the next six years. Since Funk was the society's president in 1975, it was also very nice to have him on my side.

The dangerous years of scholarly transition were safely over by 1973, and my focus remained on the parables of Jesus throughout that decade. I was still experimenting with literary criticism, problems of method, and postmodern theory. But one event in 1976 shocked me into reconsidering my long-range plans. Norman Perrin took me aside at the Society of Biblical Literature's annual meeting. He saw my recent book, *Raid on the Articulate,* about parables in Jesus and Borges, he said, and since I was leaving New Testament studies for literary criticism, and since Nathan Scott was leaving the University of Chicago for the University of Virginia, he wanted to propose me as his replacement; I was to send him my résumé as soon as I got home. That was pure Norman, generous, supportive, enthusiastic, but very, very wrong. I had not the slightest intention of leaving New Testament studies. I was simply probing the limits of theory and method in studying the parables. I decided to say nothing, send him my résumé, and presume Chicago's good sense would let it go appropriately nowhere. Norman died a few weeks later, and Joe Kitagawa, dean of the divinity school, called me sometime afterward.

"There is," he said, "a copy of your résumé sitting on Norman's desk. Is that important?"

"No," I replied. "Just slip it into the wastepaper basket."

Despite Norman's very complimentary but equally inaccurate interpretation of what I was doing, I never had the slightest intention of moving from historical Jesus to literary criticism. By the mid-1980s, however, I had shifted to a much larger understanding of what was involved in that reconstruction.

When I began work on the historical Jesus in the late 1960s and early 1970s, such scholarship was focused almost exclusively on the words, but not the deeds of Jesus, not even on the words and deeds together. The reason for that emphasis on Jesus as speaker and nothing else can probably be traced back to the German Lutheran theologian Rudolf Bultmann, for whom Jesus was a historical preacher lost forever inside sermons written about him by others. The word about Jesus was all, and the life of Jesus was unknown at best and irrelevant at worst. The focus was not on the life, not even on the life and death as a whole. Jesus was primarily a talking head of parables and aphorisms. That is what was going on, that was where I came in, and that is what I concentrated on doing. I was not even particularly aware that such a focus was extremely limited, since parables and aphorisms, in any case, were giving me more than enough to do. But as the 1980s proceeded, I became slowly aware that a focus that was initial and functional for me was ideological and theological for others. For them the words of Jesus were not a first step or just one step, but the whole pathway.

It was my participation in the Jesus Seminar that made me finally aware of that difference. In the mid-1980s Bob Funk issued an open invitation to scholars of the historical Jesus to hold four-day meetings twice annually, to debate whether Jesus did or did not say this or that unit attributed to him by the tradition, to vote on our conclusions according to levels of certainty (sure, less sure, unsure, very unsure), and to publish the results as soon as possible. We all agreed, of course, on the validity of critical historical investigation, but as the years progressed I became aware of a very basic difference between myself and Bob as codirectors of the group. He was still working in the Bultmannian tradition's emphasis on Jesus' words, and I was slowly but surely shifting to a non-Bultmannian emphasis on Jesus' life. That was probably indicative of the difference between a radical Protestant and a radical Catholic sensibility, but it would result eventually in very different reconstructions of the historical Jesus.

If, on that issue, I moved from initial agreement to eventual disagreement, there was another on which I moved in the opposite direction. Bob argued hard on two points. One was that we scholars had an ethical obligation to do our work in public and to make sure that nonscholars knew what was happening, knew not only the past of our discussions but especially the present cutting-edge options and debates, uncertainties and difficulties. The other was that there were many, many Christians eager to participate in such a program. I was much less convinced by that second claim at the time because of our divergent academic experience. He taught at a state university where many students were interested in taking religion courses. I taught at a Roman Catholic university where most were not. Catholic students had enough of religion from grade-school and high-school classes, from pulpit sermons and confessional lectures, and did not want more of the same at the university. I was, however, completely convinced by his first, or public-discourse, argument. He was right: we should do our work in public even if nobody out there listened to us. We had to stop talking only to ourselves in a language and style no outsider could penetrate. We had a public responsibility to be public. It was, after all, only public interest in the Bible that gave jobs to so many biblical scholars. There were very few openings for curators of ancient Hellenistic museums. There were very few best-sellers on the order of *The Historical Augustus: The Life of a Mediterranean Roman Emperor.*

It was only after *The Historical Jesus* was published in late 1991 that I realized that Bob was absolutely correct on that second claim as well. That book was the climax of over twenty years' work, it was written for my scholarly peers, and it was intended to start a major debate on methodology (of all things)—it was never intended for normal human consumption. But when it became a *Publishers Weekly* best-seller, I had a strong suspicion that more people bought it than finished it, and I noted exactly where and when my wife's bookmark stopped moving, so I wrote the shorter *Jesus: A Revolutionary Biography* as an apology for all those incomplete readings. But I knew by then that Bob Funk was quite correct. There were many people out there eager to give very serious thought to their faith and ready to do very serious work as part of its renewal.

As the 1990s progressed, reconstructing the historical Jesus was not just a study of the past but, as he himself had been, a critique of the present. It was, indeed, a way of doing necessary open-heart surgery on Christianity itself. For newspapers, Christmas and Easter generated repeated coverage of that subject. I had decided early on that public education was part of our scholarly duty, so I gave any journalists who called as much as they wanted, as long as they wanted, and as often as they wanted. I regretted reports that presented a certain overemphasis, not always but often, on negation, sensation, and confrontation.

Twice, on later occasions years apart, Peter Steinfels of the *New York Times* replied to my criticism of such media presentations by asking if I had ever seen the press releases sent out by the Jesus Seminar itself. I admitted that I had not, that they came out of the administrative offices, and that even if I had received copies, I would probably not have read them. I should know, he said, that they themselves emphasize negation, sensation, and confrontation. I presumed the truth of that charge but countered immediately on two points. I asked if he was unable, as a professional, to discriminate between the self-serving or hysteria-promoting aspects of a press release and whatever valid news it may contain. Besides, he had interviewed me, so he knew how I presented things, and yet I was so often portrayed as having only negative or pejorative things to say. But to be fair to the media, I found that inability to hear the positive also in fundamentalist replies and even in scholarly responses as well.

I tried, in my own case, to pay close attention to what I thought of as the ethics of one-liners, the morality of sound bites. I did not mind that necessity of modern high-speed communications for one major reason—I had been studying a superb exponent of that art for almost thirty years. What were the aphorisms and even parables of Jesus but magnificent sound bites, ones, that is, where style and substance were equally respected, where, if time were available, a one-liner could be expanded into an entire program? What were the stories and parables of earliest Christianity about Jesus but magnificent video bites just as carefully created and deliberately crafted to make certain very precise points and carry very clear messages? That was, I thought, the ethics of the sound bite or video bite. It was not just any bite, but a bite that perfectly summarized or symbolized the whole. I usually had to do it on the spur of the moment; sometimes it worked, sometimes it did not, and sometimes I cannot even remember what I actually said.

I told *Time* magazine something like this: "There's good news and bad news from the historical Jesus. The good news: God says Caesar sucks. The bad news: God says Caesar's us." It reported, accurately but not completely, "Crossan has summarized [Jesus'] message as 'God says, "Caesar sucks"'"(April 8, 1996, p. 55). That was Monday of Easter week. The preceding day, Easter Sunday, the ABC evening news had another scholar and myself comment on the historical Jesus. They had taped me for a few hours, but we all knew it was necessarily sound-bite time, a minute or two on the air at most. Toward the end we were deliberately working on a summary one-liner, and my best one was this: "As a historian, I reconstruct the historical Jesus as a peasant with an attitude. As a Christian, I believe his attitude to be the attitude of God." What aired was only the first half once again, accurate of course but still incomplete: "Jesus was a peasant with an attitude." Maybe one-liners can have only one line; sound bites can have only one part.

As my own historical Jesus project developed in the late 1980s, I was starting to focus on the life of Jesus as a whole, on words *and* deeds, on sayings *and* stories, on life as protest *and* death as execution. New materials, such as recently discovered gospels not in the New Testament, pushed me in that direction, and so also did changed methods, such as the use of cross-cultural anthropology. In both those areas I was strongly influenced and deeply grateful for pioneering work by other scholars. But there was something else operative as well, something even more basic in my own life that made it impossible any longer to think of Jesus in terms only of talk, words, or sayings, something that made it imperative to think of Jesus in terms of a total lived life.

In March 1998, a journalist who had interviewed me several times before and knew me personally was finishing an Easter interview on my recently published book, *The Birth of Christianity*. He asked what my next project was, what I was working on at the moment. I told him about this book and about some of its content. At one point he interrupted me, "Oh, of course, that's right. Sarah is your second wife." We were on the phone, so he could not see my face, but I went quietly cold inside and responded with flat and noncommittal chronology. Yes, Margaret died in 1983, and I married Sarah in 1986. And so the interview dribbled to an end.

First and *second* were terms I never would have used, never could have used for that transition. It was not just respect for the dignity and particularity of another person. It was terribly untrue to my own experience of those years. It was, for me, much more like starting all over again, starting all over again as a different person, starting all over again with a very different sense of death and therefore of life. To have even thought of *first* and *second* would have presumed an easy continuity of self I had not experienced between 1983 and 1986. Continuation was there, of course, in place, profession, and research, and I do not minimize the retaining power of those continuities. Nor do I think of them as minor or insignificant retentions, but although I had never taken Margaret for granted, I had taken our time together and our life together for granted, and I could never take time or life like that again.

After Margaret died, I had to learn how to live alone. I had never done that before. I had moved from home to boarding school to monastery to marriage. I did not even know the basics of cooking for myself. Margaret was a superb cook and loved dinner parties, and I had operated as her instructed helper. It was easier and lazier to help an expert than to educate myself. After Margaret's death, I learned to cook and even to put on sit-down dinner parties for seven as Margaret and I used to do for eight. My first and most immediate questions had been whether and how I could live alone. By the first anniversary of Margaret's death I knew for sure that I could do so and would, if necessary, survive like that.

I met Sarah several years before Margaret's death. She was an older student (she says "returning scholar" is more polite) taking an undergraduate degree as part of DePaul University's School for New Learning, which adapts requirements to fit more closely a later student's past experiences, present needs, and future goals. She was project director in symbolic catechesis for learning-disabled students with the archdiocese of Chicago, and that salary allowed her to pursue her degree. We first met in a basic New Testament course in fall 1979, where she was one of twenty students, and then in a more advanced class in spring 1980, where she was one of two. But whether with twenty or with two, Sarah stood out, as was typical of School for New Learning students. She was a joy to have amid young undergraduates taking a required general education course. She asked questions about meaning and implication, she discussed back and forth, and all of that encouraged the silent majority to open up a little. I loved having School for New Learning students in class for just that reason. (The only comparison was with Theater School students. They were usually young, of course, and did not ask such probing questions, but, oh my, they were on stage all the time, and when they stood up to pose a problem, it was an Oscar, not an answer they had in mind.)

I knew Sarah much better than the hundreds of other students I had each year at DePaul. In addition to the usual high maintenance required from teachers for all School for New Learning students as over against required-course undergraduates just wanting to get finished, get graded, and get gone, Sarah had emergency surgery toward the end of that course in which she represented half the class, and that meant individual sessions and examinations. She graduated in 1981, but when I heard in fall 1984 that she was getting a divorce, I remembered exactly who she was and knew I was very, very interested in seeing her again. I phoned her, and we went to dinner. We started dating, and after about a year, we knew that we were deeply in love and that it was time to plan our future. We were married in August 1986, and that was our very first good decision.

The second one was almost accidental, or at least indirect. We decided to rent a summer house on Bass Lake in northwestern Indiana so that Sarah's two late-teenage children, Frank and Michelle, could visit us there along with their friends and even vacation there the following summer. It was also just a few miles from her parents' home in Knox, Indiana. We ended up buying a permanent vacation home instead of renting a transient summer cottage. It was totally empty and totally ours. Margaret and I had lived in a lakefront condominium in Chicago, and its every inch bore our common imprint. Sarah and I continued to live there, but now, as we slowly realized, we also had a place of our own to create from scratch. We called it "Innisfree" and went there every weekend, every vacation, every summer, and every other time we had a chance. It was important to us for the children's visits, but it was also important to us for ourselves. That was the second very good decision.

The third one occurred a decade later. In 1995 I took early retirement from DePaul University, as did Sarah from her job as a school social worker in Westchester. When I am asked why, I usually say that in 1994 DePaul offered a one-time inducement of a full year's pay for anyone with a quotient of eighty-five units (for example, sixty years of age and twenty-five years of service) who wished to retire at the end of the academic year 1994–1995. I was sixty-one with twenty-six years, so I took it. That keeps it simple, and it is true, but it is not the whole truth.

In fact, I had talked to the Dean of Faculties six months earlier, told him I was considering early retirement, asked him what package he could offer me, and was told to wait until the general offer was made later in the fall. That, of course, was perfectly acceptable. I told him I intended early retirement to be more free for lectures around the country or abroad, and, in general, to have more time for research and publication. That kept it simple, and it was true, but it was not the whole truth.

This is the whole truth, or at least as close to it as I can get. I had known about death firsthand since I was fourteen years old and had attended Auntie Mary's funeral, looking thereafter, as you will recall, with very different eyes at her brother, who was my father. Even after that early experience and even later, after my parents' deaths, I still took time and life for granted. I did so, as I said, with Margaret. I never thought, viscerally and emotionally, about something happening to me, to her, to us. Maybe, in any case, that is not a thought you think beforehand, but a loss you suffer afterward. I could never again take life for granted and never again presume a love would last forever. So I am now Professor Emeritus, and *Emeritus* is a Latin word that means "more time with Sarah." And that, in ways that I do not fully understand and at levels deeper down than I know, must also have influenced my reconstruction of Jesus, must have influenced it inevitably toward an emphasis on life over talk. *The Historical Jesus* of 1991 was subtitled, therefore, *The Life of a Mediterranean Jewish Peasant.* The most important word there was *Life.* I was no longer satisfied with a talking head or even with theology of the Word. I was reconstructing a lived life and not just a preached sermon.

CHAPTER 8

Mine Eyes Decline the Glory

Sarah and I moved to central Florida in 1995 because of its weather, its lakes, and its twin coasts each less than two hours away from our home. I had lived for twenty-six years on Chicago's lakefront and on winter mornings walked westward to DePaul's downtown campus. It was a wake-up walk in a heavy parka hooded against the icy wind with glasses freezing over from my breath. I enjoyed it then, but one day after it was not necessary, it was not needed. We left immediately, swiftly, and happily. But living in central Florida, half an hour due west of Orlando and half an hour northwest of Disney World, has given me unique insight into one recent debate. Since I have been talking so much about parables, and since I gave you one entitled "The Aesopic Fallacy" a few chapters back, here is another one, called "A Modest Disposal," to begin this final chapter:

> Once upon a time there was a group called the Southern Baptist Convention, which locked horns (possibly an unfortunate metaphor) every year with another group called Walt Disney Incorporated. The media reported that the issue was the sexual content of movies made by Disney subsidiaries or the equal respect it showed to both gay and straight employees at its theme parks. The Southern Baptist Convention held that gays should repent, change, and go straight. Gays responded that such was not possible, that they had never met such transformed individuals, but that they had often met fundamentalists who had

repented, changed, and become Christian. Be that as it may, the media got it completely wrong. The debate was not over morality or even over differing views of morality. It was not over the Bible, the New Testament, or the Gospels, over where they were permanently valid ("Love your enemies") and where they were socially relative ("Slaves, obey your masters"). It was actually over the global control of fantasy.

The contest was between two giant corporations over the worldwide missionary expansion of illusional entertainment. Both were, at least in large doses, equally if differently dangerous. With Walt Disney Incorporated it was sometimes difficult to tell reality from fantasy as cartoon characters, literary figures, historical events, geographical places, and eventually religious traditions disappeared into animated illusion. With the Southern Baptist Convention it was difficult to distinguish between religion and Prozac, Christianity and chloroform, baptism and lobotomy. But, locked together, the object of the battle was obvious. Who, for the next century or even the next millennium, would control the transmutation of reality into fantasy, of religious reality into religious fantasy, and of secular reality into secular fantasy?

The only solution was to bring in a conflict-management arbitrator to negotiate a final solution before the parties destroyed one another. She spoke about the dangers of giant corporations fighting to the death rather than arranging sensible compromise. She said she wished that Apple and IBM had combined forces to make the original personal computer and that Microsoft had died aborning. (She admitted that last comment might have been unfair, because she realized the difficulty of reinventing the wheel without infringing on its first patent. It did, however, make the final product more complicated than the original.)

After only a few weeks, the deal was concluded. Walt Disney Incorporated and the Southern Baptist Convention amalgamated freely and evenly—not a hostile takeover or even a friendly buyout, but an absolutely equal combination. It was like, as the arbitrator said, Harper and Collins becoming HarperCollins-*Publishers*. The two erstwhile enemies became BaptistDisney-*Entertainments*.

MINE EYES DECLINE THE GLORY

They started immediately to plan for the future. There would be a new giant theme park, wiping out any recent gains made by Universal Studios' Escape and taking up all the rest of central Florida, from sea to shining sea. It would have an interactive Garden of Eden, where visitors could create different original sins and divergent histories of the world, and an interactive Rapture Ride and Millennial Slaughter, where visitors could invent alternative atrocities to exterminate the ungodly. The possibilities were endless.

There was only one cloud on the horizon. The U.S. Justice Department moved immediately to forbid the merger and to prevent BaptistDisney*Entertainments* from obtaining a monopoly on world fantasy. But a good legal defense was easily able to overturn that prohibition. Clearly, there were still other major contenders in the market. There were Hollywood's special-effects wizards, England's royal family, Rome's Vatican City, and Israel's National Parks Authority, which, according to *Time* magazine for February 22, 1999, "has approved a 262-ft.-long transparent bridge to be built just below the surface of the Sea of Galilee so visitors can follow in the footsteps of Christ. . . . After it opens in August, [the contractor Ron Major] expects up to 800,000 people a year to pay a minimum fee to walk on water. And, yes, lifeguards will be on hand in case anyone strays from the true path." That issue was actually introduced as an exhibit for the defense.

Eventually, the Justice Department agreed: BaptistDisney-*Entertainments* would not be a monopoly, just number one. Everything was now perfect, although an op-ed in the *New York Times* warned, from somewhere in William Butler Yeats's poetry, that when a heart grows up on fantasy, it often grows old on brutality.

During the last few hundred years, the ideological war was between religion and science or, in its most degenerate form, between religious fundamentalism and secular rationalism. In that warfare science did not lose, and religion did not win. But the next few hundred years will see a different ideological war, one between religion and fantasy. As all things become entertainment, and all entertainment becomes sensation, and all sensation becomes illusion, religion will have to distinguish itself very clearly from fantasy or else become a minor subsidiary of that overwhelming trivialization of the human imagination. I think now, after twenty years of monastic life and thirty years of religious scholarship, about what I have left behind and what I have kept from Christianity and Roman Catholicism in separating history and parable, religion and illusion, faith and fantasy.

Much in the Gospels was intended, as I have argued, to be taken parabolically and symbolically rather than factually and historically. And much of that, even if mistakenly accepted as historical by moderns, is more a matter for indifference and unconcern than for opposition and disbelief. But what about apocalyptic consummation, divine ethnic cleansing, and terminal annihilation of the evil and the unjust? I write as this terrible century lurches toward its conclusion amid a religious lust for millennial consummation. That hope for ultimate termination raises questions about the character of the Christian religion, the Christian Jesus, and above all the Christian God.

Sometimes even that can be funny, even if macabre as much as amusing. An example about the end of life as 1999 became 2000. At the conclusion of that down-under lecture tour, Sarah and I were standing with our luggage outside the Hyatt Regency Hotel in Auckland, New Zealand, waiting for a car to take us to a plane that would get us home to America. We were chatting with a doorman in his early twenties about the crowds expected at Gisborne, located where the North Island juts eastward toward the international date line and one of the first large cities to greet the dawn of the new millennium. I give him more or less verbatim:

There will be huge concerts and very big crowds. We expect a lot of Christians coming there to off themselves. The government may demand everyone who comes has a return ticket home. If that does not work, they won't have enough hearses, so they are planning to use refrigerated trucks for all the corpses. Of course, the dead will all be foreigners. There will be no New Zealanders. We are not a religious people.

No irony, no sarcasm, serene seriousness. I presume (and hope) he had simply got the rapture wrong. In any case, here is ending as offing, but only for religious people, only for Christians.

Is it always enough to laugh, to ignore illusion and delusion, or are there fantasies that infect the imagination in dangerous and obscene ways even when they do not lead immediately to action, to suicide or murder, to genocide or holocaust? Do we not at least have to say this, as I will now: Mine eyes decline the glory of the coming of the Lord who will trample out the vintage made of human beings as grapes. I decline the first or second coming of such a Jesus and, even more emphatically, of a God whose final solution to the existence of evil and the problem of injustice is the extermination of all those considered evil or unjust. I reject, and I think we should all reject, that vision from the final book of the Christian Bible, from the book of Revelation, where "the wine press was trodden outside the city, and blood flowed from the wine press, as high as a horse's bridle, for a distance of about two hundred miles."

My own experience growing up amid Ireland's first postcolonial generation may have sensitized me to the distinction between vengeance and justice. But I have also spent a lifetime studying the Christian Old and New Testaments, meditating on the continuity rather than dichotomy between their Gods, and especially thinking about the character of that God. But I prefer to begin with the darkness of the human heart and to look at myself before I look at others.

I find vengeance and justice lying wedded and bedded in my own heart. In theory, I recognize the distinction. Vengeance is swift, merciless, and violent. Justice is slow, merciful, and nonviolent. It is merciful precisely because it is slow; it allows time for past repentance, present restitution, and future reversal. In practice, I find that distinction more difficult to retain. For example, is the death penalty ever justice or always at least residual vengeance? When I look at other countries and cultures, usually far away in place or time, I easily judge them vengeful rather than just. But closer to home, I sense the distinction dissolving. Vengeance and justice are desperately easy to see as twin sides of the one coin and desperately hard to see as two distinct coins. And that is precisely my present question about the character of God. Is God a God of vengeance or of justice, and if of both, is that possible?

Knowing how often vengeance and justice intertwine inextricably in our humanity, I am not surprised to see them projected in similar mix onto our divinity. There is an ancient libel out there that the Old Testament God (or the God of Judaism) is a God of vengeance and the New Testament God (or the God of Christianity) is a God of love. I do not see any simple equation of vengeance with the Old Testament God and love with the New Testament God, but I do see an interweave of vengeance and justice across *both* Testaments and, indeed, across two thousand years of the Christianity that grew out of them. You can often even find vengeance or justice announced side by side in the very same book. They are not reconciled, just juxtaposed. They are simply both there, just as they are both there so often in our own heart.

Look at the book of the prophet Micah, for example. The vengeance side is quite clear in one place:

In that day, says the Lord, I will cut off your horses from among you and will destroy your chariots; and I will cut off the cities of your land and throw down all your strongholds; and I will cut off sorceries from your hand, and you shall have no more soothsayers; and I will cut off your images and your pillars from among you, and you shall bow down no more to the work of your hands; and I will uproot your sacred poles from among you and destroy your towns. And in anger and wrath I will execute vengeance on the nations that did not obey.

On that day of ultimate wrath, God will destroy the nations and their gods that have oppressed Israel.

But the justice side is equally clear in this very famous quotation.

In days to come the mountain of the Lord's house shall be established as the highest of the mountains, and shall be raised up above the hills. Peoples shall stream to it, and many nations shall come and say: "Come, let us go up to the mountain of the Lord, to the house of the God of Jacob; that he may teach us his ways and that we may walk in his paths." For out of Zion shall go forth instruction, and the word of the Lord from Jerusalem. He shall judge between many peoples, and shall arbitrate between strong nations far away; they shall beat their swords into plowshares, and their spears into pruning hooks; nation shall not lift up sword against nation, neither shall they learn war any more; but they shall all sit under their own vines and under their own fig trees, and no one shall make them afraid; for the mouth of the Lord of hosts has spoken.

Those are fascinatingly different outcomes, different final solutions to the problem of evil and injustice: positive or negative, conversion or extermination, justice or vengeance. I do not find them reconcilable. It is a question not just of human choice, but of divine character. Either/or.

You can go through the Bible, *all* the way from one end to the other, and draw up a long list of texts about God as vengeance. You can also go through it, *all* the way from one end to the other, and draw up a long list of texts about God as justice. Maybe, you can equate them or conflate them as two words for the same reaction? Or maybe you have to choose one or the other? But, first of all, on the presumption that we know more clearly the meaning of vengeance (swift, violent, merciless), what exactly is the meaning of justice (slow, nonviolent, merciful)?

Over and over again throughout the Old Testament, God is emphasized as a God of justice and righteousness, one who does what is just and does what is right. That in itself is not very impressive. I know of no God or Goddess, group or community, nation or state that asserts itself in favor of injustice and unrighteousness. It's not the manifesto, but the case law that counts, not the covenant's preamble, but its small print that matters. And here things are very clear. Here things, however mythologically expressed, are magnificently clear.

It is almost all contained in one single book, in one single chapter, in one single verse, and this is the most significant verse in the entire Bible. In Leviticus 25:23 God says, "The land shall not be sold in perpetuity, for the land is mine; with me you are but aliens and tenants." The land in immediate question is, of course, the land of Israel, the Jewish homeland. But the Israelites considered their God the God of all the earth, so what was said *to* them was said *for* all, and the character of their God did not change across time and space. The land, explicitly, and the earth, implicitly, belongs not to us, but to God. We hold whatever we hold as resident aliens in Another's country and tenant farmers on Another's land. God, in their understanding, had given the land to this people under covenant and law, and at the beginning it was divided up fairly, evenly, justly, rightly among the tribes, clans, and families of Israel. Therefore, decreed the law, you were not allowed to *sell* your ancestral inheritance; for example, in Deuteronomy 19:14, "You must not move your neighbor's boundary marker, set up by former generations, on the property that will be allotted to you in the land that the Lord your God is giving you to possess." That is not about creeping out at night and moving another's boundary stones. It is about buying and selling land as if it were just another commercial commodity. The distribution of land is about the preservation of human life and so it must be treated with very special care.

There is a fascinating practical example of this in 1 Kings 21. King Ahab approached a man called Naboth to acquire his vineyard. He did not simply say, "You have a vineyard. I want it. I am king and I will take it. You have a problem with that?" Instead, he was very fair and polite. "Give me your vineyard, so that I may have it for a vegetable garden, because it is near my house; I will give you a better vineyard for it; or, if it seems good to you, I will give you its value in money." But Naboth knows the law and has to refuse: "The Lord forbid that I should give you my ancestral inheritance." Ahab's queen, Jezebel, is a pagan princess who comes from a different economic theology and believes in free trade. So she has Naboth killed and gives her husband his vineyard. But behind all of that theory and practice is the attempt to protect the peasantry of Israel, to preserve distributive justice, to prevent the buying and selling of land, lest the few get more and more of it and the many have less and less of it. That tradition knew that would happen if land, that is, the very material basis of life, was treated like any other commercial object. It was summed up in Isaiah 5:8: "Ah, you who join house to house, who add field to field, until there is room for no one but you, and you are left to live alone in the midst of the land!"

That is also why there is so much in Mosaic law about debt. If you cannot buy and sell land, you can still lose or acquire it by loans, defaults, and foreclosures. Hence these five safeguards to control the creeping growth of crippling debt. No interest is to be allowed on loans. Collateral is to be carefully controlled and delimited. Loans are to be liquidated after seven years. People sold into slavery for debt are to be freed after seven years. Finally, there was to be a Jubilee Year. Every fiftieth year all peasant lands and rural houses must revert to their original owners. It is often hard to know how much of that is utopian idealism and how much is practical realism, but, in any case, it is all in the official law of God, and if it was there and not obeyed, that could always raise problems about everything else that was. Be careful, I suppose, about what you put in your covenant and law (or Constitution and Bill of Rights), as it may come home to haunt you.

Justice, then, is about distribution rather than retribution and about systemic or structural rather than just personal and individual justice. It is about the equitable sharing of the material basis of life itself. A God of such justice is worth worshiping, worth living for and even dying for, if unfortunately necessary. It is not just a question of whether God exists or not, but about the character of the God one believes in.

In October 1994 I was debating publicly with a conservative scholar in Moody Bible Church in Chicago. I had accepted the invitation in the hope that we could lessen somewhat the mutual contempt between opposing Christian groups. In the event, that did not work since he presented himself as a theological hit man opposing and refuting me as an "atheist" (see how these Christians hate one another). The moderator was William F. Buckley, Jr. He wanted to talk about logical arguments for the existence of God, and I did not, because a God that could be proved or disproved by human logic is already within its sway and under its power. We were supposed to be discussing the historical Jesus, but if we were to talk of God, I wanted much more to ask about the character of one's (mine, his) God. We were never able to do that because I, as an "atheist," wanted to talk about faith and he, as a theist, wanted to talk about proof. I wanted, all evening, to thank him for confirming, once again, that he could be moderator without being moderate and for proving, once again, that wit was not the same as wisdom. But I was on my very best behavior throughout, and despite his insistent provocation, I remained what he called "ingratiating" and what I would have called gracious.

But, as I read the biblical texts, I do not see them asking logical questions about the existence of God or philosophical questions about the nature of God, about omnipotence, omniscience, and other abstract subjects. I see them asking a simple question about the character of my, your, our, their God. Is that God about vengeance and retribution or about justice and distribution? Maybe retribution is what happens when distribution is unjust, maybe it is built intrinsically into it? Maybe retribution is but another name for, if I may invent a word, *dy*stribution?

I know that brutality brutalizes, and before I criticize the overt violence of colonial reprisal, I must criticize first the covert violence of imperial control. That is but minimally human and minimally moral. I can understand when marginalized minorities or small countries under discrimination, oppression, and persecution lash out in any way they can, not just with open battle, but with guerrilla warfare or even terrorist action. If they are too small to imagine fighting their oppressors or if they have been too long under their boot, I can understand a thirst for final vindication and ultimate revenge. If, therefore, their God is a God of vengeance, I understand their hopes for apocalyptic destruction and expectations of millennial consummation—and very soon. I understand, but I do not agree. It is, once again, about the character of one's God.

How does the Jewish first century in general and the Jewish Jesus in particular fit into all of that? A venerable and ancient religion was then pressed hard by Greek cultural internationalism and Roman military imperialism. Reactions, as might be expected, spanned the entire spectrum of possibility. On the far right, a Jew could declare it the will of God that Israel be a priest-led theocracy under Roman imperial control. "Do not resist and do not use violence," said the Jewish historian Josephus, "or you oppose the will of God." On the far left, a Jew could declare it the will of the same God that Israel take up arms and push the Romans into the sea. "We have no Lord but God," said Judas the Galilean, as he prepared to lead rebellion against Rome.

In the middle were two other options. One response did not imagine the violence of human revolt, but the vengeance of divine intervention. It announced an apocalyptic consummation in which God and God alone would soon establish a utopian world of prosperity and fertility, justice and peace here below on a transformed earth. It announced not the end of the material earth, but the end of the unjust world, not the annihilation of creation, but the abandonment of oppression. Here is the climax of one such prophecy from about the time of Jesus' birth, from a Jewish text called the *Sibylline Oracles* (2):

The earth will belong equally to all, undivided by walls
or fences. . . . Lives will be in common and wealth will have no
    division.
For there will be no poor man there, no rich, and no tyrant,
no slave. Further, no one will be either great or small anymore.
No kings, no leaders. All will be on a par together.

It is important, especially against the background of Hollywood's millennial vulgarity (the meteor is coming, and only Bruce Willis can save us), to emphasize that Jewish and Christian apocalypses, even when replete with transcendental violence, were trying to imagine a perfect world of equality here below. But there is still always this danger: If God's final solution is violent elimination of evil, why can we ourselves not start now on the evildoers?

There was, however, another option proposed in that terrible first century. It insisted on resistance, but on nonviolent resistance, and it was ready for martyrdom if necessary. We know of at least two very clear cases, one from before the death of Jesus and one from after it. Unarmed Jews gathered before the prefect Pilate at the Roman headquarters in Caesarea, probably in 26 or 27 C.E., to protest his introduction of imperial images on military standards into Jerusalem itself. After five days of peaceful demonstration, Pilate called in his troops, but according to Josephus, "the Jews, as by concerted action, flung themselves in a body on the ground, and exclaimed that they were ready rather to die than to transgress the law." Unarmed Jews gathered before the governor Petronius who planned, with a force of two or three legions, to place a statue of the emperor Caligula in Jerusalem's Temple. Faced with that impending desecration in 40 C.E., a "vast multitude" of men, women, and children confronted Petronius at Tiberias in Lower Galilee. They told him, again according to Josephus, that to proceed he would first have "to sacrifice the entire Jewish nation; and that they presented themselves, their wives and their children, ready for the slaughter." That type of nonviolent protest and resistance does not just happen. Somebody was organizing those people, leading them, controlling them. Unlike Josephus, the pro-Roman historian, it affirms resistance, but unlike Judas, the anti-Roman revolutionary, it denies violence. Such nonviolent resistance had to be ready for martyrdom as its logical and inevitable consummation.

It is precisely in that latter movement that I locate the historical Jesus. He said that, on the one hand, God called for resistance to oppression. The Torah, the law of God, the Jewish tradition spoke of land and debt. It had emphasized the fair distribution of land, the careful control of debt, and the protection of the peasantry, who formed the vast majority of the population (say, 80–90 percent). But the Lord's Prayer spoke rather of food ("give us this day our daily bread") and debt ("forgive us our debts as we forgive others theirs"), about enough food for today and no debt for tomorrow. It said that the Kingdom of God ("thy Kingdom come") involved such justice and that it involved it here below on earth ("thy will be done on earth, as it is in heaven"). Jesus was repeating God's demand for the just distribution of land, but in more straitened circumstances. It was now only fair distribution of food that many could envisage. In Lower Galilee by the 20s, as Herod Antipas's romanization and urbanization program (Tiberias as the new capital!) expanded through rural commercialization, as peasants were forced off their lands by debt and foreclosure, as the village safety nets of kinship and location were broken, sharing food became a divine imperative when holding land was no longer possible. But whether it was land or food, it was still a question of the material basis of life and how it was to be equally shared and fairly distributed. And it was still about distributing what is God's equitably and not about distributing what is ours charitably.

On the other hand, Jesus also insisted that such resistance be nonviolent. He interpreted the well-known Golden Rule both offensively and defensively. It said, for all: "Since you do not want to be attacked, do not attack others." But it also said, for him: "Since you do not want to be attacked, do not attack back even when you are attacked." That was rather more radical, and it led to this equally radical complex:

Love your enemies, do good to those who hate you, bless those who curse you, pray for those who abuse you. If anyone strikes you on the cheek, offer the other also; and from anyone who takes away your coat do not withhold even your shirt. Give to everyone who begs from you; and if anyone takes away your goods, do not ask for them again. Do to others as you would have them do to you.

I often receive very strong audience reactions for speaking about Jesus and *justice* rather than Christianity and *love*. The New Testament *agape,* which we translate as "love" and often interpret as charity, is best translated as "sharing," as a commitment to share the goods of this world as belonging to God and not ourselves, as a theology of creation and not just of emotion. That is why the common shared meal of earliest Christianity was called an *agape*. It was the Lord's Supper, not ours. In other words, love (as *agape*) is simply another word for that divine justice discussed above. "Then why," one objector insisted, "can't you say love rather than justice? If they are the same, say love, not justice!" They *are* the same, but maybe *love* is a word so abused by two thousand years of Christian history that it needs to be warmed in the hands of God for another two thousand before it is safe for further use.

Around fifty years ago in secondary-school English class I learned by heart a poem of John Keats called "Ode on a Grecian Urn." Its last lines asserted that beauty was truth, truth beauty, and claimed that such equivalence was all we know on earth and all we need to know. That message came from "a friend to man," or, more inclusively, from a friend of our humanity. I would like to rewrite those last lines, with apologies to the poet, as a conclusion to a new "Ode on a Jewish Urn." They come from God or Jesus or, if you prefer, from a friend of our humanity:

"Justice is love, love justice,"—that is all
Ye (better) know on earth, and all ye need to know.

The inevitable result of such nonviolent resistance was, as always, martyrdom. Jesus died eventually on a Roman cross, officially and formally executed by legal authority for opposing Roman imperialism. Had he not done so, he would have lived. Had he done so violently, many of his companions would have died with him. Crucifixion meant that imperial power had won. Resurrection meant that divine justice had won. It was simply a conflict of Gods, the Roman God of power against the Jewish

God of justice. Resurrection was not about the body coming out of the tomb even if that had actually happened. It was not about visions of the beloved dead even though that must surely have happened. It was, however, about the real, historical body of Jesus, about that body that had lived and died for justice, that had been flogged, tortured, and crucified not as idea, but as flesh. It was also about the similar bodies of all those Jewish martyrs who had died before Jesus because they had refused to deny their God or disobey their law. Resurrection meant, for the first Christian Jews, that all those martyrs were vindicated by God in Jesus. How? Not by a sudden end of the unjust world and a judicial vindication of the martyrs. Insofar as that was expected literally, it simply did not happen. But what did happen was this. Slowly but surely, more and more people turned from Caesar to Jesus, turned from the unity of the great Roman Empire to small cells of nonviolent resistance, to small communities that shared life and especially food together and that did so in unity with the life and death of Jesus as the incarnate revelation of God's character. A Christian *ecclesia* was forming over, under, and around the Roman *imperium,* and it did so as its subversive opposite.

In all of that, watch for the marks of Roman crucifixion on the body of Jesus, watch for those wounds that can never heal, fade, or disappear. Recall, as mentioned earlier, those Easter issues of *Newsweek, Time,* and *U.S. News & World Report,* April 8, 1996, all with cover stories on the historical Jesus. *Newsweek* had the caption "Rethinking the Resurrection: A New Debate About the Risen Christ." It was written across a picture of Jesus rising heavenward, arms uplifted, hands facing outward. What struck me immediately as strange was the complete absence of any wounds on those clearly visible hands and feet. I failed to realize that they had mistakenly taken Jesus from a Transfiguration instead of a resurrection painting. There were, of course, no wounds in that Vatican work by Raphael because it depicted an event before the death of Jesus. *U.S. News & World Report,* on the other hand (no pun intended), had a correct picture. Its cover had the caption "In Search of Jesus: Who Was He? New Appraisals of His Life and Meaning" written across Jesus from a Bellini painting of the resurrection with the wound in Jesus' right hand clearly visible. In Christian Gospel, art, and mysticism, the resurrected body is always the crucified body. Resurrection is always about a life for justice that led to a death for justice and to the question of which side you are on—power or justice?

A confessional postscript is necessary here. I am not myself capable of living by absolute nonviolence if placed under serious danger or lethal attack. But I consider violence as always evil, as always a separation from God. I never consider it as good but, at very best, as the lesser of two evils, and I recognize that as a pale justification for it. It is never, under any circumstances, the will of God, but simply the lesser degree of separation from the God who is nonviolent justice and whose patience is far beyond my own capacity. My only hope is that we can eventually eliminate violence from our world before the separation from God entailed in it becomes finally fatal.

In December 1991 I was interviewed by *Christian Century* about my just published book *The Historical Jesus*. The interview was in question-and-answer format, and the final question asked me how that reconstruction of Jesus related to "God viewed as loving, forgiving, merciful, and so on." I replied,

Of course, the God of my reconstructed historical Jesus is loving, just, forgiving, merciful, but I am deeply aware that, when a boot presses on someone's neck, all those beautiful adjectives change a little as seen by the boot, or as seen by the neck. I do not want to use terms that could be loaded with complacent piety to eviscerate the message of Jesus. And I include myself quite emphatically in that complacency. Let me conclude, therefore, by imagining a conversation between myself and Jesus.

"I've read your book, Dominic, and it's quite good. So now you're ready to live by my vision and join me in my program?"

"I don't think I have the courage, Jesus, but I did describe it quite well, didn't I, and the method was especially good, wasn't it?"

"Thank you, Dominic, for not falsifying the message to suit your own incapacity. That at least is something."

"Is it enough, Jesus?"

"No, Dominic, it is not."

It is surely better to admit that I cannot live by a message I think is absolutely true or imitate a life I think was absolutely divine than to cut both down to my own inadequacy. I repeated that interchange at the start of a later book, *Jesus: A Revolutionary Biography,* and I received a letter telling me, "You should not feel guilty. You have done more than enough in writing that book." But guilt had never even entered my mind. And nothing I have said above about Jesus and justice should make anyone ever feel guilty. As you know full well by now, I spent almost twenty years in a Roman Catholic monastery, and I was worked on by experts. Sarah tells me that they failed dismally. Guilt is totally inoperative for me, and I suggest it should be for all of us. Think of it as you think of gas. Get rid of it. It is the flatulence of conscience. It is a spiritual waste product, and more important, it distracts us or excuses us from such absolutely necessary attitudes as honesty and integrity, clarity and accuracy, accountability and responsibility.

Just before Easter 1994 I did a taped interview with Terry Gross for her National Public Radio show *Fresh Air*. I was in a Chicago studio, she in a Philadelphia studio, and the interview was finished, but the tape was still running.

"Will you," she asked, "go to church this Easter?"

"No."

"Why not?"

"I prorated the many years I spent four hours a day in prayer in monastic church," I replied, "and figure I am still way ahead of the national average."

That was just being facetious; the serious reason came next. In 1969 I left monastery and priesthood; I did not leave the Roman Catholic community or tradition. I would not know how to do that, and even if I tried, it would be only a matter of externals. But I did deliberately decide to stay as far away as possible from the Roman Catholic hierarchy, and that, for me, meant no participation in church activities. That was originally, as I explained to Terry Gross, a negative decision. I wanted to do my own research and publish what I found without becoming trapped in disputes with church authority, without becoming involved in its agenda, without ending with nothing to say but an attack on its vacuity. When I finished, she asked me if that could be used in the interview. I said, "Of course." It was an honest question and deserved an honest answer.

Over the last few years I have come to recognize another reason as well. I have not "fallen away" from the church—I have "stayed away" from the hierarchy. It is simply a small way not just of disobeying papal commands quietly and internally, but of protesting papal power still quietly but externally. Compared to the abuse of physical power in this century, the abuse of spiritual power may seem insignificant. Compared to crimes against humanity, crimes against divinity may seem unimportant. But they are all abuses of power, and that, I have come more and more to understand, is what God stands against, a stance incarnated in the historical Jesus, a stance always present when Christianity is faithful to both. It was inevitable and understandable that militant secularism would beget its twin opposite in militant fundamentalism. It was inevitable and understandable that against secular rationalism would arise counterstrains of religious rationalism. If science and reason claimed a monopoly on truth, Christianity trumped them with biblical inerrancy, traditional conformity, and papal infallibility. Those were, of course, the supreme victories of rationalism, the ultimate submission of sanctity to certitude.

Secularism and fundamentalism deserve one another, and each is about equally capable of destroying our humanity. I recognize, however, that if the latter were given power, it, unlike the former, would come after people like me. But I focus here on papal fundamentalism within the Roman Catholic church. As an altar boy in a church at eight, a student in a priest-run boarding school at eleven, a novice in a monastery at sixteen, a priest in an order at twenty-three, and a professor in a seminary at twenty-seven, my earlier life was deeply involved in that specific community, tradition, church. I do not forget any of that because it is an irrevocable part of me. I even remember what it was like to walk into the papal palace at the right of St. Peter's Basilica in Rome ready (and very scared) for my oral examinations before the Pontifical Biblical Commission and to have the Swiss guards snap to attention at the sight of my habit (full mantle and all). But certain things must be said at least this one time.

We have just completed a century that has seen more atrocities and obscenities against humanity than in any previous era. One defense offered by many at the bar of justice is that they only did what they were told, they were only obeying orders. Is it not clear, yet, that obedience never excuses injustice? It seems absurd, on the one hand, to parallel physical abuse of power with spiritual abuse of power. Yet, on the other, what happens in the spiritual realm often models and justifies what happens in the physical realm. Therefore, I maintain that the mode of authority, the style of leadership, the primacy of obedience demanded by the Roman Catholic hierarchy is a crime, if not against humanity, then at least against divinity.

There is also here a terrible irony. The present pope has talked out regularly against the injustice to our common humanity, against the full spectrum of that injustice, religious, political, social, economic, and technological. Externally, yes, but internally, no. About injustice inside the church, he is silent. About what others should do, he is eloquent and often correct. About what *he* should do, about what *he* can do, he is culpably negligent. I do not mind a line drawn in the sand, even a line drawn sometimes too absolutely and sometimes too inaccurately, but such can only be drawn by somebody (like Jesus) who stands on the sand to draw it. Abuse of power outside the church is rightly criticized; abuse of power inside the church is generally ignored (think about the issue of women as priests). Against that abuse of internal power there is much private disobedience, but no public protest. Among the packed episcopacy, there is no loyal opposition, nobody to say, loudly and clearly, "I am the pope's good servant, but God's first."

Remember that incident in which Jesus was asked to take a stand for or against Roman tribute? "I myself," he said, "do not carry Caesar's coinage, so show me yours, and I'll tell you where to put it" (that's my own translation). He gets it and says, "Right, then, since this is Caesar's image, give it back to him." He and his companions walked away holding back their laughter while the puzzled questioners argued about his answer. Was it yes or no? Did it mean they were to pay their coins dutifully into Caesar's coffers or cast them defiantly into Caesar's face?

What happened afterward is only recorded by a fragmentary Irish gospel carved in runic characters on a weathered monolith in northern Donegal:

> Said Mary of Magdala, "Did you notice, Jesus, that the emperor Tiberius was called 'Son of God' on the front of that silver denarius?"
>
> Jesus said nothing, but only smiled gently.
>
> Peter of Capernaum immediately interrupted them, as he always did whenever Mary and Jesus got into conversation. Said he, "Did you notice, Jesus, that he was called 'Supreme Pontiff' on the back?"
>
> Once again Jesus said nothing, but this time he started to laugh. He laughed and laughed and laughed. He was hardly able to stop. But he never told his companions what was so funny.

One final question, not about Roman Catholicism in particular, but about Christianity in general. Why do we need a church, any church? The usual answer is that we are social beings and we do things together; therefore we worship together. That is a good answer unless you rephrase the question. Is religion like sex or like politics? Sex is completely natural, utterly human, and profoundly holy. Yet, despite being social beings, we usually do not congregate to make love together at some designated place and time. Why is religion not like sex, something terribly important, socially necessary, but privately performed? Religion could, after all, be passed on and performed within the family, in the privacy of the home, as the supreme family value. We have a bedroom and a bathroom—why couldn't we have a godroom?

Politics, on the other hand, is intensely social, fully organized, and abundantly funded. Despite our individualism, this country has never splintered into multiple political parties, not even creating one or two small ones with swing-vote power over the larger ones. We have two parties which, whatever their declared differences, are basically the Ins and the Outs, the basic and adequate minimum for efficient political life. Politics is about getting something done, even if only about getting what *we* want done, so it is fully social. We are, in other words, serious about politics, but not about religion. Or, conversely, religion is not about getting something done. So we can splinter and splinter and splinter until every Christian has his or her own church.

But, in my faith, the God of the Bible and the Jesus of the New Testament *are* about getting something done. That something to be done is bringing our world into union with a God who is Justice itself, a Justice that involves the fair distribution of the material bases of life, a Justice that was incarnated in the life and execution of Jesus, a Justice that was vindicated by his resurrection within a community continuing that incarnation. It is also enough for me, actually much more than enough, to have been one small, tiny (and relatively safe) part of that dangerous process.

Wait a moment, what about heaven and hell, what about terminal rewards and punishments, what about eternity and the afterlife? First, let me be very blunt: I refuse to accept heaven from a God who could invent hell. At the end of this terrible century, I cannot think about Nazi Germany, for example, without wondering whether, if I had been there, I would have had the courage to deny, resist, or protest its atrocities. I can only hope that I would have recognized its evil and not cooperated with its program internally, at the very least, even if not externally, at the very best. The God of hell is a divinity to fear but not to love, to dread but not to worship, and it is morally necessary to say that loudly and clearly. I will not hide behind divine mystery or human finitude. Hell is an obscenity, one more example of crimes against divinity that down deep justify our own crimes against humanity. For such a Supreme Being, Mrs. Job had the only proper answer: Curse God, and die.

In postlecture discussions today, however, I find that many more Christians believe in heaven than in hell. But heaven and hell were always a pair since first they arrived in Jewish and Christian consciousness. Is it possible now simply to erase one and not thereby endanger the other? For myself, I consider heaven and hell as options for life here below, options for a life based on justice or injustice in this world. They are not actualities for afterlife on high, but possibilities for this life on earth. They are not locations created by God in the future, but options created by us in the present. In that sense, of course, hell does seem to be winning out hands down over heaven.

For myself, therefore, I admit a total disinterest in afterlife options, either to affirm or to deny them. Either way, they distract from what I understand to be the challenge of Jesus about the Kingdom of God, that is, as Matthew glossed it, the will of God for this earth. On earth, as in heaven. Heaven is in very good shape; it is earth that is our responsibility, and I am convinced that we cannot establish justice here below without union with the God who is Justice itself. I speak much less of social justice, although we could use a lot more of it, than of divine justice, a rather more formidable challenge. I can both love and worship a transcendental voice that says: "The earth is mine, with me you are all aliens and tenants." That is a God worth living for and, if unfortunately necessary, a God worth dying for. Sarah says she hopes I am wrong about that afterlife stuff. But, be that as it may, my own hope is for a church empowered by divine justice that will take on the systemic normalcy of human violence. A church, in other words, that will oppose rather than join that process. That is more than enough hope for me. The rest, I am afraid, is parable at best and fantasy at worst.

On Sunday, July 25, during that 1999 New Zealand lecture tour, Sarah and I were guests at the home of Jan and Jim Veitch in Masterton, a couple of hours northeast of Wellington. That morning we watched them assist some newborn lambs that had difficulty nursing. That evening they had invited about forty people for a potluck supper to discuss the historical Jesus and how such research might strengthen a Christian faith that needed brains as well as hearts, minds as well as emotions. After dinner, we were seated in a very large circle extending around both living and dining rooms. Among the guests was a minister who had stayed away from the church for almost thirty years after the heresy trial of a fellow minister in which so many who agreed with the "heretic" had remained silent and allowed it to proceed without strong protest and stern resistance. Toward the end, Jim, who has long experience as both professor and pastor, noted that the minister had been very quiet the whole evening and asked if he had any questions he wanted to discuss "before we close." He responded, in a soft-spoken voice, that he had no questions, but did want to say something.

He talked at length about what had happened years before and how he had felt about the church all those years ever since. He saw now that there might be hope for a church that would never do such things again, that would not demand people believe literally stories that were intended metaphorically, and that would insist on justice inside and outside itself. About ten minutes later, as the discussion was ending, he slipped quietly, gently, almost unobtrusively to the floor. He was dead by the time he reached it, and help from his wife, from a nurse who was present, and from the paramedics who arrived shortly could do nothing but confirm that fact. I do not know what hope he had for the next life because he never mentioned it. It seemed more important, at least in his final words, that he had refound hope for this one and for the church he had loved and lost.

In conclusion, this is what I have learned between Ireland and America, monastery and university, priesthood and marriage, academic scholarship and public discourse. I have learned that God is more radical than we can ever imagine, that a divine utopia on this earth is more subversive than we can ever accept, and that Pilate acted for all of us when he executed Jesus. But let me repeat that in an autobiographical anecdote.

Sarah and I are good friends with Marianne Borg, a canon of Portland's Trinity Episcopal Cathedral, and her husband, Marcus Borg, who holds an endowed chair at Oregon State University. Marcus is also one of the handful of scholars who have spent their professional life in historical Jesus research. In early March 1999 they invited Sarah and me to Oregon, first for a Thursday class and lecture at the university and then for a Friday through Sunday seminar at the cathedral. After the opening session on Friday night, I was seated at a small table signing books. As I finished one book's inscription, its owner said, "My pastor told me not to come here tonight because you are even to the left of Borg."

"Give your pastor my best regards," I replied, "and tell him that is the good news. The bad news is that both Borg and Crossan are to the right of Jesus. And worse still, if he will recall Psalm 110, Jesus is to the right of God."

INDEX

Haggard, H. Rider, 7
Harnack, Adolf, 150
Harper & Row (HarperCollins), 170
Heaven and hell, 201–2
Hell's Foundations, 143
Hero and Leander, 142–43
Herod Antipas, 193
Herod the Great, 50, 51
Hill, Anita, 141
*Historical Jesus, The: The Life of a
  Mediterranean Jewish Peasant*
  (Crossan), xv–xvi, 15, 112, 175,
  180, 196
Holmes, Paul, 169
How Green Was My Valley, 28
Humanae Vitae (encyclical, 1968),
  88–89

Ibiza, 108–9, 110; patronal society
  in, 113, 114–15; Villa Aisling,
  107, 110–11, 113–20, 127
In Fragments (Crossan), 125, 127,
  128
*In Parables: The Challenge of the
  Historical Jesus* (Crossan), 170–71
"In Search of Jesus: Who Was He?
  New Appraisals of His Life and
  Meaning" (*U. S. News & World
  Report*), 195
Incident-in-character, 136
Infancy Gospel of Thomas, 169–70
Injustice: difference between individ-
  ual, personal, national and struc-
  tural, systemic, and imperial, 49;
  social class and awareness of, xvii;
  vengeance and justice and,
  185–86
International Herald Tribune, xv
Ireland: ancient provincial divisions,
  32; Ballybofey, County Donegal, 4,

9–10, 13–14; banking in, 8–10;
  Benburb, 54; Black & Tans, 47;
  brown bread of, 15; civil war of
  1922, 49; Cromwell's armies in,
  54; farming, 14–15; history as a
  European colony, xviii, 151; history in song, 144–45; Inishowen
  Peninsula, 17; injustice and, 16;
  Letterkenny, County Donegal, 17,
  30, 48; Naas, County Kildare,
  3–7, 34; partition, 49; rebellion of
  1916, 143; rural, 1940s, 25–26;
  Trim, County Meath, 32, 84;
  "troubles" of 1916 to1922, 47–48
Isaiah: 5:8, 189; 7:14, 140
Israel: ancient, Roman occupation of,
  49–52; Mandelbaum Gate, ix, xii;
  Nazareth, Galilee, x, xxi, 50–52;
  1967 war, ix–xii

Jensen, George, 115, 117
Jerusalem, Roman rule, 50
Jesus: aphorisms of, 125; Barabbas
  story, 161–62; as bastard, 45–46,
  47; birth, date of, 51; birth stories,
  39, 137–40, 148–49; brokerage
  material used in study of, 112;
  Caesar's coin and, 199–200; crucifixion of, 194; divine or human,
  149; environment as first century
  Roman colony, 39, 47, 49–52;
  "face at the bottom of the well"
  argument and study of historical,
  xvi–xvii, 150, 151, 158–59; God
  as Father, 33, 37; historical, study
  of, xiii–xiv, xv–xvi, 60, 150–51,
  158–59; impact of Joseph's
  absence on, 32–33, 37, 38–39, 45;
  incarnation, 104, 149; justice and,
  xvii, 52, 168, 191–204; in Mark,

identified as "son of Mary," 38; in
Mark, Jesus sought by his mother
and brothers, 37–38; "negative
campaigning against," 46–47; nonviolent resistance and martyrdom,
192–94; radicalism of, 193–94,
203–4; as redeemer, 52; resurrection, 164–66, 194–96; Roman
Empire and, 49–52, 194–95;
sense of systemic evil and, 49; sib-
lings, 32, 38; social class and
study of, xvii; as Son, 104; virginal
and divine conception of, 137–40,
142, 148–49
"Jesus and Faith: Theologians in
Conversation with the Work of
John Dominic Crossan," 157–58
Jesus: A Revolutionary Biography
(Crossan), 175, 197
Jesus Seminar, 173–74, 175–76
Jesus Under Fire, 165–66
Jesus Wars, xv
JFK (film), 141–42
John (Gospel of), 149; loaves and
fishes (6:5–13), 167–68; race to
empty tomb, 164–65
John Paul II, 199
Jordan, ix–xii
Joseph: as absent or unimportant fig-
ure, 32–33, 38–39, 45; God as
father and, 37
Josephus, 50, 191, 192
Journal of Biblical Literature, 93, 172
Journal of Religion, 93
Joyce, James, 69, 110
Juarroz, Roberto, 128
Judaism: attacks on Jesus by diver-
gent factions within, 46; firstborn
son and, 104; Jesus as incarnation
of god's justice on earth, 52, 112,

140, 149, 168, 191–204; Mosaic
law, 189; nonviolent resistance,
192; Pharisees, Sadducees,
Qunram Essenes, 46; under
Roman rule, 50–51
Justin Martyr, 137–38

Keane, James, O.S.M., 27–28
"Kelly the Boy from Killane," 145
King Solomon's Mines (Haggard), 7
Kings (I) 21, 188–89
Kipling, Rudyard, 11
Kitagawa, Joe, 173

Lagrange, Father Marie-Joseph, 65
Last of the Mohicans, The (Cooper),
58
"Les Jeunes Filles en Fleur" (Paul),
109
Leviticus 25:23, 188
Life and Death of a Spanish Town, The
(Paul), 108, 109–10
Liturgical Year, The (Guéranger), 60
Long Loneliness, The (Day), 83
Lord's Prayer, 193
Los Angeles Times, xix
Loyola University (Chicago), 70, 77,
83, 91
Luke (Gospel of): 1:2, 137; 1:27–31,
140; good Samaritan story, 164;
historical Jesus and, 149;
Magnificat, 51; meeting of
Elizabeth and Mary, 51

Magnificat, 51
Maritain, Jacques, 83
Mark (Gospel of): Barabbas story,
162–63; historical Jesus and, 149;
Jesus identified as "son of Mary,"
38; Jesus sought by his mother

Scarlet Pimpernel, The (Orczy), 58
Scholasticism, 72–73, 83
Scott, Nathan, 172
Secularism, xvi, 165, 183, 198
Semeia: An Experimental Journal for Biblical Criticism, 172
Sepphoris, 50
Service, Robert, 10–11
Servite Order (Order of Servants of Mary): adventure offered by, 28; decisions concerning John Crossan, 81–86; dress, 55, 70; food, 54; Gelsenkirchen-Buer parish, Germany, 57; governing structure and decisions, 80–86, 87–90; history of, 27, 32–33; isolation of, 69–70, 74; Marianum College, Rome, 65; monastery rules, 20–21; 1950 novice class, 63, 81; novitiate year, 55–60, 63; Our Lady of Benburb Priory, 20, 27, 54–55; patronal society and, 112–13; peculium (monthly subsidy), 62; priory, Belgium, 67; Stonebridge Priory, 63–64, 69–70, 82; in Rome, 62; vow of poverty and care of members, x, 62–67. *See also* Crossan, John Dominic
Seven Pillars of Wisdom (Lawrence), 66
Seven Storey Mountain, The (Merton), 83
"Shooting of Dan McGrew, The" (Service), 10
Sibylline Oracles (2), 191
Simon of Cyrene, 132
Simpson, O. J., 141, 148
Sisters of Mercy, 66, 124
Sky Hawk, 7

Society: patronal or influential, 111–14; universal or functional, 111; violence of 20th century, 199
Society of Biblical Literature, 93, 171–72; journals, 172; Parables Seminar, 171
Spain, 108–9. *See also* Ibiza
Spanish Main, The, 58
Speech-in-character, 51–52; Magnificat as, 51; Tacitus and, 51–52
Stations of the Cross, 132
Steinfels, Peter, xv, 175–76
Stonebridge Priory, Chicago, 63–64, 69–70, 82
Story, 146; Irish history, 145–46; lie versus, 163, 168; literalness of, 145 *See also* Biblical stories
Suetonius, 139–40

Tacitus, 51–52
Tarzan (Burroughs), 7
Theological Studies, 162
Thomas, Clarence, 141
Time magazine, xvi, 75, 176–7
Titanic, xvii
Toronto Star, 165–66
Tracy, David, 171
Trinity, 102–6; locality, 104; metaphoricity, 103–4; particularity, 104–5
Trinity Episcopal Church, Portland, Oregon, 203
Twenty Thousand Leagues Under the Sea (Verne), 7–8
Tyrell, George, 150

University of Chicago, 171, 172–73; Oriental Institute, 85
University of Louvain, Belgium, 67

p.66